Countering Terrorism

Countering Terrorism

Can We Meet the Threat of
Global Violence?

Michael Chandler and Rohan Gunaratna

REAKTION BOOKS

Published by Reaktion Books Ltd
33 Great Sutton Street
London EC1V 0DX, UK
www.reaktionbooks.co.uk

First published 2007

Printed and Bound in Great Britain
by William Clowes Limited, Beccles, Suffolk

British Library Cataloguing in Publication Data
Chandler, Michael
    Countering terrorism: can we meet the threat of global violence?
    1. Terrorism – Prevention   2. Terrorism – Prevention – International
    cooperation   3. War on Terrorism, 2001–   4. Security, International
    I. Title   II. Gunaratna, Rohan, 1961–
    363.3′25

    ISBN-13: 978 1 86189 308 6
    ISBN-10: 1 86189 308 6

Contents

Introduction

The blasts came at ten minutes to nine in the morning rush hour. Within fifty seconds of each other, three bombs exploded, one each on separate trains on the Underground railway system – the Tube: the first on a Circle Line train between Liverpool Street and Aldgate stations; the next on a Piccadilly Line train, deep under the city, travelling from King's Cross towards Russell Square; and the third on another Circle Line train in Edgware Road station. Fifty-seven minutes later, at 9.47 a.m., a crowded Number 30 bus heading for Hackney was blown apart in Tavistock Square. This was the 'breaking news' in London on the morning of 7 July 2005. The 'inevitable' had happened.

As far back as 2003 the head of MI5, the UK's Security Service, Dame Eliza Manningham-Buller, and London's Metropolitan Police Commissioner, Sir John Stevens, had both warned that it was not a case of 'if' but 'when' there would be an attack in the United Kingdom by militant extremists associated with the al-Qaida terrorist network. The London '7/7' attacks bore all the hallmarks of an al-Qaida style atrocity. Multiple, simultaneous explosions, with no prior warning given, designed to cause mass casualties, achieve maximum publicity and have a seriously adverse impact on the morale of the nation's population and its economy. Although the terrorists may have had some success with the first two aspects of their intended aim, they missed out on the third.

Those responsible for planning and executing these attacks had totally underestimated the indomitable spirit of the people of London. Through this fortitude, taken together with the UK's counter-terrorism strategy and the London Resilience programme, many lives were saved, with most of the injured rescued and treated relatively quickly.[1] This ability to reduce the impact of the attacks was due to a considerable amount of planning and rehearsals by all the agencies that have to work together in the event of major incidents in the capital. Within minutes of reality dawning that morning as to what was actually happening in central London, the emergency services swung into action. Police, fire and ambulance services, doctors and paramedical teams, and London's transport staff all had roles to play, as did the Accident and Emergency (A&E) departments at key London hospitals. Given the confined spaces in which the terrorists detonated their bombs, the casualties could have been much worse. In the end 56 people were killed and it was estimated that more than 600 were injured. Although traffic on much of London's public transport and mass-transit systems, particularly the Underground network in central London, was temporarily suspended on 7 July, by the next morning it was almost 'business as usual'. Understandably, this was not the case at the locations of the terrorist attacks: as 'scenes of crime' (SOC) they were being subjected to intensive forensic examination.

Using a known Islamic website, a previously unknown group calling itself 'The Secret Organization of Al-Qaeda in Europe' claimed responsibility for the attacks. In the words of the website, the attacks were reprisals for the British involvement in Afghanistan and Iraq. However, the origin and authenticity of the group has not been confirmed. Also this so-called 'secret organization' made no mention in its statement with respect to the G-8 summit, which, coincidentally or not, was starting its first day on 7 July at Gleneagles in Scotland. Britain's Prime Minister, Tony Blair, was swift in his condemnation of the atrocities and those behind the blasts. In view of the seriousness of the atrocities perpetrated that morning in London, Blair broke off his chairing of the summit to fly to London and be briefed by ministers and key government officials. Before departing, however, he gave a sombre but strident response to the terrorists and their sponsors: Britain would not be bowed by terrorists. Flanked by all the heads of state and dignitaries attending the summit conference – many of whom later gave their own responses of support and solidarity with the British at this outrage – Blair made it clear that no stone would be left unturned until all those responsible, in any way, for the attacks had been brought to justice.

The attacks that morning in London almost hijacked the agenda of the summit just at a time when the G-8 and representatives of certain African countries were debating significant financial assistance from which a number of countries in the 'global south' would benefit. To add to the irony of the situation, the sort of countries that would be beneficiaries are similar to those from which terrorists of the type responsible for the blasts that morning originate.

There are a variety of causes that have contributed or continue to contribute to this phenomenon of terrorism. Poverty, perceived injustices and double standards on which terrorism can feed are but a few. Poor living standards, unemployment and inadequate or non-existent education systems leading to futures without hope all provide fertile ground on which terrorism easily breeds. Corrupt and/or dictatorial governments denying populations even the most basic form of democracy can exaggerate their peoples' frustrations and accelerate their radicalization by extremist clerics. Humanitarian assistance accompanied by the encouragement to convert to Islam can make the difference between surviving and starving to death. The 'club of the eight most industrialized nations', despite its ideals and rhetoric, has been slow to reach out to the 'global south'; that is until this G-8 Summit of 7 July 2005 agreed a number of measures aimed at alleviating poverty in at least eighteen African nations. However, the G-8 nations have not responded to the global threat from transnational terrorism in ways that might be more pertinent and, in the longer term, have a much more positive impact. Because the commitments and responses from the nations of the 'industrialized north' have fallen short of the investment needed, financial vacuums have developed. Depending on the country in question, these have often been filled by Islamic-based charities, invariably with strings attached.

For vested reasons insufficient pressure has been applied to such states as Saudi Arabia. Many Muslim humanitarian organizations or charities, with their head offices in the Saudi kingdom, have knowingly or unwittingly been abused downstream to provide financial support to terrorist organizations. The fact, so often trotted out, that this was a political expedient in the West's not-so-clandestine efforts that resulted in the end of the Soviet occupation of Afghanistan no longer holds water. Nor does the fact that there was a certain ambivalence on the part of some Western governments to the misuse of NGOs, such as the Third World Relief Agency (TWRA), to assist covertly beleaguered

Muslims in the Bosnian conflict (1992–5) with war-like materiel. Just because it suited the situations at the time is no excuse for the process to be allowed to continue as an accepted practice, particularly in support of terrorist groups. Humanitarian organizations have an important role to play in conflict zones to assist the displaced, the needy, the injured and the sick. These functions must stand apart from any assistance to the belligerents to ensure the neutrality of the NGOs is not compromised.

At the same time, extremist Muslim clerics proclaiming a Wahabist or Salafist strain of Islam, with little if any understanding of the real world, have been left, *carte blanche*, to encourage an extreme and 'un-Islamic' interpretation of their faith. They have been free to preach and ferment aggression towards the Jews, the United States and its allies. But in addition to these more widespread and general causes, which encourage a radical, extreme and fundamentalist form of Islam, the London bombings have taken on a much more sinister aspect. For the first time in Western Europe, Islamist terrorists have resorted to suicide attacks. Suicide attacks are the nightmare scenario that security services and law enforcement agencies hope they will not have to confront. The attacks on London's transport system and its population on 7 July 2005 were particularly significant and demonstrated a serious turning point in the threat posed by transnational Islamist terrorism.

On this occasion the security services had little or no real warning of the impending attacks. Clearly, the terrorists' operation had been well planned and coordinated in the utmost secrecy, achieving one of the oldest military 'principles of war' – surprise. Despite the intensity of the ensuing manhunt and the speed with which the Metropolitan Police Anti-terrorist Branch identified the bombers and key aspects of the operation, just two weeks later, on Thursday, 21 July, another team of bombers attempted an almost identical series of strikes. Again the bombers targeted three Tube trains and a bus in London. Fortunately, none of the explosive charges was initiated. Although it appears that the detonators went off, the main charges did not explode, denying four would-be homicide terrorists their moment of misplaced publicity.

Before these second attacks failed, however, evidence had come to light proving that at least two of the '7/7' bombers, Mohammed Siddeque Khan and Shehzad Tanweer, had flown from the UK on

Turkish Airlines flights via Istanbul to Karachi, Pakistan, on 19 November 2004. They had then remained in Pakistan for some months before flying back by the reverse route on 8 February 2005. Their families, back in the Leeds area of Yorkshire, said that they had gone to Pakistan to undertake religious studies. However, even 'religious studies' in Pakistan, with its *madrassas* and Sunni extremist groups, can have other connotations.

Then, at a time when a number of individuals had been telling the media what a community-spirited person Khan had been, the Qatar-based Arabic satellite television channel, al-Jazeera, showed an al-Qaida videotape in which Khan explained his reasons for the attacks.[2] Although Khan did not personally claim responsibility for the London attacks, Ayman al-Zawahiri, generally accepted as al-Qaida's deputy leader and leading ideologue, who appears on the same tape, 'characterized the blasts as a response to UK foreign policy'.[3] Khan's appearance, even though it is not clear when he recorded his part of the tape, is synonymous with the behaviour of contemporary Islamist terrorist suicide bombers. Clearly his speech was intended for British audiences, being delivered in English with what al-Jazeera described as 'a heavy Yorkshire accent'.

But perhaps of greater significance is the home-grown nature of the young Muslims who perpetrated the London attacks. The London bombers were not terrorists who had come especially to the UK to carry out their atrocities. Those who committed the suicide blasts on 7 July had all been born and raised in England. Similarly, at least two of those responsible for the failed attempts on 21 July had been young immigrants and/or asylum seekers who had come to Britain to find a better life in a freer, easier and more prosperous society than the ones they had left behind in such war-torn countries as Eritrea and Somalia. They were able to benefit from the social system, receiving a free education and being provided with state housing. Instead, they chose to 'bite the hand that fed them'.

Many young Muslims interviewed in Britain in the wake of 7 July, while condemning the attacks and the killing of innocent people, nonetheless blamed the British Government for its role in Iraq, in going to war in support of the United States. However, in a lengthy briefing to the media on 26 July 2005, Prime Minister Blair said that Iraq was, incorrectly, being used as an excuse for the London bombings. He reminded his audience that there was no war in Iraq on 11

September 2001, when the World Trade Center and the Pentagon had been attacked. True as this statement is, an increasing number of young Muslims, both male and female, have become more radicalized by the actions of the US and its allies in Iraq and also in Afghanistan. It would be wise to take due consideration of these feelings but also to keep them in perspective.

According to an ICM opinion poll, commissioned in early 2006 by the British *Sunday Telegraph* newspaper, 40 per cent of Muslims want shariah law in the UK. However, the article did go on to point out that 41 per cent were not in favour.[4] Nonetheless, these figures were perhaps somewhat at odds with another of the poll's questions. Whereas 7 per cent of the interviewees felt that 'Western society is decadent and immoral and Muslims should seek to bring it to an end, if necessary by violent means', 80 per cent felt that 'Western society may not be perfect but Muslims should live within it and not seek to bring it to an end'. Taken together, these reflections emphasize key points that are rarely appropriately aired during public debates. The United Kingdom is a Christian country founded on values that have been cherished and upheld for centuries. They may not be perfect but they are what native Britons like and believe in. They include religious tolerance, within which individuals are free to practise whatever religion they wish. That does not mean they are free to preach religious or ethnic hatred, nor, we would suggest, inciting violence in the name of their chosen religion. In this, the UK is not alone. There are many other European countries in which similar feelings exist.

Similarly, if a Muslim, or any other individual for that matter, chooses to live in a country that has a different legal and judicial system from that of the country of his or her origin, then he or she should abide by the system applicable to the country in which he or she chooses to live. After all, if an individual does not wish to respect the laws, cultures and customs of a country he/she is always free to leave it. If one prefers to live under shariah law, then one should live in an Islamic state that is governed by such laws. If people from Christian countries opt to live and/or work in countries with religious and legal systems alien to that of their country of origin, they are expected to abide by the laws and customs of those countries, like it or not. How often do we hear a politician from a Western industrialized Christian country speaking out about the fact that there is no religious tolerance, for example, in Saudi Arabia? Rarely, is the reality:

although Edmund Stoiber, the Minister President of Germany's Freistatt Bayern (Free State of Bavaria), in a speech to his Christlich-Sozialen Union (CSU) party, said that 'Tolerance is not a one-way street . . . Those who demand the call from the minarets [be allowed] in Berlin, should allow the bells to ring out in Riyadh and Tehran!'⁵

Whereas Muslims from many states are free to practise their religion within Christian countries, if Christians are found practising their religion in Saudi Arabia, even in private, they are likely to be arrested and punished. The reason given is that Saudi Arabia is custodian of such important religious sites as Mecca and Medina. These discussions have become much too one-sided and do not fully address all aspects of the debate.

Unfortunately, the one-sided debate was also emphasized as a result of the reactions around the Muslim world to the cartoons depicting the Prophet Muhammad published on 30 September 2005 by the Danish newspaper *Jyllands-Posten*.⁶ Contrary to the mayhem and indignation that appeared on the streets in Bangladesh, Pakistan, Palestine, Iran, Syria and Indonesia when the situation erupted on a global scale in January 2006, there had been no reaction when six of the cartoons had been printed on the front page of one of Egypt's most respectable newspapers, *al-Fajr*, on 17 October 2005.⁷ Neither the readers, the public, other countries nor even the Egyptian Government had reacted. The public outcry that erupted in January and February 2006 had clearly been orchestrated by radical Muslim clerics. Having failed to get their way following complaints to the authorities in Denmark when the cartoons were first published, the clerics then went on a 'tour' of countries in the Middle East to whip up anti-Christian and anti-Western sentiment. Clearly it was an ideal opportunity that the extremists were able to exploit for a very short term. It soon became history and vanished quickly off television screens, unlike the daily carnage emanating from Iraq.

The roots of extremism that translate into the threat posed today by transnational terrorism run much deeper and have to be confronted globally, at every level of the problem. As many of us have been saying for a very long time: this is a multi-faceted problem that demands a multi-pronged approach. Mr Blair referred to the attacks in the USA on 11 September 2001 as a wake-up call for the international community, which then, as he so eloquently put it, 'turned over and went back to sleep again'. It is important to see why so many 'went back to sleep' and what needs now to be done to overcome this political malaise.[8]

The fight against global terrorism and extremism will be the most defining challenge of the early twenty-first century. More than ever before, international consensus and action are gravely needed to combat the unprecedented wave of terrorism and extremism that has emerged after 9/11. No longer are we fighting terrorism generated from individual threat groups. The era of network terrorism has come of age. Terrorism is no longer one nation's problem. Without exception, the contemporary wave of terrorism violates the sovereignty of each and every nation. The postmodern terrorist is highly mobile. He or she moves from country to country to disseminate propaganda and recruit; to seek sanctuary and safe haven; to raise funds and move money; to procure weapons and other supplies; to communicate and meet, and finally, to reconnoitre targets and mount attacks. The transnational Islamist extremist terrorist is adept at recruiting in one theatre, training in a second theatre, planning and preparing attacks in a third theatre and striking in a fourth. No single nation could or can, in reality, comprehend the threat and meet the challenges it poses. Al-Qaida's iconic attacks on 9/11 demonstrated that, no matter how strong economically or militarily the United States might be, it had to build an effective coalition to fight terrorism.

Defeating the contemporary wave of terrorists and terrorism requires a concerted, coordinated and collaborative effort from the international community. If ever there was a time for the United Nations to rise to the occasion then this should have been that moment. The direct kinetic action has failed to reduce the terrorist threat in the first five years after 9/11. While investment in operational counter-terrorism is still essential to reduce the immediate threat, it is necessary to craft a long-term strategic response.

Reactive measures by individual governments, particularly the overreaction of the United States of America and its allies, have not appreciably reduced the threat. On the contrary, the threat in the global south has continued to grow significantly. The threat has increased in the Middle East and spread both eastwards into Asia and westwards across Europe. To develop an appropriate, comprehensive and robust response – both proactive and reactive – it is necessary to develop a comprehensive understanding of the threat.

Has there been a failure? Until 9/11 the international community took far too little interest in Afghanistan, a country that was providing training for between 30 and 40 terrorist groups from around the world. The international neglect of Afghanistan culminated in 9/11. Even after the atrocities on that date, the response has been largely military. Trade and economic investment, the most valuable weapons in the inventory of the developed nations, particularly of the West, have not been used. Similarly, investment by the Western industrialized nations in public affairs and diplomacy, to build bridges with the Muslim world, has been slow, inadequate or, in some instances, non-existent. Finally, a true multi-pronged approach against a multi-dimensional threat has yet to be developed.

Why then, with what should have been such a golden opportunity after 9/11 to kick-start a truly international response to terrorism, has the overall response been so abysmal, slow, piecemeal and to a large extent far from effective? Why is it that countries that have shown leadership and willingness to cooperate in other areas of the international arena have failed to meet their obligations fully and fulfil their responsibilities with regard to countering terrorism? Why has it been that only a few countries have taken firm decisive actions within the law? Why have some states, even at the expense of criticism from the more timorous, challenged accepted humanitarian norms in the manner in which they deal with such an unusual and uncompromising scourge of the new millennium?

The reasons proffered, if not the answers to these questions, are equally numerous and diverse. In examining them we will look at some of the underlying problems that cause this inertia. We will examine some historical facts and what the international community needs to do to be in a better position to counter, not only the current threat from transnational terrorism, but others that may erupt in future years. Much of the discussion will deal with basic facts. One of these that so often appears not to be fully understood is the threat. Understanding it and appreciating its severity are fundamental to the whole process.

I

The Current and Future Terrorist Threat

Since 9/11 there have been a number of very profound developments in the landscape of global terrorism. First, al-Qaida has transformed from a group into a movement. In addition to al-Qaida, some three dozen groups are willing and able to stage al-Qaida-style attacks. Western law enforcement and intelligence agencies are focusing on al-Qaida, but the threat has grown much larger. It is far more widespread. Second, the violent Islamists have declared Iraq the new 'land of *jihād*'. The groups in Iraq have built robust support and operational cells in the Levant and beyond. Using Iraq as a launching pad, terrorist leaders have been planning and preparing attacks in countries outside and well beyond Iraq. Third, Muslims worldwide, including moderate Muslims, are angered by the US invasion of Iraq. They see no justification for it. Many Islamist groups are aggressively harnessing the resentment among the Muslims including those living in the migrant communities and diasporas of the West. These extremist groups are calling upon Muslims in North America, Europe and Australasia to provide recruits and other support. In particular, after the US invasion of Iraq, Islamist groups have found a significant amount of support to continue the fight against the USA, its allies and friends.

These three significant developments characterize the new threat environment in which we live. The emergence of Sunni Islamic extremism since the early 1980s has demonstrated a steady and sus-tained development. The actions of governments targeting the operational infrastructure of the Sunni extremist movement have not been very successful. The Sunni extremist movement gained a new impetus after 9/11. Its vanguard is al-Qaida, the child of the multinational campaign against the Soviet occupation of Afghanistan. But it also draws significant support, albeit of a somewhat covert nature, from the Muslim Brotherhood.

THE CONTEXT

Despite concerted action worldwide, al-Qaida, the most hunted group in history, has survived. Several years after 9/11 the core leadership is still intact. Although many of the operational commanders have been apprehended or killed, many of the founders, the key ideological and spiritual leaders, are alive and at large. Furthermore, to survive the current and continuing threat to it from the international community, al-Qaida has evolved from a group into a movement. In order to remain relevant and to survive, the core group of al-Qaida led by Usama bin Laden, along with the associated groups and entities that comprise the movement or network, will further transform and mutate.

The threat of terrorism has grown far beyond the original al-Qaida. Nonetheless, close examination is necessary to understand the ideological and operational dimensions of the threat that has evolved. An examination of al-Qaida's history reveals that the group has a remarkable ability to survive and evolve under pressure. This is the true strength of the adversary.

BACKGROUND

Historically, al-Qaida has undergone three distinct transformations:

Phase One: Following the Soviet withdrawal from Afghanistan in 1989, al-Qaida al-Sulbah ('The Solid Base') began as a group to support and assist local jihad movements and associated groups or to target directly opposing governments, mostly in Muslim countries. By providing finance, weapons and trainers the group played or attempted to play critical roles in what were then the lands of jihad: Algeria, Bosnia, Chechnya, Egypt, the disputed areas of Kashmir and Mindanao (southern Philippines), Tajikistan and Uzbekistan.

Phase Two: Al-Qaida developed its own capability to mount operations throughout the 1990s, due largely to close cooperation with Egyptian groups – Egyptian Islamic Jihad and the Islamic Group of

Egypt – which culminated with the 11 September 2001 attacks against the USA. By recruiting Western-educated Islamists such as Khalid Sheikh Muhammad, al-Qaida was able to strike deep inside the West.

Phase Three: Due to security measures in Western countries taken immediately after the 2001 attacks, al-Qaida and its associated groups were no longer able to mount attacks, with the same ease, on Western soil. From September 2001 onwards al-Qaida, its associated groups and affiliated cells switched their attention to targets in countries where it was easier to operate. Attacks were staged in Indonesia, Kenya, Morocco, Pakistan, Tunisia and in Russia, including Caucasian states such as Chechnya and Ingushetia. Western facilities have been targeted in Saudi Arabia, Turkey and Iraq. In this latter phase, most of the attacks were not staged by al-Qaida per se but by entities associated with it. Since these associated groups lack the same level of expertise as the founding organization, the numbers of casualties and fatalities the entities have suffered have climbed – in some instances quite significantly. The loss of bases in which to train and rehearse in Afghanistan has forced al-Qaida to change from a hierarchical organization into a movement comprised of loosely affiliated groups and entities. In order to survive and continue the spread of its ideology and operational stance it has resorted to intensive networking.

THE CONTEMPORARY WAVE OF ISLAMISM

Against the backdrop of the global rise of Islamism and worldwide terrorism,[1] al-Qaida originated as a vicious by-product of the multi-national, anti-Soviet campaign. Although it started out quite small, mostly as a group that supported the Arabs who went to fight the Soviets in Afghanistan, al-Qaida grew into prominence within a decade. The contemporary origins of the current Islamic movement date back to two landmark events, both of which occurred in 1979. First, the newly created Islamic Republic of Iran defied the USA, a superpower, by holding a group of Americans hostage for 444 days. Second, a number of Afghans, assisted by volunteers from across the Arab world, defeated the mighty Soviet army, which in 1979 had invaded a Muslim country. The successes of the Iranian revolution (1979) and the multinational campaign in Afghanistan from 1979 to

1989 against another superpower, the Union of Socialist Soviet Republics, instilled the belief among a significant segment of Muslim youth that they could take on the United States of America. They had defeated one superpower, so why not another?

A year before the Soviet army, the world's largest army, withdrew in humiliation from Afghanistan, al-Qaida al-Sulbah was born. Its creator, Dr Abdullah Azzam, the principal ideologue of the anti-Soviet Afghan campaign, was a Jordanian-Palestinian religious cleric from Jenin in the West Bank. At its very formation in March 1988, al-Qaida was thought of as the vanguard of the Islamic movements. Azzam and his deputy and protégé, Usama bin Laden, wanted the group to play the lead role in conflict zones where Muslims were suffering.[2]

Al-Qaida arose out of the Afghan Service Bureau (Maktab-il-Khidamat), an organization established in 1984 by Azzam and bin Laden at the height of the campaign against the Soviet occupation of Afghanistan. From these roots, al-Qaida rank and file benefited directly from an earlier generation of organizational and operational expertise and experience. However, the true strength of al-Qaida is in an ideology of global jihad that appeals to a wide and disparate following in the Muslim world, including a number of Islamist parties and groups. To date, the ideology drawn from historical events, and tested under fire in Afghanistan, Bosnia, Chechnya and Iraq, continues to resonate in the Muslim world. These 'battlegrounds' continue as principal sources of inspiration to the Islamist rank and file directly engaged in the fight. These 'battlegrounds', and the Islamist rhetoric that promotes their existence, appeal to a wide support base that sustains their perceived global aspirations. In addition, the Iranian revolution, the anti-Soviet campaign, the subsequent rise of the Taliban and, more recently, events in Iraq have politicized and radicalized a few hundred thousand Muslims worldwide. The fallout from these campaigns continues to radicalize and mobilize Muslim territorial and migrant communities. Even today, after the total destruction of its training and operational infrastructure in Afghanistan, neither al-Qaida nor other Islamist groups has difficulty in recruitment or replenishment. They have no difficulty in replacing losses of personnel, due to death, injuries or arrests, or replenishing their logistic resources, whether weapons or finances. Al-Qaida and its associated entities have managed to build, in the utmost secrecy, a robust, diffuse and highly resilient organization. It has changed from that of a tightly knit organization with a hierarchical – even bureaucratic – management structure to a loose affiliation of like-minded groups. Bound together by the same ideology espoused by bin Laden and the *éminence grise* of al-Qaida, Dr Ayman al-Zawahiri, the world must now confront a network that is not constrained by national borders. The world is now faced with *terrorisme sans frontières.*

Some five years after 9/11, the 'core al-Qaida' (a group of 3–4,000 members, as estimated in October 2001) is operationally weak. Western security and intelligence services believe that this core group, led by bin Laden, is no longer able to mount '9/11' style attacks on Western soil. Nonetheless, several African, Middle Eastern and Central, South and Southeast Asian groups have adopted al-Qaida-style tactics and technologies. Although the strength of al-Qaida is now limited to a few hundred members , its ideology of global jihad is widespread, inspiring dozens of Islamist groups worldwide.

What has been al-Qaida's single biggest contribution? Al-Qaida has been able to inspire and instigate Islamist groups worldwide to fight at two levels. First, groups have attacked the near or domestic enemy: their own governments. Second, the fight has been taken against the far or distant enemy: the US, its allies and its friends. While refusing to die, the most hunted terrorist group or movement in history continues to fuel a global uprising among extremist elements in the Muslim world. In the post-9/11 strategic era, especially the period after the invasion of Iraq, many new groups have emerged. They are expanding the Islamist space and increasing the threat exponentially. Intent on reducing the terrorist threat, the international community forged and implemented a wide range of security and counter-terrorism measures after 9/11. They offer no permanent solution. Nonetheless, military action in Afghanistan dismantled the safe-haven and training infrastructure of the Islamist terrorists. Stepping up intelligence and law enforcement measures in target countries has reduced the immediate threat (1–2 years). The capabilities of the terrorists have suffered, but their overall intentions and commitment to their interpretation of jihad remain unchanged.

This was clearly demonstrated by the bombings of the morning commuter trains in Madrid on 11 March 2004 and eighteen months later the attacks in central London. After painstakingly identifying the post-9/l11 security architecture, the terrorists found gaps in its armour. They effectively exploited these loopholes and attacked iconic capitals in Western Europe. The terrorists mounted their attacks in countries that were fully supportive of, and participating in, the US-led coalition offensive in Iraq. However, it is important not to overlook the fact that Spain and the UK had both been active and effective supporters of the United Nations' peacekeeping efforts in Bosnia in the early 1990s. Later, as key participants in the NATO-led implementation (I-FOR) and stabilization (S-FOR) forces, they had continued to provide significant troop contributions during Bosnia's post-conflict stabilization period. Spain and the UK have also been major contributors to the process of reconstruction in 'post Taliban' Afghanistan. Spain, in particular, has suffered significant casualties – seventeen Spanish soldiers dying as a result of a helicopter crash in August 2005 near Herat in north-western Afghanistan, and sixty-two killed two years earlier, when one of their trooping flights crashed in Turkey.

As a result of the intervention in Afghanistan by the US-led coalition, al-Qaida and its associates have been dispersed from their core base there and in Pakistan. They have spread into lawless zones around the world: Iraq, in particular its border areas with Iran and Syria; Somalia, a conflict of international neglect; Yemen, where only 35 per cent of the country is under government control; Kashmir, a conflict zone involving India; the Myanmar–Bangladesh border; the southern Philippines; and other areas in conflict. Al-Qaida is using bases in these areas to launch attacks against the US and/or its allies. The sustained efforts of those nations that take a more robust and pro-active stance on counter-terrorism has led to a substantial number of key al-Qaida 'commanders' being killed or captured. One of the most significant of these was Khalid Sheikh Muhammad (or KSM as he is often referred to 'in the trade'), the head of the al-Qaida military committee, who was captured in Pakistan by the Inter-Services Intelligence on 1 March 2003. In his place, two leaders emerged. One of these, Faraj al-Libi (Libby), the coordinator of domestic operations, was arrested in Pakistan in May 2005. The other, Hamzah al-Rabiyyah, the coordinator for external operations, was killed in the Afghanistan/Pakistan border areas by Pakistan security forces in December 2005. Despite his death a new 'operations chief' will emerge. It is highly likely that he already existed, ready to take over, or has done so by now.

Over the years several commanders have emerged in South and Southeast Asia, the Arabian Gulf, North Africa, the Horn of Africa, the Levant, the Caucasus and other regions. Some of them have already been killed or captured. Others are alive and continue to organize or engage in attacks against their proclaimed enemies. For instance, Isamuddin Riduan, alias Hambali, was captured by the Thai Special Branch II in Central Thailand on 11 August 2003. Khalid Ali Abu Ali-Haj, alias Hazim al-Sh'ir, a senior leader, was killed by Saudi security forces in Saudi Arabia on 15 March 2004. But Fazul Abdullah Muhammad, alias Haroon, the Chief of East Africa operations, remains at large. Just as infantry squares in the Napoleonic wars closed ranks, filling the gaps caused by shot, shell and musketry fire, so too does al-Qaida, rapidly replacing losses of its key commanders. Of greater importance was the emergence of Abu Musab al-Zarqawi as the de facto commander of operations of a network of groups in Iraq associated with the al-Qaida movement.

After 9/11, and more specifically the US-led invasion and subsequent occupation of Iraq, Ahmad Fadil Nazal al-Khalayleh, alias Abu Musab al-Zarqawi, a Jordanian from Zarka, imposed himself as a rising figure in the network. A particular milestone in his rise to international prominence was the gruesome beheading of Nick Berg. But he had the blood on his hands of many other hundreds of people in Iraq and beyond. In Iraq he appeared to take delight in the daily slaughter, not just of members of the coalition forces, but of Kurds, Shia and even Sunnis. Although his main base was in Iraq, the tentacles of the network he built extend deeply into the Middle East and well into Europe and North America. Given the extent of the networks he was able to assemble after 9/11, he was considered as the de facto operational chief for the al-Qaida movement until his death in Bakuba in June 2006. Despite his differences with Usama bin Laden over the targeting of Shia Muslims, al-Zarqawi managed to absorb numerous Islamist support networks or transform them into operational ones.

Al-Zarqawi, a veteran of the anti-Soviet multinational Afghan jihad, was unknown in the 1980s. He came to the attention, internationally, of intelligence and security services in the late 1990s after he started to work with al-Qaida. From 1992 to 1997, while in jail in Jordan, he was indoctrinated by Abu Muhammad Maqdisi. Although they did not meet, this process continued between al-Zarqawi and Abu Qatada, the religious leader of al-Tawhid, by communicating through Maqdisi. Between 1997 and 1999 al-Zarqawi planned to overthrow the regime in Jordan and conduct operations against Israel.

Countering Terrorism

Like some three dozen other Islamist groups, that of al-Zarqawi also received funds and support from al-Qaida to train Jordanians and Palestinians. Recruits from these two nationalities had not previously featured prominently in relation to al-Qaida.

Al-Zarqawi became an important operational leader within al-Tawhid, which had cells in a number of European countries, including Great Britain and Germany. Through these cells, links were established with Ansar al-Islam in Iraq and with several other groups in the region and beyond. For instance, a cell connected to al-Zarqawi, operating in the Pankisi valley in Georgia, provided training for both Chechens and North Africans with the intention of conducting chemical and biological attacks in Russia, France and the UK.[3] As part of the preparation for attacks on targets in Europe and beyond, training and experiments in building chemical and biological weapons were also conducted in the Khurmal chemical plant and training camp. This was situated in the Halabja district of Suleimaniyeh province in Kurdish Iraq, an area controlled by Ansar al-Islam.[4] In addition to Iraq, al-Zarqawi either absorbed or began to influence several other networks in Europe. As such, the Salafist jihad networks influenced and/or controlled by al-Zarqawi became one of the most serious terrorist threats to the European continent and beyond to North America. Due to excessive focus by governments worldwide on the core elements of al-Qaida, other groups have emerged, including the Islamic Group of the Moroccan Combatants (GICM) and the Libyan Islamic Fighters Group (LIFG). More recently, new networks that had been led by Zarqawi, such as Tawhid Wal Jihad (known as 'al-Qaida of the Two Rivers' or 'al-Qaida in Mesopotamia'), have come into prominence.

THE NEW FACE OF AL-QAIDA

In waging global jihad, al-Qaida has a specific role. Larger than life, it seeks to promote a clash of civilizations between the West and Islam. As the proclaimed vanguard of the Islamic movements, al-Qaida's intermittent attacks on symbolic, strategic and high-profile targets are intended to inspire and incite the Islamists and the wider Muslim community to enter into perpetual conflict with the West. Having attacked America's most iconic targets on 9/11 it had achieved its aim. Both the strikes by al-Qaida and the US reaction and response mobilized dozens of violent Islamist extremist groups into periodically attacking US interests, its allies and its friends. While the period before September 2001 witnessed an average of one attack every year by al-Qaida, the post-9/11 environment witnessed an attack by it or one of the groups associated with it once every three months. With 9/11, both the frequency and the scale of the threat posed by terrorist groups changed dramatically. Before, terrorism was perceived as a public nuisance and a law-and-order problem. After al-Qaida attacked New York's landmark World Trade Center for the second time, along with the Pentagon, terrorism became a national security issue. Due to the potential for mass destruction and mass disruption, terrorism remains on the national agendas or at least on the political agendas of those countries that consider themselves most threatened. In order of priority, most national security agencies in the industrialized groups of nations place terrorism first, followed by organized crime and then proliferation.

Although most governments and a significant proportion of the international media continue to focus on al-Qaida as a formed group, the real terrorist threat has moved to the al-Qaida network or movement. Since 9/11 few terrorist attacks have been conducted by al-Qaida. Instead they are carried out by its associates: such groups as Jemmah Islamiyah, Ansar al-Islami, Tawhid wal Jihad (an al-Zarqawi group), Le Groupe Salafiste pour la Predition et le Combat (GSPC), Abu Sayyaf Group, Special Purpose Islamic Regiment, Islamic International Brigade, Riyudes-Salikhin Reconnaissance and Sabotage Battalion of Chechen Martyrs, Lashkar-e-Toiba and Jaish-e-Muhammad have all been active in various attacks. Many of these groups were ideologized, armed, trained and financed by al-Qaida and also by the Taliban in Afghanistan. In other conflict zones the required support throughout the 1990s came from al-Qaida. Although al-Qaida per se has lost operational control of many of the groups it assisted when Afghanistan was a terrorist Disneyland (February 1989 to October 2001), these Islamist associates still utilize the ideological and logistics infrastructure built by al-Qaida during the last decade.

In addition to their strengthened intention and capabilities to attack the West, the violent Islamists are determined to target some of the Middle Eastern regimes they perceive as un-Islamic. The Islamist extremist movement is becoming stronger in Saudi Arabia and Yemen, two countries that have produced the largest number of al-Qaida members. On average, before 9/11 Saudi Arabia witnessed one terrorist attack each year. Since the US invasion of Iraq in March 2003, the country has witnessed a terrorist encounter or attack every month.

Although there are marked differences in ideology and strategy between the disparate Islamist groups, many of them feed off each other, and more importantly, learn from one another. To create a civil war within Iraq, al-Zarqawi wanted to target the Shia Muslims, even though Usama bin Laden has always campaigned for an inclusive rather than an exclusive policy. Nonetheless, al-Qaida and especially its leader Bin Laden are still held in respect and awe by many Muslims who have been with al-Zarqawi. Faraj Ahmad Najmuddin (alias Saleh Krekar, alias Abu Sayed Fateh, alias Fateh Krekar, alias Mullah Krekar), the founder of al-Ansar al-Islam, currently living in Norway, said in 2000 that bin Laden represented the crown of the Islamic nation. Ansar al-Islam was established by the merger of Jund al-Islam ('Soldiers of Islam') and the Islamic Unity Movement, a faction of the Islamic Movement of Iraq, based in Kurdistan.[5]

Similarly, the late Ibn al-Khattab, the long-time commander of the Islamic International Brigade in Chechnya, described Usama bin Laden as 'one of the major scholars of jihad, as well as being a main, worldwide commander of the *mujāhidīn*'. He added:

> the West, and the rest of the world, are accusing Usama bin Laden of being the primary sponsor and organizer of what they call 'international terrorism' today. But as far as we are concerned, he is our brother in Islam. He is someone with knowledge and a *mujahid* fighting with his wealth and his self for the sake of Allah. He is a sincere brother and he is completely opposite to what the disbelievers are accusing him of. We know that he is well established with the *mujāhidīn* in Afghanistan and other places in the world. What the Americans are saying is not true. However, it is an obligation for all Muslims to help each other in order to promote the religion of Islam . . . He fought for many years against the communists and is now engaged in a war against American imperialism.[6]

The penetration of local and regional conflicts by transnational Islamist groups such as those of al-Zarqawi and Jemmah Islamiyah have given the domestic groups new capabilities and increased the staying power of the transnational groups. Until recently, many in the West perceived the conflict in Chechnya not as an Islamist but as a separatist campaign. To date, many Western governments have permitted Chechen groups to disseminate propaganda, raise funds and procure supplies on Western soil. Similarly, Kashmir, Algeria, Mindanao (the Philippines), Iraq and other conflict zones have been effectively penetrated by al-Qaida and other transnational terrorist entities. Little did governments realize that these conflict zones would be used by the Islamists to compensate partially for the loss of Afghanistan!

Today, it is often difficult to separate many of the regional conflicts, rooted as they are in local political, religious or ethnic grievances, from the global jihad. Local areas of conflict from Kashmir to the Philippines, from Yemen to Somalia, Algeria and beyond have been, and continue to be, exploited by al-Qaida and its associated groups. It was the ideology of al-Qaida that influenced the Southeast Asian groups to attack not only their government forces, administrative and civilian infrastructures, but also the US interests in the area and those of its allies. After al-Qaida provided them with training, funding and ideological support, some of these groups took to behaving like al-Qaida itself: Ma Salamat Kasthari, for example, the Singapore leader of Jemmah Islamiyah (JI), planned to hijack an Aeroflot aircraft from Bangkok in Thailand and crash it onto Changi International Airport in Singapore. This is just one example of a typical al-Qaida tactic being adopted by a group active in the Southeast Asian region.

Many locally based Islamist groups never even considered mass casualty or suicide attacks as a tactic against Western targets until they came into contact with al-Qaida. As a direct result of its influence, Islamist groups across the globe are becoming more violent: in some instances they are becoming as violent as mainstream al-Qaida. Usama bin Laden has built an organization that functions both operationally and ideologically at every level, be it local, national, regional or global. Defeating al-Qaida and its associated groups tactically will be a major challenge for the international security and intelligence community and for law enforcement authorities. The global fight against Islamist extremism and terrorism will be the defining conflict of the early twenty-first century.

The asymmetric threat posed by transnational terrorism will also be a major challenge for military forces and will engage a range of other actors, especially politicians and religious leaders, for a very long time to come. To terrorize Western governments, their societies and their friends in the Muslim world, violent-minded fundamentalist ideologues such as Abu Qatada al-Filastini, Abu Hamza al-Masri, Abu Muhammad al-Masri, Safar al-Hawali and Salman al-Ouda have recruited and generated support from among territorial and migrant Muslim communities worldwide.

Even after troops of the US-led coalition destroyed its training and operational infrastructure in Afghanistan, the new al-Qaida movement continues to pose an unprecedented terrorist threat to international peace and security. Although bin Laden is likely to be killed or die of illness, he has crafted and popularized an ideology that continues to inspire, motivate and incite his followers to oppose the 'enemies of Islam'. The significant military response from members of the international community during the first two-and half years after 9/11 failed to reduce the threat. In fact, the terrorist threat has increased several times over since those defining moments in modern history.

The response of governments and societies to the threat that evolved after 9/11 has done little to reduce the contemporary wave of terrorism. Rather, it will gather momentum. Since there is no standard textbook for tackling this threat, the international community should maximize its successes and minimize its failures. Not only has combating transnational terrorism become a national security priority, it now transcends national boundaries and has become an important collaborative necessity. It requires a comprehensive versus a single-pronged response: a shared not a unilateral response.

AL-QAIDA ADAPTS

Many security and intelligence agencies worldwide were somewhat surprised that al-Qaida survived after the US-led intervention in Afghanistan. Similarly, al-Qaida itself did not anticipate that the US would go as far as putting ground troops into Afghanistan. Since then core al-Qaida has suffered severe and significant disruption, albeit to varying degrees. Dispersal of its members before and after 9/11, however, has enabled the organization to survive. By taking advantage of its traditional and well-established links with other Islamist groups it has modified its modus operandi. Before 9/11, al-Qaida had conducted an average of one attack every two years. Since then, al-Qaida and its associated groups – that should now be redefined as the 'al-Qaida movement' – have mounted an attack on average every three months. The successes of the US-led global campaign in disrupting the al-Qaida network have also dispersed its operatives. Organizers, operatives, financiers and other key individuals of the movement who had been based in Afghanistan and Pakistan have moved out to lawless zones in Asia, the Horn of Africa, the Middle East and the Caucasus. To compensate for the loss of its training and operational infrastructure in Afghanistan, al-Qaida has sought to establish new bases in Yemen, the Philippines, the disputed regions of Kashmir, even Chechnya and Georgia. Subsequently, it became the turn of Somalia and Sudan in East Africa.

The threat to global peace and security caused by the extensive dispersal and diffusion of al-Qaida members has increased dramatically. This is a consequence of the US-led coalition's intervention in Afghanistan and even more of the US invasion of Iraq. The implications of these actions do not appear to have been fully anticipated by the US administration, despite warnings emanating from areas of expert knowledge and individuals inside US government departments with a better understanding of the psyche involved. The situation in Iraq deteriorated rapidly after the invasion and the half-hearted cooperation of some Muslim governments has only encouraged the terrorist. As a result, the Islamists have become more brazen and their attacks more violent. For sure, Washington's decision to intervene in Iraq, rather than reducing the threat from transnational terrorism, has made the global security environment more complicated, more dangerous and more widespread.

Having performed its vanguard role, successfully mounting a series of coordinated operations against iconic US targets, a hunted al-Qaida has turned to investing in an ideological role, using the internet and the media. As a result of this sustained propaganda, several groups not operationally linked to al-Qaida have taken to following the al-Qaida model. These groups, even though they have not benefited from al-Qaida money, training or weapons, have been inspired and motivated to the extent that they conform to its ideology and are affiliated to the movement. The Madrid bombing in March 2004 was not conducted by al-Qaida or an associated group but by an ideologically linked affiliated cell. While Western governments have tended to invest their resources in fighting al-Qaida per se, the centre of gravity has shifted towards its associated and affiliated groups, posing varying scales of threat in different regions. As has been the case time and time again, there are no hard and fast rules with regard to the ideology and the behaviour it inspires. Furthermore, since the London attacks Usama bin Laden and his deputy Ayman al-Zawahiri have wasted no opportunities to infer their support for the actions of the extremists and to warn of more to come. They have demonstrated a similar desire to remain 'in the frame' with regard to terrorist activity in Iraq, especially when al-Zarqawi was, rightly or wrongly, the main beneficiary of the media attention and the ensuing publicity. As more information has come to light concerning the London attacks of July 2005, some connections to al-Qaida are being claimed.

GLOBAL PHENOMENON

In contrast to the success of the US-led coalition in Afghanistan after the attacks of 11 September 2001, which gravely weakened al-Qaida, the US intervention in Iraq has facilitated the growth of existing Islamist political parties and terrorist groups and the emergence of new ones. The resurgence of the Taliban, Hizb-i-Islami and al-Qaida in Afghanistan has magnified the threat. The resistance of secular Saddam Hussein loyalists and Tawhid wal Jihad, an al-Qaida associate group, means that violence will continue for some considerable time. Al-Qaida and its associate groups are aggressively harnessing resentment among Muslims living in the West and elsewhere. In Iraq's immediate region and beyond, the growing anger directed towards the USA and its partners has provided Islamist groups with the opportunity to exercise greater influence among Muslim communities. This resentment was heightened by the 'Danish cartoons' affair, which erupted across large tracts of the Muslim world in January/February 2006.[7] Tragically, this situation, which will be discussed later, was blown out of all proportion, partly by some elements in the media and also by Islamist extremists who were provided with a theme they could readily exploit to their own violent ends.

Unprecedented security, intelligence and law enforcement cooperation, however, heightened public vigilance and an aggressive hunt for al–Qaida and cells associated with the movement has so far prevented terrorists from mounting another large-scale operation on Western soil. Although the capabilities of terrorist groups to attack the USA, Western Europe and Australasia have suffered, the intention to mount an attack within those areas has not diminished. The double suicide bombings in Istanbul in November 2003, the March 2004 carnage in Madrid and the suicide attacks in London in July 2005 are grim reminders that terrorists can strike despite comprehensive security measures. The targets from which terrorists can choose are too numerous for them all to be protected. As terrorists, determined to survive and succeed, continue to adapt to the hostile security environment that has developed since 9/11, they are proving adept at identifying loopholes in Western security architectures. Harnessing this capability enables them to exploit the gaps and breach security measures.

The frequency of attacks in the Middle East, the Horn of Africa and across the Asian continent will continue, but as the terrorists aim for greater impact they will attempt to kill, maim and injure more people. To achieve this, they will continue to attack economic, religious and population targets using the tactic of coordinated simultaneous suicide operations. Sustained global action against al-Qaida will further force the mother group into the background. This will empower its associate groups and affiliated cells to come to the fore. Consequently, intelligence and law enforcement agencies will find it more difficult to monitor and respond to a larger number of Islamist 'target' groups. The US intervention in Iraq has weakened the resolve of Muslim leaders and their governments and publics to fight terrorism. The failure of the international community to provide more grants and aid to Afghanistan and Pakistan ensures the support for extremist ideologies and the survival of the al–Qaida ideological leadership. Furthermore, Iran is likely to develop into a safe zone for al–Qaida unless the West strengthens the hand of the moderates over the hardliners in Tehran. Since the election of President Mahmoud Ahmadinejad and the defiant response of Iran to international reactions to its intention to enrich uranium – for peaceful purposes – supporting the moderates and expecting a regime to emerge that is friendlier to the West is likely to prove much more difficult.

Islamist terrorist groups from Asia, the Middle East, the Horn of Africa and the Caucasus will conduct the bulk of the terrorist attacks, most of which will be conducted in Muslim countries against targets symbolic of the USA and its partners. Due to the increased protection of US facilities abroad likely to be terrorist targets, and the enhancement by governments of the security of military and diplomatic targets, the terrorists are shifting their attention to allies and friends of the USA. The terrorists are concentrating on 'soft' targets, such as hotels and banks, religious gatherings and places of worship, centres of population and tourist resorts. A prime example of the latter was the attack that focused on Australian tourists in Bali on 12 October 2002. Another example was the bombing of tourist targets in the Red Sea resort of Sharm el-Sheikh on 23 July 2005.[8] In such cases one cannot overlook the terrorists' aims of also damaging the local economies of the peoples concerned. In the main, the tendency will be towards suicide attacks. These will be either vehicle-borne or by individuals wearing improvised explosive devices – both hallmarks of al-Qaida and certain other Islamist terrorist groups, such as Hamas. The result will be mass casualties, including the deaths of Muslims. Nonetheless, despite the collateral damage, Islamist groups will find sufficient support to continue the fight against the USA and its allies.

As the London attacks in July 2005 led by Mohammed Siddique Khan demonstrated, the movement is still capable of operating in the style of 'classic' al-Qaida. Nonetheless, due to the sustained pressure and focus on the movement, bin Laden's immediate group will be able to conduct far fewer attacks. But, come to think of it, with what they have set in-train globally, do they need to expose themselves to those seeking to bring them to justice or to promote their medieval notion of an Islamic caliphate? Al-Qaida is likely, primarily, to remain in the background inspiring, inciting and, occasionally, coordinating attacks. Meanwhile, the number of groups trained, armed, financed and indoctrinated by al-Qaida will grow and become the greater threat. In particular, associated entities such as Tawhid Wal Jihad in Iraq; Le Groupe Salafiste pour la Prédition et le Combat (GSPC) in Algeria and elsewhere; the Libyan Islamic Fighters Group; the Pakistan-based Lashkar-e-Toiba and Jaish-e-Mohammed; Chechen Islamist groups in Russia; Hizb-i-Islami, the Islamic Movement of the Taliban; and Jemaah Islamiyah in Southeast Asia will conduct al-Qaida-style attacks as well as conducting more 'conventional' guerilla-style operations.

Al-Qaida and its most active associates are predominantly concentrated in four specific geographical areas: Iraq and its border regions; Yemen and the Horn of Africa; the Afghan–Pakistan border areas; and the Indonesian and Philippine archipelagos. Since the US-led action in Afghanistan in October 2001, the threat posed by al-Qaida and the evolving movement has become diffused and much more global.

Iraq: Like Afghanistan during the Soviet occupation, Iraq became a magnet, as well as a lightning rod, for politicized and radicalized Muslims worldwide. Islamists have declared Iraq the 'new land of jihad'. In the short term, the scale and intensity of fighting there will increase because of the flow of budding *mujāhidīn* into Iraq through Iran, Syria and Saudi Arabia; collaboration between foreign *mujāhidīn* and Iraqi Islamists; and increased support from angry Muslims worldwide. Add to all these ingredients the tacit and active sanctuary and covert support from Iraq's neighbours and the theatre is assured the dangerous cocktail of terrorist activity with which it has become synonymous.

Unless Western and Islamic governments invest more resources and personnel, the situation in Iraq will deteriorate even further. The situation there is already producing the current and, in all probability, the next generation of *mujāhidīn*. Western security services are concerned about the number of 'fighters' returning from Iraq particularly, but not only, to countries in Europe. The same trend that was observed during and after the anti-Soviet and Taliban campaigns is being repeated. Currently, the bulk of the foreign *mujāhidīn* in Iraq has originated from the Middle East and the Levant. As time passed youths from North Africa and the Gulf, the Horn of Africa and the Caucasus have entered the Iraqi 'battleground'. They have been joined by young European Muslims, by Europeans converted to Islam and by Asian Muslims. The year 2005 even saw a young Belgian female suicide bomber die in an attack against a US military convoy. In 2004 and 2005 they have exported their deadly craft to attack targets in the neighbouring Hashemite Kingdom of Jordan.

Yemen and Africa: Al-Qaida has developed significant infrastructure in the Horn of Africa, including Somalia, and is using the region as a base to launch operations in the Gulf and in Africa. Several hundred al-Qaida members in Yemen move back and forth to

East Africa, developing the Horn as a sanctuary. In the coming years, East African Islamist groups influenced by al-Qaida will increasingly participate in international terrorism. Meanwhile, sub-Saharan Africa will remain the 'Achilles heel' for Western security and intelligence agencies. The defeat of a coalition of secular warlords in Somalia by the Islamist 'Council of Islamic Courts' and its assumption of power in the capital, Mogadishu, in June 2006 could be the grounding of another extremist state. Despite initial denials on the part of its leaders, there are concerns internationally that this group is likely to be sympathetic towards al-Qaida and its supporters. Concerns within the international community that the Council for Islamic Courts could develop into a 'Taliban look-alike' were given some credibility when, on Tuesday, 4 July 2006, Islamist militiamen forcibly prevented a large group of Somalis from watching a World Cup soccer semi-final in a cinema in the town of Dusa Mareb, killing the cinema owner and a young girl in the process.[9] Dusa Mareb is, according to the Reuters report, 'the home area of the Islamists' hardline leader Sheikh Hassan Dahir Aweys'.

Afghanistan: In the period between the Soviet withdrawal in February 1989 and the US intervention in October 2001, Afghanistan was a terrorist haven. Al-Qaida, the Taliban and other Islamist groups trained tens of thousands of *mujāhidīn*. Although nearly 600 members of al-Qaida and their associates who fled to Pakistan have been arrested, the reservoir of trained *mujāhidīn* is huge. Many remain concentrated in the Afghan–Pakistan border area. Hizb-i-Islami, the Taliban and al-Qaida are using Pakistan's Northwest Frontier Province (NWFP) as a launch pad for conducting operations into Afghanistan, making Pakistan one of the most pivotal states in the global effort to combat transnational terrorism.

Pakistan: As President Pervez Musharraf continues to target members of al-Qaida and the Taliban in his country, support for Islamist ideals and opposition to his regime has grown. To prevent an Islamist government taking power, sustained Western assistance to President Musharraf and his government, improved Pakistan–Afghanistan relations and an international resolution of the Indo–Pakistan dispute over Kashmir are all essential.

Indonesia: While existing Islamist groups have grown stronger, several new ones have emerged in Indonesia. After democracy returned to Indonesia in 1998, the Islamists are exploiting the political space to grow. Of the 14,500 Islamic schools, some 200 preach violent jihad and 40 have produced terrorists. Some of the graduates travel to Mindanao, in the Philippines, where terrorist training camps are still active. In its camps, the Moro Islamic Liberation Front (MILF) trains fighters not only for their own Muslim separatist cause, but also individuals intending to join the Abu Sayyaf terrorist group. However, unless Indonesia's political leadership and the national elite develop a robust legal framework to combat terrorism and extremism, violence will grow and spill over to the rest of Southeast Asia.

Iran: Hardliners in Iran have advocated support for the anti-US insurgency in Iraq. Many al-Qaida leaders and members moved to Iran or Pakistan in late 2001 and early 2002. Western intelligence sources claim that several hundred al-Qaida operatives, led by Saif al-Adel and Saad bin Laden, are located in Iran. Although Iranian moderates have called for tougher action against al-Qaida, the duality of Iran's response to it is likely to continue. Defining Iran as 'evil', the US Administration has done little, if anything, to assist the efforts of the West in combating terrorism. In addition, the US has not helped moderate elements in that country. The stance being taken by Iran's ultra-hardline and ultra-conservative President Mahmoud Ahmadinejad, elected in late 2005, is likely only to compound the situation for the foreseeable future.

THE ROAD AHEAD

The fight against al-Qaida and its associated groups, as spearheaded by the USA, has met with partial successes and some failures. To succeed, it is paramount that the USA maintains a robust anti-terrorism coalition, particularly with the support of Middle Eastern and Asian Muslim governments. By resolving the Israeli-Palestinian dispute and by investing in public diplomacy (as opposed to government-to-government relations), the USA must seek to change its image from that of an aggressor to that of a friend in the Muslim world.

The first four years of combating terrorism after 9/11 demonstrated that no one country or a Western coalition can manage the threat with which we are now faced. The effectiveness of the fight against al-Qaida and its associated groups is strictly dependent on long-term international cooperation, coordination and collaboration. As the threat posed by transnational terrorism has 'globally

Countering Terrorism

matured', an organization is now needed to challenge and neutralize it. Such an organization will require a worldwide reach if it is to be effective in countering evolving Islamist extremism and the networked terrorism it invokes.

While governments can share intelligence and conduct operations against terrorist groups planning and preparing attacks, the community of nations must think of ways to address the problem, strategically. International organizations, particularly the United Nations, should reflect upon its own successes and failures in countering terrorism. To defeat the contemporary wave of terrorism and Islamist extremism, the United Nations must seek to build capabilities and the capacities that individual governments are incapable of, or are unwilling to seed, nurture and sustain. The United Nations must look beyond just the operational response necessary to counter terrorism. The organization needs to develop a strategic framework for reducing and eventually eradicating the threat. But in order to start this process the organization, whose credibility has been severely undermined by US unilateralism in recent times, will need to demonstrate greater political cohesion. As will be discussed later, such an approach is constantly subject to national interests. Nonetheless, that has to be the ultimate aim. Before the United Nations as the body corporate, however, can start to tackle this difficult and complex subject, its members as a whole have to appreciate the threat fully. This understanding has to transcend national borders. It is not enough to know to what extent the threat affects any individual state, but its impact on neighbouring states, regionally and further afield, must also be fully understood.

2

To Know and Understand One's Enemy

In military circles, a well-established and widely acknowledged principle is the need 'to know one's enemy'.[1] But knowledge of one's enemy is not enough. In the context of today's asymmetric threat from transnational terrorism, *understanding* the enemy is even more important. In fact, understanding the enemy is probably now more important than knowing it. Knowledge and understanding are keys to being able to counter the enemy successfully and eventually eradicating the threat. In meeting the challenge militarily of conventional or unconventional threats, one must develop a robust knowledge and understanding of the intentions, capabilities and the opportunities for attack from our adversaries. These requirements are equally applicable and important when ascribed to how countries tackle terrorism. Several months after 9/11 the US government did not know the mastermind behind the suicide attacks that obliterated the World Trade Center, America's most iconic landmark, and damaged the Pentagon, the heart of US military power. If it had not been for a group of courageous passengers, there was also an intended suicide strike on the US Congress as it sat in session that morning in September 2001.

The US Government was not shadowing the threat groups closely enough. Consequently, the US was faced with a strategic surprise from its adversaries. Immediately after 9/11, a great deal needed to be found out about those involved in the attacks and the individuals behind them. The initial investigations indicated links between Mohammed Atta's group and locations and individuals in Europe, the Middle East, South and Southeast Asia. Gradually, al-Qaida and its associated groups became the principal target of many governments worldwide. 9/11 itself had a catalytic effect. Governments began to

extend their observation and surveillance of politicized and radicalized segments of their Muslim communities. As a result of increased
alertness, a Singaporean Muslim provided information in October
2001 that led to the detection of a terrorist network in Southeast Asia
and Australia with links to al-Qaida. In December 2001 thirteen
members of Jemmah Islamiyah were arrested in Singapore while
planning to blow up the diplomatic missions of Australia, Israel and
the United Kingdom, along with a number of commercial targets,
using 21 tonnes of ammonium nitrate.[2]

Meanwhile, the coalition offensive against the Taliban regime
in Afghanistan, which began on 7 October 2001, uncovered more
information emphasizing the extent and global reach of the al-Qaida
network. These new sources provided important leads, some of
which helped foil attacks elsewhere in the world. The discoveries in
Afghanistan, and also in Pakistan, prompted arrests of more al-Qaida
supporters and operatives. Among these sources were documents,
manuals and video material produced by al-Qaida in camps in
Afghanistan and confirming its intent to produce chemical or biological weapons.[3] Piecing together all this information, like a giant jigsaw
puzzle, produced an image of a transnational terrorist network emerging rapidly from what had previously been seen as a tightly structured
organization. The emerging network had an extensive following, with
significant geographic coverage.

In November 2001 the rout of the Taliban regime became a
reality. At the same time the coalition intensified its efforts to catch
Usama bin Laden in the rugged mountainous area of Tora Bora.
Many of the Taliban's al-Qaida supporters and their 'Afghan–Arab'
guests left Afghanistan. A large number made their way out
through Pakistan's Federally Administered Tribal Areas (FATA), and
over time the Pakistani authorities detained more than 700 of these
Afghan–Arabs as they were trying to make good their escape.
Others made their way to Iran, either directly from Afghanistan or
through the western border regions of Baluchistan. Often they
were assisted by heroin and opium smugglers, who knew best how
to avoid the Iranian border guards. Some of the fugitives then
crossed by boat or dhow to make landfall on the Arabian peninsula
or continued north through Iran. Others were apprehended by the
Iranian authorities and eventually handed over to their countries of
origin after protracted diplomatic negotiations. But many, by way of

Turkey, Iraq and other routes, found their way to points further west and elsewhere.

'WHO RUNS AWAY . . . LIVES TO FIGHT ANOTHER DAY!'

Looking back, it was like a bomb-burst – with al-Qaida operatives, supporters and sympathizers dispersing across the globe. They went to countries in Africa, Europe, the Middle East, Central, South and Southeast Asia and even North America, directly or via Canada.[4] Some joined like-minded groups that already existed and had established links to al-Qaida. Others went to ground and formed small cells from which to continue their support for the global jihad called for by bin Laden. Many of these were young people who had gone to Afghanistan, where they had been trained to fight and indoctrinated into the extremist way of thinking in the al-Qaida camps. They had then fought alongside the Taliban, or gone on to fight in the disputed area of Kashmir or with the Chechen rebels in Russia. But others had been selected by key members of the al-Qaida command structure, the *shaura majlis*, for training in more specialist tactics and techniques used by terrorists, such as bomb-making, assassinations and kidnappings. It is these individuals that continue to pose the gravest threat. In the camps that had existed in Afghanistan – in Darunta, Khalden and Herat – members of al-Qaida and its associated groups had experimented with the production of crude forms of chemical and biological weapons. After the loss of these camps some of these al-Qaida 'specialists' went on to continue their crude experiments in Georgia's Pankisi valley and in Iraqi Kurdistan.

Meanwhile, other individuals had been hand-picked to return to countries where they had citizenship, particularly in Europe, with the aim of recruiting young men. These in turn would found a new 'generation' of al-Qaida, both as new members of the network and as the new generation of self-styled 'holy warriors' or jihadists. It is these individuals, in the overall al-Qaida strategy, who are the ones that surface every so often and are identified as being involved in, or connected with, post-9/11 attacks or foiled attempts carried out in the name of jihad.[5]

Despite the many arrests that have taken place around the world since 9/11 and the adverse impact these have had on the operational capabilities of the network, many more followers of al-Qaida still remain at large. Many other individuals, identified with the network more recently, never went to camps in Afghanistan. These are the ones referred to in a report of the United Nations Monitoring Group, overseeing the implementation of sanctions against the Taliban and the al-Qaida network, as a 'third generation al-Qaida, which is becoming self perpetuating'.[6] By 2004–5 al-Qaida-related cells existed in some 60–70 countries around the globe.

One way of looking at this particular phenomenon is to compare the two sets of attacks that took place in Riyadh and Casablanca in May 2003. Most of the suicide bombers connected with the attacks in Riyadh had been trained in camps and/or fought in Afghanistan. After their return to Saudi Arabia they had been able to move around freely in local society, until coming together to carry out the suicide attacks on three residential compounds, accommodating mostly Westerners, on the night of 12 May.

In the case of the five almost simultaneous suicide attacks in Casablanca on the evening of 16 May 2003, however, none of the attackers was believed to have been to Afghanistan. Some were exposed to al-Qaida ideology and ideologues, from whom they had received indoctrination and, possibly, some instruction. The suicide bombers all came from the same rundown, deprived area of Thomas, situated in a part of Casablanca known as Sidi Moumen, and were members of a previously little-known group called the Salafia Jihadia. A more detailed examination of these two terrorist operations highlights the problems clearly connected with knowing and understanding one's enemy that impact on national efforts to combat the phenomenon of transnational Islamic terrorism. If the threat is not clearly understood nationally, this in turn will be reflected in the international response to the terrorists. Unfortunately, the word 'al-Qaida' is bandied about too often and too readily when terrorist events arise. The media use it sometimes to good effect, but sometimes as the 'all-encompassing bad guys', thus clouding the issue. In such circumstances it becomes an emotive definition of the threat to which politicians and governments are particularly sensitive. Consequently, many governments prefer to distance themselves from 'al-Qaida' per se. This is an important point that will be discussed later, but, in short, it results in governments preferring not to recognize the presence of the network, or elements of it, within their borders. In so doing the countries concerned tend to ignore the reality of the threat and how, over time, it might develop. There are states, even in Europe, in which transnational Islamist terrorists and their support cells, whether or not they are connected to al-Qaida, are able to exist without too much oversight from law enforcement or security services. When questioned on the presence of such cells or their individual membership, the official response is that they are not causing any problems to the state in which they reside and are therefore not perceived as a threat. True, the threat may well not be to that state. The reality is, however, that with the excellent freedom of movement that now exists in Europe for citizens within and between the Schengen and Swiss free trade areas and for holders of a visa for these areas, it is very easy for terrorists and their supporters also to move around freely. This borderless way of operating – *terrorisme sans frontières* – has been clearly demonstrated in Europe by a number of events, both before and after September 2001, and now encompasses 'home grown' groups spawned independently by the extremist ideology and radicalization.

One of the first of these events was an attempt by a group of Islamists to bomb the Christmas market in front of the cathedral in Strasbourg in France in December 2000. The five men of Algerian origin suspected of attempting this foiled attack were detained by police in Frankfurt, Germany. As a result of subsequent investigations it appeared that they had links to like-minded extremists in Italy and Great Britain. They were subsequently tried by Frankfurt's higher regional court. Four of the Algerians were convicted on charges of conspiring to commit murder and carry out a bombing and, in March 2003, were given prison sentences ranging from ten to twelve years.[7] Interestingly, the court is reported as having found that the defendants were not directly linked to al-Qaida, despite the fact that on 16 December 2004 a court in France sentenced ten Algerian or Franco-Algerian individuals to varying prison sentences for being involved in the same Strasbourg plot.[8] Two of the group's leaders were given terms of up to ten years, one was given eight years and the fourth, who was already being detained in England at 'Her Majesty's Pleasure', was sentenced *in absentia* to six years in prison in France. The remaining six were given shorter sentences for providing logistics support for the would-be perpetrators, primarily with respect to furnishing false documents. This is a common factor that surfaces regularly when cells are discovered and investigated.

Meanwhile, in January 2003 officers from a number of police forces in the United Kingdom, in a coordinated anti-terrorism operation, raided premises in north London and other cities and arrested a number of individuals. In the course of this operation, the police mistakenly believed that they had recovered equipment for making the deadly agent ricin in one of the apartments raided. These raids in the United Kingdom followed the arrest in the Paris suburb of Courneuve of four terrorist suspects, one of whom, a Franco-Algerian, was also allegedly connected with the Frankfurt cell accused of the attempted bombing of the Strasbourg Christmas market. These two cases highlight the dispersal of these like-minded individuals and how they are able to link up freely as they plan and prepare to commit their murderous and senseless atrocities. While these are just two examples of cells that have been discovered and disrupted in Europe, both before and after 9/11, there are many more around, as well as examples of ongoing operations that have been successful in thwarting the terrorists and their sympathizers.

Subsequent anti-terrorist operations in Germany, Italy and Spain disrupted cells that were recruiting would-be suicide bombers to go to Iraq to fight with the 'insurgents' – terrorists by another name – against the US coalition and its Iraqi government, army and police allies. On 12 January 2005, in a major operation involving around 700 police officers from a number of Germany's *Länder* (states) and officials from the Office for the Protection of the Constitution (*Verfassungsschutz*), some 57 apartments were raided in and around the cities of Bonn, Düsseldorf, Frankfurt, Freiburg, Ulm and Neu-Ulm. Eleven of the twenty-two people initially detained were eventually kept in custody. According to initial reports, some of those arrested had ties to Ansar al-Islam and al-Tawhid, and allegedly they had been recruiting individuals to go to Iraq to fight against the US and its allies.[9] They like to refer to it as their jihad or 'holy war', but there is nothing 'holy' about blowing up men, women and children who are trying to carry on a normal life. In reality, attacking such soft and innocent targets only emphasizes the cowardice of the terrorists.

Two weeks later the authorities in Germany arrested two more individuals on grounds of supporting al-Qaida-related terrorist activities. One was suspected of attempting to acquire 48 grams of enriched uranium, while the other, Mohammed 'K', was arrested on charges related to a life insurance scam. During the latter part of 2004 he had married a German woman. He then approached ten insurance companies with a view to taking out low-value life insurance policies, clearly in the hopes of not attracting too much attention. In the end only five of the companies responded positively to his enquiries, yet the total value of the policies on redemption was in excess of €800,000, a contemporary equivalent in excess of $1.13 million. It was the intention of Mohammed 'κ' to travel to Egypt, where he would buy a dead body, fake a fatal car accident and, with the aid of a corrupt official, have his death certified. His relations in Germany would then collect on the policies, a significant proportion of which was to be handed over to other representatives of the terrorist support organization. Mohammed 'κ', meanwhile, was to have headed off to Iraq to undertake his jihad, carrying out a suicide bomb attack for one of the groups of 'foreign fighters'.

POST–SADDAM PERIOD

Until the invasion of Iraq by the US-led coalition in 2003, governments worldwide, including Islamic governments, had tended to cooperate with the US and its European allies in their responses to terrorism. Since Muslims perceived the US invasion as unjust, the US occupation of Iraq had a markedly negative impact on the international efforts intended to counter transnational terrorism, particularly the brand associated with al-Qaida. Many states, not just Islamic ones, had expressed their concerns about an invasion of Iraq for some considerable time during the run-up to the actual event. Many people with knowledge of al-Qaida and a feeling for how the intentions of the United States of America are perceived throughout the Muslim world warned that an invasion, with or without the legitimacy of a UN Security Council resolution, was likely to trigger an adverse reaction from members of the al-Qaida network and their sympathizers. What form such a reaction might take was not necessarily clear at the time, a status that also applied to any attempt at forecasting the eventual outcome of events in Iraq following an invasion.

The fact that the people of Iraq and the world are better off without Saddam Hussein and his barbaric, evil and sadistic regime is not in question. To what extent the blood-letting, carnage and totally unnecessary loss of life could have been avoided, particularly among the Iraqi population, is another question altogether. The enthusiasm demonstrated by such a large number of Shiites and Kurds at being able to cast their votes on 30 January 2005 cannot be underestimated, however 'free and fair' some might describe the elections. The message of even more Iraqis was 'loud and clear' when they voted for their first government in December 2005. Even the Sunnis, who had for the most part boycotted the earlier election, were persuaded to go to the polls. Again, there were some complaints of electoral fraud, but even these cries of 'foul', especially when compared to the standards that have been observed in recent years in other fledgling democracies, could not diminish the long-term political significance of the event for the Iraqi people. Some said at the time that achieving Iraq's first proper election was worth the sacrifice. Few lasting democracies have been achieved without civil conflict, and often bloody and violent ones at that. But however legitimate or otherwise the actual US-led invasion, if certain basic military principles that have stood the test of time had been followed, then there is every chance that the loss of life and the sacrifices made on all sides might have been considerably less.

There are those who would argue that giving Hans Blix and his United Nations Monitoring, Verification and Inspection Commission (UNMOVIK) teams and the International Atomic Energy Agency (IAEA) inspectors more time to prove the presence or not of weapons of mass destruction (WMD) should have been the correct path to follow. Even if this path had prolonged the start date of any offensive, the penalty the delay might have imposed would have been outweighed by the legitimization for the subsequent invasion that could more easily have been achieved. But the results of such an UNMOVIK inspection, providing it did not allow itself to be compromised by Saddam or find itself unable to proceed because of Iraqi intransigence, would have made it much more difficult for the 'antis' to argue against more deliberate action. Instead, with the inspection process incomplete and hence inconclusive, the doors were wide open, for governments, populations and, by all accounts, the members of the UN Security Council, to have been deceived as to the truth. After Saddam had been toppled, the Iraqi Survey Group (ISG) – the coalition's own inspectors – sought in vain to find the illusive WMD. In the end David Kay, the leader of the ISG, could only say when briefing the Senate Armed Services Committee, 'We were almost *all* wrong!'[10] Who exactly he was speaking for when he said 'all' is not exactly clear, when there were such diverse views and scepticism on this subject in the first place. Nonetheless, he did qualify his statement by indicating that they had come across many instances of activities that were prohibited under the appropriate UN resolutions and that had not been reported, as required, under UN resolution 1441 (2002). But the findings of the US Commission into the role of the intelligence community in the run-up to this Iraq War were singularly unambiguous. At the press conference on 29 March 2005,[11] in advance of the report being released, the Commission said that the intelligence was 'dead wrong'.[12] Similarly, attempts to prove a connection between Usama bin Laden and Saddam Hussein have met with an equal lack of success. The report of the US '9/11' Commission refers to a memo from the office of Richard Clark, the US National Counter-terrorism Coordinator at the time (September 2001), which concluded 'that only some anecdotal evidence linked Iraq to Al-Qaida . . . The memo found no "compelling case" that Iraq had either planned or perpetrated the [11 September] attacks'.[13]

Many, many people still feel that more time should have been spent on finding a diplomatic solution – one that would have forged a much broader 'consensus of the willing' to achieve the necessary regime change. There are few who could argue against the necessity to remove such a sadistic and cruel dictator as Saddam Hussein. He had served the needs of America and some of her allies in trying to topple the Ayatollahs in the Iran–Iraq War of 1982–5. His annexation of Kuwait in 1990, however, and his arrogance and repressive treatment of so many Iraqis, despite losing the first Gulf War in 1991, should have been beyond international tolerance. If greater support for such a venture had been won from within the international community before it was put in train, then it might have been possible to manage it with greater consent, wider participation and in a less destructive manner. It might also have set the precedent for dealing with other unpopular cruel regimes, for example in Central Asia. Finding a diplomatically acceptable solution would have taken much longer to accomplish. The urgency for the invasion taking place when it did was based very much on the flawed threat of the presence of WMD and the possibility that the Iraqi regime would provide such weapons to terrorist groups. However, one cannot overlook the desire to have any ground offensive completed and a new democratic government installed in Iraq in good time before the US presidential election of 2004. But once again one needs to look at what had been taking place for the previous twelve years.

Countering Terrorism

SANCTIONS END

Iraq was ostensibly subject to sanctions, which would be lifted only with the confirmation that Saddam had destroyed all stocks of chemical and biological weapons, as well as dismantling any programmes for their development and those for nuclear or radiological weapons. But clearly, as investigations into the UN 'Oil-for-Food' programme found, the sanctions were being violated on a daily basis. It was no secret that more than 200,000 barrels of oil were being pumped through a pipeline to Syria. Oil was knowingly being smuggled into Jordan to avoid that country's economic collapse. Nor was it possible to hide the kilometre-long tailbacks of Kurdish tankers at Iraq's borders with Turkey, waiting to transport oil from the north of Iraq. Despite all these violations being public knowledge, there appears to have been no political will to bring the situation under control. If anything it was the opposite. The question is, who was supposed to be monitoring the sanctions, as opposed to overseeing the administration of the programme intended to relieve the suffering of the Iraqi people? In a world where conspiracy theories abound, one might come to the conclusion that another reason for the United States and the United Kingdom to proceed with the invasion, despite the vehement opposition from France, Russia and Germany, and others in the Security Council, was to end the sanctions regime. There have been suggestions that these latter three countries, or persons within them, were all benefiting from the violation of the Iraq sanctions, while the US and the UK were having to pay for maintenance of the 'deny flight' operations over Iraqi airspace. Invading Iraq would kill two birds with one stone – namely, close down the sanctions from which Saddam and some others, but not the majority of his own people, appeared to be benefiting and bring an end to an expensive counter air operation. It is to be hoped that time will tell! In this modern day and age it is important that the truth be told: the whole truth and nothing but the truth.

GOODWILL ENDS

If the Bush administration had expended more time on good diplomacy in order to win a consensus to implement the desired regime change, then the US, and to some extent the UK, would not have squandered all the post-9/11 goodwill that existed in the international community towards combating transnational terrorism. Use, throughout this book, of the phrase 'war on terror' has purposely been avoided. Terror is a tactic. One does not wage war against a tactic. But prior to the US and the UK, along with the 'coalition of the willing', deciding to 'go it alone' in Iraq, there was significant support throughout the international community for the so-called 'war on terror', even if most countries were at odds with the term. There was support, even though that support varied from country to country, for the requirements laid down in UN resolution 1373, the over-arching counter-terrorism resolution, and those resolutions requiring the implementation of sanctions measures against al-Qaida, the Taliban and their associates. However, once the invasion became a fact, many of those states, particularly those known to have difficulties implementing the resolutions, now had a custom-made excuse for withdrawing or diluting whatever support might have been forthcoming. Certainly the members of the UN's Monitoring Group on sanctions against al-Qaida, the Taliban and their associates sensed a cooling of attitudes in a number of states visited during 2003 when compared with their reception during the previous year. The work of this group and its contribution to the international response to the al-Qaida network is discussed in detail later in this book. Suffice it to say that in some of the Arab countries visited there appeared to be no concern that, due to incomplete implementation of the called-for measures, they were likely to feature by name in the Group's next report to the Security Council. Then there was the conduct of the war itself and the impact this has had on confronting transnational terrorism, despite the threat it poses to global peace and security.

It is very easy to be critical after the event or at a long range from it. For servicemen and women committed to a war by their government, there is nothing worse than hearing about the course of the war and what one might expect to happen next from a string of 'armchair generals'. These erudite military experts are trotted out by television channels, vying for viewers and improved ratings, on their early morning and evening news programmes. Despite the interesting information and analysis they impart, some are too inclined to say too much, thus providing the 'enemy' of the day with useful intelligence of the 'possible intent' of 'friendly forces'. However, there are some very basic principles of war that have stood the test of time, but do not appear to have been followed. As a result we have witnessed disastrous results that with better and more comprehensive planning and a much greater understanding of the 'enemy' could have been avoided.

GROUND PRESENCE

No matter how proficient armed forces are with all the latest 'high-tech' communications, surveillance and weapons systems, when it comes to occupying a country there is no substitute for 'boots-on-the-ground'. It is crucial, especially in the early stages of such a conflict, to be able to dominate 'vital ground' – a military term, the definition of which, in an asymmetric context, has more than mere topographical connotations. This was as true for the 'invasion' of Iraq in 2003 as it had been for so many military campaigns down the ages. In Iraq, even if the population had been as welcoming as the coalition would have liked and was led to believe it would be, and given a standing army the size of Saddam's, it and its weapons and munitions dumps would have to be secured. That takes troops and lots of them. The next point is that if you want to have the structures of government and security working reasonably well as soon as possible after the 'war fighting' is concluded, then you don't disperse the 'defeated army' by sending them all home. It makes much more sense to keep them in their barracks, retaining them in 'formed bodies' with their command structure in place and giving them gainful employment. By giving them a purpose in life they are able to retain, or, if lost, rapidly regain their self esteem. This is an important aspect of the Arab psyche that was tragically misunderstood. The Iraqi armed forces were not all members of the Ba'ath Party, just as not all the officers and soldiers in Germany's Wehrmacht in the Second World War were Nazis.[14] As it happened, even some of the latter were called upon to fill positions in Germany's post-war armed forces, when they were eventually re-formed in 1955 as the Bundeswehr.

In addition to establishing some measure of control over such a significant source of manpower, there would be long-term dividends from keeping much of its command structure in place. By including them in the immediate post-conflict stabilization and reconstruction phases, they would have been much less inclined to the insurgency that they founded and have supported. Also, securing the many weapons storage sites around the country would have made the task of the Iraq Survey Group just a little bit easier and would have reduced the availability of weapons and explosives to terrorist groups. After all, the fear, verging on paranoia, of weapons falling into the hands of terrorists had, we were all told, been one of the compelling reasons for invading Iraq sooner rather than later. In the light of such facts, it would not seem unreasonable or illogical to have expected the invasion plans to have included such a contingency being given a very high priority. As well as securing the oil fields and other elements of critical infrastructure, the allocation of 'troops to tasks' is, once again, a basic principle of sound operational military planning. In fairness to all concerned, the extent and the ferocity of the looting that took place in the immediate aftermath of the regime's demise could not necessarily have been foreseen: but for there not to have been an effective police force in the country in the immediate aftermath of the invasion should have been anticipated. Therefore, large numbers of military police units should have been included in the order of battle. These should have been close behind the advancing 'war fighting' elements, ready and positioned to establish law and order rapidly and to start working with whatever police were still around, at least until it was clear as to how and when the civil structures were to be re-established. Close on their heels, ready 'in the wings', should have been civilian police – advisers and trainers – ready to assist in the immediate post-conflict stabilization phase. Concurrent with the civilian police specialists, there should have been other specialist post-conflict reconstruction experts and civil engineering (CE) resources. These reconstruction and stabilization elements should have had the capability, even if only locally, of repairing, maintaining and running the basic life-support utilities for the civilian populations, such as electricity, water and sewage. Coalition support for the other basic human needs such as petrol, diesel, paraffin and bottled gas, and a significant medical capability, should also have been 'factored-in' to the planning processes.

The reaction from dissident elements in Iraq, so soon after the invasion, should not have come as such a great surprise. If there had been a better understanding of the in-country situation at the time and, more to the point, a detailed knowledge of the tribal/political dispositions, then it should have been possible for the situation to have been managed better than it was. Armed with this knowledge, the lack of links between Saddam's regime in Iraq and al-Qaida might have been more apparent. Even if the information, in the absence of sound, irrefutable intelligence available in the run-up to the invasion, with respect to the situation on the ground had been better, preparations could have been in place to deal with a negative response from the local population. Whether this response was triggered or instigated by terrorists or 'insurgent elements' is immaterial. The planning prior to the invasion should have taken these possibilities into account and the required troops to contain such eventualities factored in to the force deployment. This approach would have given the ground commanders greater flexibility and the means to respond appropriately.

As many of the coalition's junior commanders and soldiers have found, the reality of dealing with such an unpredictable, ruthless and elusive enemy is far removed from all the preparations and training to which they had been subjected. Tragically, the transnational terrorists were able to exploit the situation from very early on in the campaign. Listening to all the reports coming out of Iraq, the definition of those hostile elements, with which the coalition troops and the newly formed Iraqi security forces have been engaged, has varied considerably. It has included such terms as insurgents, militants, Sunni Ba'athists and common criminals (both angry at their loss of power and/or status), Islamic extremists and 'foreign fighters', linked or not to al-Qaida. No matter how people would like to describe them, for whatever ethnic, political or religious reasons, they are terrorists – common-or-garden terrorists – and should therefore, first and foremost, be treated as such: nothing more and nothing less. The fact that it may be politically convenient to use the word 'insurgent', in case the need arises to negotiate with them, is a false premise. Being dogmatic about not negotiating or conferring with terrorists is an extremely short-sighted approach to a complex problem, but failing to categorize correctly those who resort to terror for political ends sends the wrong message and only prolongs the deadly campaign.

NEW BATTLEGROUND

Contrary to statements from one or two leading politicians, just because Saddam Hussein is under lock and key, the invasion of Iraq has not made the world a safer place, even though 'hope flares eternal' for the people of Iraq and their future. Instead, we have seen a violent upsurge in terrorist activity in the country. A serious and significant fallout from the occupation of Iraq has been the establishment of a new battleground for jihad for the followers of al-Qaida and other like-minded Islamic extremists. Besides the insecurity and carnage to which they have contributed, there has been a trend for some of the 'foreign fighters' to head back to their countries of origin. The same had happened after the fall of the Taliban in Afghanistan: as then, a recent cadre of seasoned and battle-hardened Islamists has left Iraq and returned home or to other countries. Once there, the likely intention is to continue attacks on their governments and/or societies not to their liking. The ranks of the al-Qaida group in Saudi Arabia, believed to be responsible for the suicide attacks of May and November 2003 and the attacks in Yanbu, Khobar and Riyadh, have been swelled by Saudi 'militants' returning from Iraq. In Iraq they are credited with, or claim to have been, fighting coalition forces – hence reference on some al-Qaida-related websites to the 'Fallujah Squadron' or 'Fallujah brigade'. The cynical attacks in Istanbul, Madrid and London were also a direct consequence of the invasion of Iraq.[15]

On 15 November 2003 suicide bombers detonated vehicle-borne improvised explosive devices (VBIED) outside the Beth Israel and Neve Shalom synagogues in Istanbul, killing 25 and wounding 303, most of whom were Turks, and causing extensive damage to the local area. Then five days later, on 20 November, two more explosions shattered the working day, one outside the Istanbul headquarters of the Hongkong and Shanghai Banking Corporation (HSBC), a British international bank, and the other outside Her Britannic Majesty's Consulate-General. In all there were 26 fatalities, including the British Consul-General, and 456 injured, plus significant damage to the local economy. It is widely believed that these were not the original targets. When first planned, the Turkish-based group responsible wanted to hit US bases in Turkey, but when they saw the extent of the defences, they opted for softer targets. However, because of the locations of the targets chosen, the terrorists ended up killing and maiming a very large number of Turkish citizens, many of whom were Muslims. The Turkish authorities moved quickly and arrested a number of individuals trained and directed by al-Qaida.

On 11 March 2004 a group of terrorists, all of whom were Muslims, bombed four commuter trains during Madrid's morning rush hour, killing 191 and wounding around 1,800. Although a direct connection to the Iraq-based groups or to al-Qaida has still to be proven, the attacks did contribute towards Spain's ruling People's Party losing the general election a few days later, letting in the Socialist Party. The latter, speaking for the vast majority of the Spanish people who were against the war in Iraq, promptly withdrew the Spanish contingent from Iraq. This unfortunate move set a trend and prompted an upsurge in the intensity of the terrorists' attacks against coalition forces in Iraq. But the response of the Spanish electorate was a reflection of the feelings of vast numbers within the populations of most European states and in many countries worldwide. The invasion of Iraq and the reasons given for it have severely damaged the credibility of many of the pro-invasion political leaders.

3

Iraq: A Strategic Defeat?

as the United States of America suffered a strategic defeat in Iraq? Will American forces eventually be forced to withdraw due to mounting fatalities and injuries and political and civil pressures back home? There are also significant pressures from Iraqi circles, especially from within the new legislature, as well as both Sunni and extremist Shia factions. The Bush administration has been at pains to emphasize that they are in for the long haul. But if the US leaves too soon, will the Islamist extremists – insurgents and/or terrorists – claim that just as they had defeated the might of the Soviet Union in Afghanistan, so too did they defeat the Americans in Iraq? The global jihad movement is bound to interpret a US withdrawal as a defeat. Just as Soviet troops withdrew from Afghanistan after a protracted conflict lasting a decade, US troops are likely to withdraw within half that time. In the same way that bin Laden spoke of the US 'running away' from Beirut, Lebanon (1983), from Aden, Yemen (1992), and from Mogadishu, Somalia (1993), ideologues of jihad will take delight in citing the 'defeat of the superpower' in the wake of heavy US fatalities and casualties in Iraq.

America's strategy is to raise a new Iraqi army and security apparatus concurrently with the development of a 'democratic' form of government, and then withdraw from Iraq. The US-led coalition strategy to raise a new Iraqi army has been partially successful, if agonizingly slow. The new Iraqi army lacks sufficient motivation, appropriate firepower and the required leadership to combat the various terrorist groups. As the Iraqi army grows and becomes militarily more capable, the intention is for US troops to assume, more and more, a supporting role. The Iraqi forces should and will slowly take the lead. As the roles reverse, without the sophisticated equipment, training and discipline of the US army, the question is: will the Iraqi army perform any better against the terrorists and insurgents? Every day, with more training and experience, the Iraqi security forces are improving. However, every day the terrorists develop new tactics and measures to counter the coalition counter-measures. On some days there have been up to 300 incidents. The Iraqi terrorists are constantly learning new tactics, developing more sophisticated methods of attack and gaining combat experience. If Iraq's new government is to survive, the US military will have to maintain a significant proportion of its 150,000 troops in Iraq for a considerable time in the future. Moves to reduce ground troops, as has been intimated, replacing them with an increasing use of airpower, could prove in the long term to be counterproductive. Despite their effect on the perceived 'enemy', 500-pound bombs and their collateral effects are not really the best way to win hearts and minds; however appealing such a course of action might be to politicians and some military commanders, it will have serious repercussions on the ground. No matter the accuracy of some of today's so-called precision weapons, guidance or delivery failures occur – often with appalling consequences. There are always going to be significant errors in targeting, in particular human errors. There have been numerous examples of such errors during both the current Afghan and Iraq campaigns. Then there is the political and ideological fallout from the collateral damage that all too often occurs. Both play into the hands of the extremists. They provide them with lurid propaganda, severely damaging coalition efforts to win the hearts and minds of moderate Muslim majorities, not just in Afghanistan and Iraq, but around the world.

'INSURGENTS' ARE 'TERRORISTS'!

After the US invasion of Iraq on 20 March 2003 the global security environment changed dramatically. No sooner had President George W. Bush, from the aircraft carrier USS *Abraham Lincoln*, declared an end to 'major combat operations in Iraq' on 1 May 2003, than attacks against troops of the US-led coalition began increasing rapidly.[1] The general deterioration of security in Iraq, especially after the killing of Saddam's sons Uday and Qusay in Mosul on 22 July 2003, was compounded by a significant increase in what has been referred to, euphemistically, as insurgency activity. The insurgency or, in reality, the terrorist activity was made possible by two factors. First, the US government disbanded the Iraqi military. As a result, several thousand experienced military personnel were 'footloose and fancy free' to form or join an insurgency in Iraq. The bulk of the insurgent leaders were former regime loyalists. Second, Saddam's last act was to release several tens of thousands of criminals from Iraqi jails. These criminal elements merged with the former regime loyalists to fight the US-led coalition troops and the new government in Iraq, albeit for slightly differing reasons.

Free from the oppressive regime and authoritarian regime of Saddam Hussein, it was relatively easy for these various elements to undertake terrorist attacks against the US-led coalition forces. This explosive mix was soon augmented by an influx of foreign jihadists, predominantly from other Arab countries, who saw this as an ideal opportunity to attack the 'occupiers' of Muslim lands. Although the foreign fighters or terrorists make up less than 1 per cent of the insurgent strength, they are the most influential. As the vanguards of the campaign, the foreign terrorists conduct highly publicized kidnappings and beheadings, assassinations of government officials, an average of one car bombing each day, and frequent suicide attacks against police recruits, police stations and other targets.

Iraq has been transformed into a new 'Land of *Jihād*'. A manmade conflict, Iraq presents a strategic threat. Iraqi Ba'athists, Fedayeen and other armed elements, indigenous and foreign, opposed to the 'occupation' and the efforts to develop a more democratic and politically stable Iraq, have sufficient individual motivation and support to sustain an insurgency of guerrilla and terrorist actions that could last for several years. When the insurgency began it was dominated by indigenous Iraqi elements and only a small percentage of attacks were attributed to Islamist extremists. Increasingly the complexion of the conflict changed. The dominance and roles of these components became reversed. Even some of the secular Ba'athists tended to be influenced, if not driven, by the very notion of jihad. But the situation is compounded by extremist Shia militias, loyal to Moqtadr al-Sadr, that are also involved in the internal power struggle and are supported by elements in Iran.

Has Iraq deflected terrorist attacks directed against the United States? Are the opportunities to fight the US in Iraq a magnet for Islamist terrorists? The US leaders and government spokespersons

Countering Terrorism

argue that Iraq is a magnet for 'jihadists'. Bush apologists argue that it is better to kill them in Iraq rather than suffer from terrorism in the USA and in other parts of the world. Instead, the very invasion of Iraq has created the conditions for the sustenance of existing groups and the emergence of new ones. Iraq is both a magnet and a lightning rod for the terrorists. Rather than dissuade potential jihadists from becoming involved in terrorism, the prosecution of the 'war on terror' in Iraq has had the opposite effect, particularly with respect to Afghanistan and the Taliban.

TALIBAN RESURGENCE

In late 2002, even before the invasion of Iraq, there were numerous reports that young Muslims were heading into the Afghan-Pakistan border area. They went there to join remnants of the former Taliban and al-Qaida fighters who were opposed to the presence of the coalition forces in Afghanistan. The coalition forces were hunting Usama bin Laden, Mullah Omar, Taliban fighters and 'Afghan-Arabs' still at large in the area. Reliable sources indicated the presence, once again, of training camps, though not like those of the pre-9/11 era, which were well established and often quite substantial in size. The new camps were small and very temporary. They were designed to be used for only a short period of time and to train a handful of recruits, making them less conspicuous to the various means of overhead surveillance.[2] Despite the numerous reports of such facilities in November and December 2002, their significance was initially played down by one or two prominent figures. Nonetheless, the frequency of attacks increased throughout 2003, and in October US Special Envoy to Afghanistan Zalmay Khalilzad reportedly warned that resurgent Taliban and al-Qaida forces were presenting a serious threat to Afghani reconstruction efforts.[3]

The resurgence of the Taliban in the summer of 2003 should therefore have come as no surprise. There have been some notable successes on the part of both US-led troops in Afghanistan and of the Pakistani army and security forces operating in the Federal Administered Tribal Areas (FATA). However, with so much attention and specialist resources diverted to the 'Iraqi Front' these 'new-Taliban' were able to make their presence felt and they have continued to be a thorn in the side of the Afghan peace process. Their activities

have severely hampered the post-conflict reconstruction and stabilization efforts of the UN and the International Stabilization Assistance
Force (ISAF). Their attacks had a serious and adverse effect on the
efforts of humanitarian non-governmental organizations (NGOs) to
deliver aid and the registration process for Afghanistan's first government and presidential elections. Nonetheless, despite the difficulties,
when the time came, the Afghan people defied the threats and attempts
by the 'bandits' to derail the elections, turning out in large numbers
across the country to try their hand at 'democracy in the making' –
albeit an Afghan style of democracy. However, although this was a
defeat for the Taliban and other Islamist extremists in Afghanistan,
Usama bin Laden and his deputy Ayman al-Zawahiri remain at large.
Unfortunately, the 'new-Taliban' has continued to make its presence
felt and to tie down significant numbers of NATO troops as well as
restricting much of their movement within the country.

Events in Iraq, taken together with the increased insecurity in
many parts of Afghanistan, may well have contributed to the early
shortfall in troop contributions from members of NATO, despite the
promises made after NATO assumed command of the International
Stabilization Assistance Force (ISAF). In retrospect the idea behind
ISAF was somewhat inconsistent with the task that had to be accom-
plished. At the time of the Bonn/Petersburg Conference in November
2001, considering the situation that had to be handled, one could
perhaps have appreciated the concerns of many likely contributing
nations. Afghans have a history of reacting violently to the occupation of their lands by foreign troops. Many had tried, the British
included, and all had suffered defeats on varying scales, the last only a
decade before with the departure of the Soviet forces and the end of
the Soviet Union itself. But 'faint heart never won fair lady!' and this
time the situation was different. The majority of the Afghan people
was singularly weary of years of war, combined with droughts and
famine. Apart perhaps from those in the 'Pashtun-belt', in the southern and eastern parts of Afghanistan, most Afghans objected to the
austere and extremist style of living that had been the hallmark of the
Taliban regime trying to run the country. This time the international
community had to demonstrate that it was there to support the people
of Afghanistan, with their transition to a peaceful coexistence of
the various tribes, without being held to ransom by the warlords or the
remnants of the Taliban.

Countering Terrorism

Given the long-term nature of the problem, it would have been better to have put a much larger force into Afghanistan. The implementation of the Dayton Accord in Bosnia by NATO in December 1995 provided a useful template from which to work – adapting lessons well learned, where appropriate, to this new set of circumstances. Notwithstanding the logistics involved, it would have been better in the long run to deploy a massive amount of troops on the ground, up-front in all the main population centres; units able to respond decisively if attacked, but also with a strong 'hearts and minds' capability.

Such units should have been capable of fanning out from the main centres (sometimes described as the 'ink stain' process). Using this methodology a working rapport could quite quickly be established with the local tribes and peoples. The deployment of a force of this magnitude would have needed to be sensitive to the independent way of thinking of the Afghans. Instead of just securing the capital, units should have been deployed as simultaneously as logistics allowed, to secure and operate out of Herat, Jelalabad, Kandahar, Kunduz and Mazar-e-Sharif. It was right to secure the capital, but the country as a whole needed to see and feel the presence of a new security environment. The logistics to achieve such a plan as this, especially while the country was still shrouded in winter, would have been a massive undertaking, especially when compared with the original IFOR deployment into Bosnia.[4] But in the long term the dividends would have been greater. Many of those who have been on the ground in Afghanistan tell of the wishes of the majority of Afghans who want to lead a normal, peaceful existence. Due to deteriorating security, even Médecins Sans Frontières (MSF) announced that it was ceasing operations in Afghanistan after having been present in the country, despite the difficulties under which they had had to work, for more than twenty years. Afghanistan was where the so-called 'war on terrorism' needed to be fought. Notwithstanding all the anticipated difficulties, there should have been an initial 'concentration of force' to facilitate the rapid transition to a secure environment in which civil governance could develop, albeit in a form appropriate to the Afghan peoples' heritage. Instead, with campaigns now being fought on two fronts, the effort in Afghanistan became secondary to Iraq, which was sucking up military resources to deal with first the invasion and then a rapidly escalating insurgency and attacks by Islamist terrorists. Meanwhile, the Taliban have continued to strengthen themselves, as well as, drawing on the al-Qaida experiences from Iraq, update their capabilities. The net result was that the UK, supported by Australia, Canada, Estonia and the Netherlands, was obliged to deploy a force of around 4,000 troops into southern Afghanistan's Helmand province. Because the province, a major opium-producing area, had for the most part been left to its own devices, the arrival of such a significant force was seen by the Taliban as a significant challenge to them and the drug barons. The reaction to the deployment by the British-led NATO force was quick and violent. It was akin to poking a stick in a hornets' nest. In a very short space of time a number of British soldiers had been killed as a result of Taliban attacks. The NATO response was equally uncompromising, with significant numbers of the Taliban being killed in the ensuing operations and firefights. The aim of the British-led force is to bring security and reconstruction to the province, but it is difficult to start winning over 'hearts and minds' when there is so much hostility being generated within the communities by the Taliban and their terror tactics. The British-led force, which took-up NATO operations in southern Afghanistan in the summer of 2006, experienced fierce resistance from the Taliban. This had not been anticipated. The British Commander described the fighting as 'extremely intense'.[5] But subsequent results indicated that the Taliban had suffered severe set-backs and that perhaps this time, the Afghani people might see a new future, rather than the 'war lords', who themselves were reluctant to lose their significant income from another bumper opium crop. Only time will tell.

ANSAR AL-ISLAM

Prior to the US invasion of Iraq, Islamist extremist groups maintained a presence in northeast Iraq. A large Islamist group, Ansar al-Islam, a breakaway faction of the Islamic Movement of Kurdistan (IMK), was ideologically close to al-Qaida. It was formed after Saddam attacked the Kurds in Halabja in March 1988. Ansar al-Islam, an associate group of al-Qaida, was opposed to Saddam, a secular dictator who had killed several thousand Kurds. When making the case to the UN Security Council in February 2003 for approval to invade Iraq, Colin Powell, then US Secretary of State, referred to the presence in Iraq of Ansar al-Islam. However, the US Government's knowledge and understanding of both IMK and Ansar al-Islam were weak. Both these groups were opposed to Saddam and were not in any way supported by him. About 600 Arabs and Kurds, many of whom had arrived from Afghanistan via Iran after the fall of the Taliban regime, sought refuge with Ansar al-Islam. Early into the invasion of Iraq, the area controlled by Ansar al-Islam was attacked by a combined force of US Special Forces and Kurdish *peshmerga* militia.

> In one of the most dramatic yet least known operations of OIF (Operation Iraq Freedom), the coalition opened a division-sized ground attack against AI (Ansar al-Islam) consisting of Kurdish *peshmerga* led by US Army Special Forces on 28 March 2003, following a preliminary attack with 64 Tomahawk Land Attack Missiles (TLAMs) and air strikes against suspected terrorist locations. Six columns of 1000 *peshmerga* each advanced along six separate axes of attack. Each column had Special Forces soldiers alongside the column commander and spread through his subordinate units. Four thousand additional *peshmerga* secured the flanks or waited in reserve. The columns advanced rapidly, forcing the AI fighters to retreat by aggressive ground maneuver and close air support. Unable to fight an effective delaying action against the coalition force, AI found itself in an all out retreat to survive. The second day of the operation witnessed the defeat of AI and the escape of its leaders into Iran as coalition forces moved forward, attacking Iranian border guards assisting the fleeing terrorists. The success of Operation Viking Hammer yielded several positive effects for the coalition. First, the operation defeated one of the largest terrorist groups in the world. Second, the operation increased the credibility of the Special Forces soldiers with the *peshmerga* after the Kurds witnessed US firepower in action in the form of cruise missiles and close air support platforms. Next, the raid upon the terrorist complex provided the *peshmerga* with confidence in their fighting ability, adding immeasurably to their morale. Finally, the operation against AI freed up an estimated 10,000 *peshmerga*, who now eagerly joined the Special Forces soldiers moving south to the Green Line for disruption operations against Iraqi forces postured on the Green Line.[6]

Much of the group's sanctuary in this remote corner of Iraq was destroyed, but many escaped and established their presence elsewhere in the Iran-Iraq border areas. One key al-Qaida figure associated and operating with this group was Ahmad Fadil Nazal al-Khalayleh or, as he became more universally known, Abu Musab al-Zarqawi. He took his alias 'al-Zarqawi' from his birthplace, the Jordanian town of Zarqa. Before 9/11 he had established his own terrorist training facility in northwest Afghanistan, near the ancient town of Herat. Herat's natural connection is towards Iran, one of the main trading routes from the town crossing the border near Dogharun en route to the northern Iranian Shia shrine city of Mashhad. There are suggestions that al-Zarqawi had set up his own camp, so far from the rest of the then 'mainstream' Taliban- and al-Qaida-linked facilities in southern and eastern Afghanistan, because he and Usama bin Laden did not see eye-to-eye on a number of issues. He is believed to have been injured in Afghanistan during the coalition offensive that caused the collapse of the Taliban regime and there were rumours at the time that, as a result of his injuries, he underwent surgery to his left leg in a Baghdad hospital. Both the US and the British intelligence communities firmly believed that Saddam was hosting al-Zarqawi, and his presence in a Baghdad hospital was quoted by some as proof of the extremely thin connection between the Iraqi regime and al-Qaida. At the time, elements within the US administration were looking for any shred of evidence that might confirm this link in order to substantiate the necessity for the invasion.[7] The intelligence and assessment were flawed. The Western intelligence community was also of the view that al-Zarqawi had his injured leg amputated while in Baghdad. This piece of information also proved eventually to be fictitious.

Al-Zarqawi proved to be an extremely implacable, ruthless and elusive foe for the coalition and its allies. He and his group, 'al-Qaida in Mesopotamia' or 'al-Qaida of the Two Rivers',[8] which evolved out of al-Tawhid, claimed responsibility for a great deal of the carnage in Iraq. The horrific reality is that everything these terrorists stand for and the atrocities they perpetrate are unbelievably callous, inexorably inhumane and totally medieval. Al-Zarqawi was credited with masterminding the suicide bombing of the UN's Canal Hotel Headquarters on 19 August 2003, in which 22 people were killed, including the UN Secretary-General's Special Representative, Sergio de Mello. It has also been claimed that he was behind the well-coordinated, but unsuccessful, attack on the Abu Ghraib prison near Baghdad at dusk on 4 April 2005. Al-Zarqawi was, reportedly, always very hardline in his approach and this has been clearly demonstrated by the ferocity of the terrorist attacks against not only the coalition 'forces of occupation', but against Iraqi men, women and children. Collateral damage that includes fellow Muslims or their being target-ed directly had no impact on his conscience or that of his followers. The depths of his fanatical vision of the world and aggression towards it encompassed not only 'Crusaders and Jews' and Shia who are not 'true believers', but Sunnis who want to see progress. This may not be the case with Jaish Ansar al-Sunnah ('The Army of the Defenders of the Traditions of the Prophet Mohammed'), a splinter group from Ansar al-Islam formed in September 2003, which con-centrates on military and government targets. Although there were past occasions when Usama bin Laden distanced himself from groups that undertook such atrocities, hence his severing ties with the Algerian GIA, this time, in a taped message broadcast by al-Jazeera Television in December 2004, he allegedly gave his blessing to al-Zarqawi and the actions of his group. In the tape he reportedly referred to al-Zarqawi as al-Qaida's 'emir' in Iraq. It remains to be seen how bin Laden will relate to al-Zarqawi's successor, as and when one becomes a confirmed reality.

ASSESSING THE IMPACT OF IRAQ

Maintaining the status quo in Iraq will mean continuity of the current level of violence. If a significant US presence remains, the conflict in Iraq could continue for many years to come. Except for the US forces fighting the insurgents and the insurgent groups fighting the new Iraqi army and the US-led coalition forces, there will be no new devel-opment. Under the current circumstances, there is no short-term solution to ending the violence in Iraq. However, there are many, both inside and outside Iraq, who suggest that a withdrawal of US and British troops may be the only way of significantly changing the situ-ation on the ground. This will mean Iraqis having rapidly to assume a greater responsibility for their own destiny and may increase, even if for a short period, the blood letting. Although it is still too early to assess the overall impact of the US invasion of Iraq, it is important to identify at least some of its implications.

The most visible and immediate effect is the extent of the death and destruction within Iraq itself. Although some 40,000 Iraqis have died during the first three to four years of the US invasion and occupation, it is hardly a consideration.[9] It is rarely discussed in Washington, DC, or London and references to it in the international press are few and far between. There are no accurate statistics, only estimates of the number of Iraqis injured or maimed and of the property destroyed. Under the current circumstances, these losses are likely to continue. At present, coalition intelligence estimates the number of Iraqi insurgents at 200,000 with another 100,000 active supporters. By the time the conflict in Iraq ends, the death toll could be several times that of the current number of deaths.

There are other losses that cannot be easily quantified. Especially since no WMD were found, the US is being cited as the source of suffering both by the affected Muslims and by many more in other countries. Across the Muslim world, the goodwill that America once enjoyed has been severely eroded. The Iraqi and Muslim anger against the US concerning Iraq will remain for a long time. Although the intentions were otherwise, the invasion and occupation of Iraq have harmed US and other Western interests in the Muslim world, both in the short and long terms. It will require a massive effort on the part of the US and other Western nations to rebuild goodwill, not only in Iraq but in many other Muslim countries and communities within some Western societies.

By the middle of 2006 the number of coalition personnel killed, maimed and injured had passed 20,000. Many of the maimed and injured will never return to active service. For the United States, force protection is always high on the agenda. Despite extensive research and development into their design and operation, improvised explosive devices (IEDs) have been the most effective weapons used against US and British troops in Iraq. In May 2005 alone there were 700 IED attacks. Although it produced only 33 deaths in May and 38 in June 2005, it demonstrated increasing sophistication, a trend that continued. Coalition forces have developed measures to counter the terrorists' (and that includes the so-called insurgents) IEDs, but the latter are constantly updating their systems to counter the countermeasures. In this they have proved to be cunning and innovative. The results have been even deadlier and more effective. Of greater concern are the weapons that have been used since the second half of 2005 against troops in the British area of responsibility (AOR) in southeast Iraq. Allied intelligence sources believed that the design of these devices indicated a connection with elements in Iran and/or Hezbollah. These weapons are proving to be effective even against heavily armoured vehicles. But the sophistication of design, demonstrated by the terrorists, extends well beyond the explosives and the shape of the charges they use. The means and methodology of initiation of the devices have proved extremely challenging for the coalition.

To counter the electronic jamming measures devised by the US to stop the IEDs from detonating, the terrorists used Passive Infra-Red (PIR) targeting systems. With expertise they have accrued within Iraq and from further afield, the terrorists' technical experts have improved the design. These improvised 'upgrades' include the use of shaped charges that concentrate the blast and give it a better chance of penetrating armoured vehicles, along with the electronic counter-countermeasures.[10] With mounting US fatalities and casualties, resulting from an increase in insurgent technologies, tactics and techniques, coupled with changes in public opinion at home towards the utility of the Iraq occupation and elections, US troops may be forced to withdraw from Iraq, or at least effect a rapid drawdown. The US are likely to reduce their strength, once it is considered that training Iraqi forces is having a positive impact on the overall security situation and the latter are proving effective. The newly trained Iraqi forces, however, will have to rely on the US for heavy weapons and close air support for some considerable time to come. Meanwhile, the campaigns being orchestrated by the terrorists and the insurgents are likely to persist. At this point, the US forces are the dominant forces and the Iraqi forces are the support forces. However, at some stage the Iraqi army, police and other forces will have to assume responsibility for their nation's security; this may prove to be a difficult and painful transition. Nor will it be assisted by the tribal pressures on the individual members of the nascent Iraqi security services.

Iraq has become the theatre to which young Muslims travel from many countries to undertake their so-called jihad. Just as the Afghanistan experience was pivotal in producing the previous generations of *mujāhidīn* or aspiring 'holy warriors', the 'Land of the Two Rivers' is the breeding ground for a new generation of Iraq-based terrorist alumni. These extremist elements have penetrated Asia, Europe, the Middle East and North America. Due to the proximity of Iraq to

Europe, the terrorist threat from the ongoing conflict in that theatre will be significant. Three of the four pilots who conducted the 9/11 operation had been recruited while living in Germany. Later, in August 2004, a cell was discovered in Britain, allegedly intent on attacking London's Heathrow Airport and having reconnaissance material on key financial institution targets in America.[11] The UK continues to be aware of the possibility of further attacks: in April 2006 'at least 400 al-Qaeda terrorist suspects – double the previous estimates – are at large in Britain, according to MI5'.[12] In a similar vein, the size and quality of the jihadist networks in Europe will impact on future security in North America. Within the first three years of the terrorist activity in Iraq, more than 300 radicalized Muslims living in Europe have travelled to Iraq and experienced the jihad. Some intelligence services have put the figure much higher. With more than four dozen cradle and convert Muslims from the US and Canada similarly travelling to fight in Iraq, it is only a question of time before foreign and even domestic Iraqi groups extend their influence into North America. Iraq has become the location to which budding *mujāhidīn* are attracted. In Iraq both physical and psychological war fighting are taking place. Just as Afghanistan spawned the first and second generations of Islamist extremist terrorists, Iraq will indubitably prove to be the breeding ground for new generations of battle-hardened international terrorists. The killing of al-Zarqawi is unlikely to make a significant difference, although in the short term, due to the intelligence found in his lair, al-Qaida-related groups in Iraq are likely to suffer severe disruption. But al-Qaida has continually demonstrated remarkable resilience and flexibility and, like the Taliban, may easily recover and continue posing a threat. It is the overall situation in Iraq that will be more defining, coupled with the efforts of the newly elected government. If the latter can deliver and the Iraqi security forces are able to stand on their own two feet there is every possibility that followers of al-Qaida will be looking for a new battleground for their jihad.

MANAGING THE THREAT

The extent of the threat to coalition forces from Muslims travelling from countries in the West to fight and die in Iraq became apparent by 2004. However, governments took little visible action until 2005. At UK airports and other points of exit, officers of MI5, the British security service, and Special Branch met several British Muslims – both British-born and UK-based – who were leaving for Iraq. Since there was no legislation to arrest them, the British officers could only meet them at points of departure and interview them as to where they were going. Only a fraction of the Muslims travelling out of the UK to Iraq, however, came to the prior notice of the authorities. Thus they could not be prevented from participating in guerrilla or terrorist attacks against coalition forces. Although the British had 8,000 troops in theatre, most of them were centred on the area around Basra, Iraq's second city, in the southeast of the country. Although the British have suffered a number of casualties from terrorist attacks, primarily from Shia militias, some most likely supported by hard-line 'conservative' elements from inside Iran, the bulk of the terrorist and guerrilla activity has been in central, northern and western Iraq.

As of 2005, the availability of legislation to prevent European or Canadian Muslims from travelling to Iraq with the intention of fighting and killing coalition forces, or anywhere else for that matter, was somewhat rare. Although the European security and intelligence community was of the view that about 200 European Muslims have gone to fight in Iraq, their governments failed to draft legislation that would effectively address the issue. Initially, the Western services were of the opinion that the foreign fighters would die in Iraq and not return to their own countries of origin or residence. Hence the problem would solve itself. Over time, however, the Western security and intelligence community realized that this was not necessarily the case. Significant numbers of European Muslims were returning from Iraq. In the security atmosphere pertaining after the Madrid bombings ('3/11'), this 'seasonal movement' of Islamist extremists between Europe and Iraq became a matter of grave concern. This 'two-way-traffic' of those going to fight in Iraq and then return to Europe, to share their experience, recruit and raise funds, alarmed Europeans. Most of them were first- and second-generation North African Muslims living in Europe. It also gave rise to concerns in the US that the main terrorist threat to the States was from Europe; these concerns were highlighted by a panel of experts testifying to the US House of Representatives Committee on International Relations on 20 April 2005.[13]

The number of radicalized Muslims in the United Kingdom tends to be quite marked since the most active clerics who supported Usama bin Laden, al-Qaida and the 'global jihad' live there. For instance, nine British Muslims, mostly captured in Afghanistan and Pakistan in 2001 and 2002, were held in detention in Guantanamo Bay. They were eventually released by the US to authorities in the United Kingdom. The post-9/11 statistics are even more alarming. Between 2001 and 2005 about five dozen British Muslims travelled overseas to conduct terrorist attacks.[14] A few of these cases were publicized. One involved Richard Reid, the 'shoe bomber', who attempted to destroy an American Airlines aircraft en route from Paris to the USA in December 2001. Then there was the case of two British Muslims, from families of Pakistani origin, Asif Muhammad Hanif (22) and Omar Khan Sharif (27), who went to Israel in 2003. On 30 April one of them managed to kill himself and three guests and wounded 50 others in a suicide attack on Mike's Bar in Tel Aviv. The body of the other bomber, having failed to detonate his device, was found later in the sea, having apparently drowned while attempting to escape. Their videotaped wills, in English, were posted on 8 March 2004 – almost a year later – by Hamas on the Eiz Adin Al-Qassam Brigade's website. In February 2005 a 40-year-old Muslim, who originated from the United Kingdom and was travelling on a French passport, killed himself in a suicide attack against coalition troops in Iraq. Although evidence of Europeans going to fight in Iraq gained wide publicity in mid-2005, when Spain, France, Germany, the Netherlands and the UK announced the questioning, detaining or arresting of their own nationals in this connection, would-be suicide bombers for Iraq were being recruited in Italy in 2004.[15] On 21 June 2005 the British police raided a rundown house in the northern city of Manchester and arrested a man who was a house-mate of a suicide bomber in Iraq.[16] In October 2005 an Ansar al-Islam cell in Iraq was conceiving a plan to attack the New York subway system. Ansar al-Islam is a group with an extensive presence in Europe, Canada and the US.

However, even when efforts are made, following due process, to clamp down on individuals recruiting fighters or suicide bombers from within Europe to go to fight against the US and its allies in Iraq, cases collapse because of sometimes incorrect or ill-informed judicial interpretations. A classic example was highlighted by the Italian newspaper *Corriere della Sera* on 16 February 2006 with the headline 'Kamikaze contro i marines, non è terrorismo' ('Suicide [attacks] against Marines is not terrorism').[17] The article concerned a Court of Appeal's upholding of an earlier subject verdict by a Milan judge in a case against three members of Ansar al-Islam accused of recruiting volunteers to go to fight against coalition forces (which includes Italian troops) in Iraq. The same day an article was posted on the 'Counterterrorism Blog' by Lorenzo Vidini, describing key elements in the case.[18] The following is an excerpt from Mr Vidini's succinct and to-the-point explanation of the articles on which it was based, not only in *Corriere della Sera* but also from an earlier article in the *New York Times*:

> 'The recruitment of volunteers to fight in Iraq against American soldiers cannot be considered under any point of view a terrorist activity.' These words, which would have been more fitting in the speech of a radical anti-war militant, were the core of the ruling with which a Milan Court of Appeals acquitted three men linked to Ansar al Islam (the motivations of the November 2005 ruling were made public only recently . . .).

As shocking as it might sound, this is nothing new in Italy. The Court of Appeals, in fact, upheld only the first-degree ruling of another Milan-based judge. In January 2005, the Judge decided that the men were indeed part of a network that was recruiting fighters for the Iraqi conflict, but that the operations taking place in Iraq constituted 'guerrilla warfare' and not terrorism. In the Judge's view, 'Ansar al-Islam was structured as an Islamic combatant organization, with a militia trained for guerrilla activities and financed by groups in Europe and orbiting in the sphere of Islamic fundamentalism, without having goals of a terrorist nature, goals probably shared by only some of its members.' Because one of the men on trial, Mohammed Tahir Hammid, conveniently declared that he did not agree with Ansar al-Islam's tactic of using suicide bombers, the Judge considered Ansar al-Islam to be a 'heterogeneous' organization whose members had conflicting opinions on the valid means to use in fighting enemy forces.

Therefore, according to the Judge, Ansar al-Islam could not be considered a terrorist organization as a whole and those who recruit and raise funds for it cannot be considered terrorists. Two men, while found guilty of minor crimes such as document forging, were acquitted of all the charges involving terrorism. The third (who, incidentally, happened to be a close friend of top 9/11 planners Ramzi Binalshibh and Said Bahaji while living in Hamburg) was cleared of all charges and now lives happily in his native Morocco (after the Italian Interior Ministry deported him).

Mr Vidini goes on, quite rightly, to point out that, in making its ruling, the appeal judge overlooked certain fundamental aspects of the case. The first is that Ansar al-Islam has been designated as a terrorist organization by the United Nations, thus calling into question the judge's understanding of Italy's obligations under a Chapter VII resolution of the UN Security Council. Secondly, by giving this ruling, the judge had either been incorrectly advised as to what constitutes terrorist acts and the situation pertaining in Iraq or failed to understand the situation for what it actually is. However, because the coalition forces refer to insurgents, rather than terrorists, the judge might be forgiven for her interpretation. But her ruling also puts Italy at odds with the UN Security Council; her ruling ignores Operative 2 of resolution 1373, which decides that all states shall 'deny safe haven to those who finance, plan, support or commit terrorist acts' and prevent those who undertake any of these activities 'from using their respective territories for those purposes against other states or citizens'. Mr Vidini, in his 'blog', goes on to record the response to the verdict by Franco Frattini, the Security and Justice Commissioner of the European Union, who commented: 'This sends a devastating signal. Fundamentalist Islamic cells can now think that there are safe havens in Europe. The judge has interpreted the law wrongly.' The Frattini statement must have echoed the thoughts of many other politicians and judicial, security and law enforcement officials throughout the European Union who were, and still are, involved in combating terrorism. Not only does it send the wrong message to the terrorists and their supporters, but it undermines the very efforts of the international community at a time when it was working to improve its response by plugging some of the gaps so often and so readily exploited by the terrorists and their supporters.

While there are significant problems, as described above, that need urgently to be addressed, there were also reports of successes. The *New York Times* article, referred to in the Vidini 'blog', dealt primarily with the breaking up of a cell in France.[19] On Monday, 24 January 2005 French police, in a number of raids, arrested eleven individuals in a northeastern suburb of Paris on suspicion of recruiting people to go to Iraq to fight alongside the terrorists. In the article a senior Interior Ministry official is quoted: 'This is a very significant operation that has shut down a ring that was beginning to supply fighters to Iraq.'[20] All nine men arrested (the eleven included two females) were French: eight of North African origin and the ninth a Christian convert to Islam. These events concerning the recruitment in Europe of would-be terrorists for Iraq and the association with Iraq-related terrorist groups are but two examples (out of many) of 'European Muslims' being radicalized by recent events in 'Mesopotamia' and the 'Land of Babylon'.

MATRIX OF TERRORISM

Before Iraq, there was no adequate public support to galvanize and spawn such a high degree of violence. The worldwide threat of terrorism has increased several-fold since the US invasion of Iraq. The Americans were unprepared for the dramatic increase in terrorism in 2003 and 2004, and for how it worsened, rather than improved, through 2005 into 2006. For several months, the US Government was reluctant to publish terrorist incidents in its *Patterns of Global Terrorism Report*. The Bush Administration decided to eliminate its nineteen-year-old US State Department report because terrorism had increased 300 per cent, largely due to the Iraq invasion. A US Congressional Research Service survey concluded that al-Qaida and its associated groups launched seven attacks killing at least 220 in 2004, up from four attacks killing 104 in 2003. Henry A. Waxman, Ranking Member, Government Reform Committee, US Congress, wrote: 'it seems inconceivable that the administration missed two-thirds of the international terrorist attacks that occurred in 2003.'[21] History has shown us that international terrorism is largely a vicious by-product of protracted regional conflicts. The support – recruits and finance – for international terrorism largely comes from the territorial communities in the 'global south' and migrant communities within some of the Western industrialized countries.

Although it is politically incorrect to mention the fact in writing or speech, Iraq has been the single most important driver in the escalation of global terrorism. Terrorism has been on the rise since 9/11 and the arena has been widening since March 2001. More Muslims worldwide have begun to perceive Islam as under attack. The most intractable of the post-Iraq developments is the morphing of al-Qaida from a group into a movement and the wide support for a decentralized Sunni extremist movement. Immediately after 9/11 a significant proportion of the international community fully supported the intervention in Afghanistan by the US-led coalition. Because the camps in Afghanistan had produced a generation of extremist Islamist terrorists, this was a step in the right direction. An unintended consequence of the intervention was the dispersal of al-Qaida members and their associates from Afghanistan and Pakistan to lawless zones in the 'global south'. Three dozen local jihadist groups in Africa, Asia and the Middle East that were trained, armed, financed and ideologized by al-Qaida started to work with these dispersed al-Qaida elements. Although they were hunted by governments worldwide, they survived with the support of local associates, entities and sympathizers. These entities received a new lease of life after the US invasion of Iraq. Exploiting the anti-American sentiments of many Muslims, these local or regional groups share al-Qaida's vision and mission of a global jihad. Compared to the jihadist groups that traditionally attacked targets specific to their immediate area of interest, 'core' al-Qaida attacked the 'distant enemy' – the United States. Post-9/11, al-Qaida's constant message to its affiliated groups was to attack both the 'nearby enemy' (local governments) as well as the 'distant enemy', by attacking US interests abroad and those of its allies.

TERRORISM'S NEW CENTRE OF GRAVITY

Until Iraq, there were definable centres of gravity for international terrorism. In the 1970s and '80s it was the Syrian-controlled Bekaa Valley in Lebanon. Then, during the 1990s and until October 2001, it swung to Afghanistan. Together these two countries served as terrorist 'Disneylands', generating nearly 30,000 jihadists, originating anywhere from Africa to the Middle East and Asia and even Latin America. But compared to the situation in Iraq, there was very limited public support for their activities or their ideology. When Lebanon and Afghanistan were the principal geographical areas in which training was conducted or there was fighting, the violence was largely confined to these areas. As a direct result of the US-led invasion of Iraq, multiple centres of international terrorism have emerged. In addition to Iraq serving as a cauldron of conflict, the situation there is politicizing and radicalizing Muslims worldwide.

Countering Terrorism

Young, hardline, extremist terrorists are often a product of the human suffering that is grounded in the ethnic rape, pillage, internal displacement and resulting destruction of communities – especially communities existing on the extremities of human existence. Besides the internal displacement of populations (IDP), these circumstances generate localized conflicts and conflict zones. Wherever ethno-political or politico-religious conflicts persist, the resulting violence has profound spillover effects. Palestine produced the Palestinian Liberation Organization and the Islamic Resistance Movement (Hamas). Lebanon produced 'The Party of God' (Hezbollah). Algeria produced the Armed Islamic Group (AIG) and the Groupe Salafiste pour la Prédition et le Combat (GSPC). The turmoil in Sri Lanka bred the Liberation Tigers of Tamil Eelam (the 'Tamil Tigers'), while the disputed territories in Kashmir spawned Lashkar-e-Toiba and Jaish-e-Muhammed. Chechnya produced the 'International Islamic Brigade'; Afghanistan produced the 'Islamic Movement of the Taliban' and al-Qaida. The killing, maiming, injury, human suffering, internal displacement and refugee flows, once publicized, had a profound impact on their ethnic or religious kind, living both within and outside these zones. If the international community is serious about ending terrorism, then solutions must be found that will address and subsequently end the violence in these conflicts. The issues must either be satisfactorily resolved or one side involved in the fighting must be defeated, which in the longer term may present further challenges.

The very presence of US troops has galvanized the Iraqi insurgency and the Islamist terrorists, and is radicalizing Muslims across the globe. This is the view of both the Americans and the Iraqis and, increasingly, of the rest of the world. For every terrorist killed, two more are joining the insurgency in Iraq or the global terrorist network. As long as the United States is seen as the dominant power in Iraq, the insurgents will have no difficulty recruiting and generating the support they need. Furthermore, al-Qaida and its associated groups will have a recruitment poster to point to and will have no difficulty in surviving.

Clearly, and not just because of the way events have unfolded in Iraq, it was in the interests of the Iraqi people and the US for the latter to have been able to leave the country soon after the successful overthrow of Saddam's regime. With this in mind, a role had been envisaged already in 2003 for the United Nations to assume certain responsibilities in the stabilization process. Tragically that intention, good as it was, came to an abrupt and violent end on 19 August 2003 with the bombing by al-Qaida-associated terrorists of the Canal Hotel in Baghdad, the headquarters of the United Nations' mission to Iraq. In all 22 members of staff were killed, including Sergio de Mello, the Special Representative of the UN Secretary-General in Iraq. Many more were wounded, some of them severely. Consequently, the UN had little alternative than to withdraw, since the security environment had deteriorated to such a point that the UN mission could no longer operate effectively.

The ramifications of this terrorist atrocity against a totally unarmed mission, deployed solely in the interests of peace and stability, supported by a Security Council mandate, proved to be far-reaching. Instead of an early and orderly withdrawal, with a UN mission assuming much of the responsibility for stabilization activities, such as the formation of a new government and the associated electoral process, the US and its coalition partners were left to shoulder much of this burden. In addition, the security situation that has continued to deteriorate also tied down huge amounts of military resources and has had a severely adverse effect on the freedom of movement of any civilian stabilization component. At the time it may have seemed ideal for the United Nations to step into the breach and do what it is good at, despite the criticism to which it is continually subjected, but the reality on the ground precluded such a move. As far as the terrorists and the insurgents are concerned, the United Nations is as much a part of the 'enemy' as the US-led occupation forces, a fact also highlighted by al-Qaida's Ayman al-Zawahiri. But there is another aspect that was significantly underestimated in the planning process for the invasion of the Iraq and its aftermath, namely the reaction of the majority Shiite population.

After years of political and religious suppression it was natural to believe that, with the overthrow of Saddam's sadistic regime, the Shia population would have welcomed their 'liberators' with open arms. In many ways they did, certainly to start with. However, the early breakdown of law and order in 2003 soon led to broad disillusionment, compounded as it was in certain parts of the country with the rise of Shiite militias and a resulting descent into anarchy. To what extent Iran is to be blamed for this militancy and the success in subsequent elections of the more conservative Shiite religious parties

Countering Terrorism

may be difficult to define accurately. However, one cannot ignore Iran's desire and need to stir its own ingredients into Iraq's new-found political cauldron, not just in support of the Shia community but also as a means of undermining US efforts at 'bringing democracy' to the region.

4

Iran – The Open Flank

In the light of the US Administration's avowed intention to deal with Saddam Hussein and effect a regime change, ensuring that *all* countries in the Middle East, particularly those bordering Iraq, were going to be 'onside' for and after any comprehensive military action was critical. It therefore begs the question, given that the decision had already been taken to invade Iraq, with or without a mandate from the UN Security Council, as to what was to be achieved by President George W. Bush's 'Axis of Evil' statement.[1] Even if Iran's nuclear ambitions had been known for some time, though not generally as public as to their extent that they are now, making such an inflammatory statement about one of Iraq's neighbours at a time when diplomacy should have been in overdrive demonstrates a gross error of judgement. Was it was based on arrogance or ignorance of the true situation – bad intelligence or bad advice; on a flawed overconfidence in the US military's ability to fight not just on two fronts, but even to be prepared to deal with a third; a gross misunderstanding of the Iranian psyche (a common US problem when dealing with peoples of other cultures and religions); or just plain ineptitude? We may never know. One thing is certain, wrapping Iran into the 'Axis of Evil' bubble reduced significantly what feeling many Iranians had towards the US prior to the invasion of Iraq and played directly into the hands of the conservative hard-line elements that run the country: the Ayatollahs' Supreme Council and the Republican Guard. The net result of the 'Evil-Axis' statement, delivered as part of the US Presidential 'State of the Union' address at the beginning of 2002, served only to erode further the efforts of moderate elements in the Iranian parliament, who were trying to 'modernize' the way in which the country was governed and produce a more liberal social and political environment.

The facts concerning Iran's nuclear ambitions, which had been of significant concern for some considerable time, and Tehran's avowed and long-established support for terrorism, specifically through Hezbollah ('The Party of God'), should have been offset against the formidable undercurrent inside Iran, from a huge swath of the population, for political reform. To any observant visitor from the 'industrialized world' to the country during 2001 and 2002, it was clear that many people wanted a more liberal and modernistic way of life. Clerics of any persuasion, like soldiers, rarely make good politicians (though clearly there are one or two notable exceptions to this rule). Satellite television, the internet, mobile phones and even heroin addiction have all made their mark on an intelligent and sophisticated society.[2] Young Iranians were yearning for change. Many who could afford it, and were prepared to 'run the gauntlet' of European immigration systems, made their escape. This was demonstrated by those entering Bosnia via the weekly Mehan Air 'charter flight' to Sarajevo in the summer of 2000, that is until twenty of them went home in body bags having been drowned by their *schleppers* in the Sava River, while trying to cross into Croatia. That particular Mehan Air flight was noted by the Bosnian State Border Service as having the single largest number of 'return passengers'. Usually each Mehan Air flight arrived at Sarajevo with 150–56 passengers, but departing flights rarely boasted more than ten. These flights were clearly being used, along with the regular Turkish Airlines flights, as a one-way trip legally into Bosnia, which then became the springboard for the various onward and illegal routes to Britain and other countries in Western Europe – if they could make it. Some even wanted to risk all to get to North America.[3]

Twenty-five per cent of Iranians have been born since the 'Khomeini Revolution'. President Khatemi, viewed by many in the world as the 'acceptable face' of the Islamic Republic of Iran, had the support of much of this large part of the population, which also supported the many reformist politicians who were trying, through being members of the Iranian parliament, to introduce change. Ranged against them were the hardliners of the Republican Guard and other religious extremists supportive of the old 'Khomeini school', who were hell-bent on retaining their power and influence, keeping the country in a religious stranglehold. For them, as is the norm for most conservative hardliners, especially in the Muslim world, change was to be avoided. That so much of the country is in the 'middle ages' is a tragedy for one that has such a great history, both before and after the coming of Islam. Despite advances in modern technology, so much of the way the country is run is archaic. The banking system, the hotels, the chaotic traffic system in a car-clogged capital, the restrictions on human rights and civil liberties: all scream out for modernization and better management. Yet Tehran, by all accounts, appears to be committed to acquiring a nuclear weapons capability. This quest has been followed, quietly and secretively, for some considerable time.

One can appreciate the reluctance of successive US administrations to come to terms with the past insults to their national pride, caused by the siege of the US Embassy in Tehran, the length of time the hostages were held and the bungled rescue attempt. Coupled with Iran's overt support for terrorism, especially Hezbollah, this has only compounded the stand-off and widened the gap that needed to be bridged to achieve some level of working, diplomatic reconciliation. However difficult a pill to swallow, there comes a time when it is better to open the door, if only a crack, and begin the long road back to better relations. Handled quietly and carefully, with due feeling for the psyche of the people to whom the overtures had to be made, this could have been a positive and supportive signal towards the reformists in Iran. More importantly, developing better relations with Tehran would have helped secure the 'right flank' for the invasion of Iraq. It might also, again with clever diplomacy, have encouraged the Iranians to be more cooperative in working with the United Nations with regard to the interdiction and apprehension of leading al-Qaida figures. Unfortunately, the Iranians have been able to play both sides of the coin.

During the early part of 2002 the Iranians indicated that they had detained a number of 'Afghan-Arab' members of al-Qaida who were attempting to flee Afghanistan.[4] Many of these, judging by the names, the countries of their nationality and the fact that they were accompanied by women and children, were some of the 'foot-soldiers' referred to earlier. But among these foot-soldiers were long-term members of the cadre that would form some of the sleeper cells. These were the 'disciples' that would carry the ideological word to young Muslims in the countries to which they were headed: to young

Muslims in the mosques and other gathering places, indoctrinating them and recruiting them to the al-Qaida way of thinking and behaviour. They would instil in them the urge to become part of a new generation of suicide bombers and jihadists. Nearly all the individuals who had escaped or fled from Afghanistan through Iran were, after protracted diplomatic discussions, released to the embassies of their countries of origin. Once 'home' they were freed into society, some to go to their homes but many to prepare for future assignments, as and when the situation presented itself.

Then, in the first few months of 2003, the Iranians detained many more. These were divided into two groups based on their origins. Those in the first group, of around 2,300, had been rounded up over a period of time and were handed back to the authorities in Pakistan, from whence they had come. The second group of about 147 is more interesting and of greater concern.[5] Like those from the previous year, they were handed over to the appropriate consular officials. These individuals hailed from a variety of Arab countries, including Saudi Arabia. However, according to a number of open source reports, perhaps too many to ignore, four or five key al-Qaida figures had also been detained, for among the names were Saad bin Laden, one of Bin Laden's sons; Sulaiman Jassem Sulaiman Abu Ghaith, a stateless Kuwaiti accredited with having been al-Qaida's 'official spokesperson'; Usama bin Laden's own deputy, the 'good doctor' Ayman al-Zawahiri; and Saif al-Adel.[6]

Saif al-Adel had originally been described as bin Laden's head of security. At the time of those reports, there was speculation in some circles that he had assumed the mantle of al-Qaida chief of operations, following the death of Mohammed Atif (a.k.a. Abu Hafs) in a coalition air strike in eastern Afghanistan in December 2001 and the arrest in Rawalpindi, Pakistan, in March 2003 of Khaled Sheikh Mohammed (KSM) – the mastermind of 9/11. Fuel was added to speculation concerning the presence of Saif al-Adel in Iran by suggestions that, according to mobile phone intercepts, the suicide bombings that took place in the Saudi capital Riyadh on 13 May 2003 had been directed by him from Iran.[7] The Iranian authorities' response, when asked for clarification of the presence in Iran of these al-Qaida 'personalities', was vacillation and stonewalling.

One body mandated to request such information was the UN Al-Qaida Sanctions Monitoring Group. All the al-Qaida individuals named in the reports were subject to the travel ban imposed under Security Council resolutions 1390 and 1455. The Monitoring Group had a number of meetings with Iran's Permanent Representative to the United Nations and his deputy to discuss the subject. Eventually, after four months or so, the Iranian response came as an official press statement in September 2003, denying the presence of the named individuals in their country – although there are many who believe that they were still being retained. Some diplomats suggested that the individuals had been detained at the pleasure of the Iranian Republican Guard, possibly as hostages to a deal to get the US to hand over certain Iranian dissidents, members of the Mujahideen Khalq Organization (MKO or MEK), or 'People's Mujahideen', who had taken refuge in Iraq after the fall of Saddam's regime.[8] However, unconfirmed stories suggested that the US would not deal on this, since they wanted to keep the MKO dissidents in place, in case they needed them in future attempts to undermine the 'Regime of the Ayatollahs'.

Needless to say, in circumstances like these conspiracy theories will always abound. It was even suggested in some diplomatic circles that the government in Tehran had been holding these individuals in the hope of doing a deal with other countries that were holding Iranian nationals. Another reason being floated was that the Iranian Interior Minister, himself a conservative hardliner, refused to hand them over, particularly to the Americans. Ignoring at this stage of the discussion the rights and wrongs of the USA and her coalition allies going to war against the Saddam regime, it would still have been much wiser and demonstrated greater statesmanlike leadership if the US Administration had found ways of diplomatically engaging with the government in Tehran, so that it was 'onside' for whatever actions would have to be taken to deal with Saddam Hussein. In retrospect, such an engagement should have been started long before, even if it would have been a bitter pill for the US to swallow. Perhaps one of the best moments in modern history would have been at a 'politically convenient' time after the first Gulf War. That military incursion into Iraq had been sanctioned by the United Nations, following on from the invasion of Kuwait. Many Arab states participated in that coalition, which, having 'freed' 'occupied Kuwait' rolled on into Iraq bringing Saddam Hussein's generals to the military surrender table. Ayatollah Ruhollah Khomeni, the leader of the Iranian Revolution, had died eighteen months earlier, in June 1989; there had thus been a sufficient cooling-off period after his death for the time to be ripe to start making the necessary overtures.

In retrospect, this might not have proved so difficult to achieve as one might at first think. Despite memories of the siege of the US Embassy in Tehran still being fresh in many American minds, and the customary 'clerical rhetoric' of the conservative hardliners, there were many Iranians who would have welcomed closer ties with the US. After Sayyed Mohammed Khatami had become president in 1997 there had been a new face to deal with in Tehran. There had been an initial thawing of the relations between Washington and Tehran, albeit predominantly from the reformists' side of the house. Later the 'second pillar' of US diplomacy appeared to be well in place in Iran in 2001 and 2002, judging by the number of US citizens travelling up and down in the lifts of the Hotel 'Azad' (the former Tehran Hyatt), one of Tehran's leading hotels. They certainly were not dressed as tourists. Iran is also a big country – roughly four times the size of Iraq – and big countries like to be respected, especially when they have good links into and around Central and South Asian republics. Being the world's fourth largest exporter of oil and gas also provides a certain economic and political clout.

Diplomatic overtures to Iran were not only important when preparing to invade Iraq, because of Iraq's majority Shia population, but also to try to ease the tension concerning Iran's nuclear ambitions. The Iranians, specifically the hardline religious clerics and the Republican Guard, have long felt threatened by the US – 'The Great Satan'. Branding Iran as part of the 'Axis of Evil' clearly did little to assuage those fears. Thus one can understand their intent to have a suitable deterrent, one that they knew the US would respect. One does not have to agree with this approach, but, when one spends time in the country and gets a feeling for their national pride, it comes as no surprise. One must also look at the country's history, both ancient and modern. At the height of its earlier zenith, between the sixth and fourth centuries BC, the Achaemenid Persian empire had extended from the Indus River to the Mediterranean. After a century or so of Greek dominance, Persian rule revived and, under the Parthians and Sassanians, lasted for another 700 years until the rise of Islam. Examples of their hydro-engineering can still be seen in parts of Oman by following the course of *qanat falaj* – the ancient semi-subterranean irrigation systems. Taking all these facts into consideration would suggest that a different approach might have had a much more positive and, in the long term, more beneficial outcome. This is not to say that some form of insurgency, of an intensity that could be managed, would not have transpired in Iraq after the invasion in 2003. But, with a more amenable Iran, the coalition might have had to deal with a few more friends and far fewer enemies. One should also not overlook the role played by Tehran during the Taliban era and the attitude the Iranians adopted towards Kandahar and Kabul.

The Consulate-General of the Islamic Republic of Iran in Mazar-e-Sharif had been attacked by the Taliban in the summer of 1998: nine Iranian diplomats were murdered, including the Consul-General. Prior to this atrocity Tehran had been trying to work with Islamabad to resolve the Afghanistan conflict, the Iranians being deeply concerned about the rise of the extremist Pashtun elements in Kabul. But after this event, which they partially blamed on Pakistan, relations cooled dramatically – the Iranian Shia approach to the Sunni Taliban being like 'chalk from cheese'. Among the Iranians there is probably the biggest Shia population opposed to radical Sunni extremism. Even if the bulk of the Iranian leadership are also fundamentalists, they are Shia fundamentalists. For a number of years Iran has had to combat the trafficking of heroin and opiates coming out of Afghanistan, not because it has any great wish to assist the West in keeping the drug flows down, but because its own population contains in excess of two million heroin addicts, creating a major internal problem. Therefore it was in the Iranians' own interests to strengthen their border services. The Iranian border guards, in their efforts to cut down on the heroin smuggling, have over a number of years suffered a large number of casualties. More than 3,000 have been killed in engagements with drug traffickers. As the weaponry and methods used by the latter became more and more sophisticated, so the Iranian security forces evolved tactics and whole systems of defences on their eastern border with Afghanistan to channel and interdict the drug smugglers. Drug enforcement agencies worldwide always admit that, no matter how successful their methods of interdiction, drugs still get through. In the case of Iran, they are the first to admit that the border defences are going to have gaps or holes in them that will be exploited by the drug-runners. Iran has made a major effort to deal with this problem. It was not surprising, therefore, with border security so high on the agenda, that so many 'Afghan-Arabs' appear to have been apprehended trying to escape the wrath of the coalition onslaught in Afghanistan against the al-Qaida bases and the Taliban regime. In addition to the repatriations, already mentioned, the Iranian government also transmitted a confidential memorandum to the UN Secretary-General, informing him by name of the people who had been detained and then handed back to their countries of origin.

In view of the earlier allegations and denials, it was thus all the more interesting to read on 17 July 2004 that Iranian TV had reported the Intelligence Minister, Ali Yunesi, as stating that his ministry had located and dismantled all branches of al-Qaida network in the country and stopped al-Qaida terrorist acts. No further details were proffered.[9] Had some of the al-Qaida people been there after all? Was this just 'Iranian spin' or was it a formal announcement of the end of another interesting 'twist' in the Iran–al-Qaida saga that surfaced on 3 March 2006, when the Pentagon released a number of documents containing the transcripts of Guantanamo Bay tribunals questioning detainees?[10] One of these contained allegations from an interview with a particular detainee, the Taliban-era Governor of Herat (name withheld in the official papers), who described a meeting in his area of responsibility in October 2001 between senior Taliban officials from Kandahar and 'Iranian officials in which Iran pledged to assist the Taliban in their war with the United States'.[11]

If this was indeed true, and not just another snippet of Taliban–al-Qaida disinformation, or even the release of unsworn testimony and uncorroborated 'evidence' by the US government, then it gives even greater credence to the allegations that senior al-Qaida officials were being given sanctuary in Iran, so long as such an arrangement was beneficial to the Iranians. One cannot ignore the likelihood that, among the hardline, 'conservative' Iranian government elements in the 'Supreme Council of Ayatollahs' and the Iranian Republican Guard, the thought of a US presence gaining a firm foothold and influential presence in the region would be of grave concern. Such unease would have been heightened by the rapid bilateral arrangements, albeit in support of their operations in Afghanistan, by which new US bases were established in the region: in Kazakhstan, Uzbekistan and, across the Gulf, in Qatar.

The July 2004 statement by the Iranian government may have been nothing more than an attempt to signal that it was doing all the right things with respect to the so-called 'war on terror'. On the other hand perhaps it was simply an attempt to allay fears of the presence of Islamist terrorists who, given the opportunity, might gain access to the 'nuclear technology', even if it was being developed only for peaceful means? Or perhaps it was just a cosmetic demonstration by the government to display its willingness to implement certain terrorism-related resolutions, albeit in its own way, and work within the framework of the United Nations? The 'political willingness' of this theory, however, is called into question in the light of Iran's reaction in February 2006 to being reported to the UN Security Council. This time the confrontation arose in connection with Iran's intention to proceed with its uranium enrichment programme, in contravention of the Nuclear Non-Proliferation Treaty and the governors of the International Atomic Energy Agency (IAEA), the UN's nuclear oversight body. Iran's unilateral intention to proceed is, in its view, a sovereign right that any nation possesses to conduct nuclear research for peaceful purposes – energy, medical and so on. The IAEA's threats only made Iran's leaders even more belligerent in their rhetoric, particularly that emanating from their radical new president, Mahmoud Ahmadinejad. Buoyed by the belief that they would be supported in their independent approach by Russia, they appeared ready to challenge the will of the international community. Rhetorical exchanges were ramped up in March 2006 by both sides. Iran threatened that the US would feel 'harm and pain' if Iran was referred to the Security Council. The US countered with threats of its own, even though they were ill-defined. Besides the nuclear concerns, US Secretary of State Condoleezza Rice added in a statement to a Senate hearing on 9 March 2006 that 'Iran . . . is the central bank of terrorism'.[12] Most experts, working at the forefront of research into the threat posed by the financing of terrorism, would not agree with this statement. Notwithstanding the extent of Iran's financial and moral support for Hezbollah and other Palestinian groups pitted against Israel, Saudi Arabia and her Gulf neighbours have spent a great deal more, funding groups involved in terrorist activities against Israel and elsewhere.

Nonetheless, it may not have been a total coincidence that Iran, on 16 March 2006, offered to engage in talks with the US with a view to improving the security situation in Iraq.[13] Besides desiring to bring its influence to bear with the majority Shia population in Iraq, especially when much of the US plans were in shreds, such a forward leaning and positive approach might help deflect some of the 'international' heat Iran was feeling. For many months the prospect of civil war had loomed over the post-Saddam-era stabilization and reconstruction efforts. Sunni insurgent terrorists, in cahoots with foreign opportunist jihadists – linked to 'al-Qaida in Mesopotamia' or 'al-Qaida in Iraq' – had tried their best, but in vain, to lower Iraq into the depths of all-out civil war. However, the destruction on 22 February 2006 of the gilded dome of the Shia Askariya shrine in Samarra, one of the most sacred Shiite places, unleashed an unprecedented wave of sectarian killings and violence, with some people considering that the country was in a state of civil war. In a BBC interview Iyad Alawi, Iraq's former Prime Minister, stated: 'It is unfortunate that we are in civil war. We are losing each day as an average 50 to 60 people throughout the country, if not more . . . If this is not civil war, then God knows what civil war is[?]'[14] But, as is so often the case, if describing the reality on the ground is at odds with the political requirements of the day, the truth will be masked with a different 'spin'. There are many, however, who appear resigned to the blood-letting as a prelude to an eventual representative democratic form of government. Some seem happy to quote history by way of giving the terrorist insurgency in Iraq an air of acceptability, rather than to have striven from the outset to provide the conditions for an environment based on reason and dialogue.

However, if there is a positive outcome from the talks between Iranian and US officials, in the short term for the benefit of the Iraqi people and the future of their country and in the long term for Iran–US relations, then at least some good will have come out of mayhem, murder and misjudgement. It will also highlight the fact that, as with good 'reconnaissance', if time had been spent securing the coalition's 'right flank' it would not have been wasted. Furthermore, if a deep and meaningful engagement with Iran had been initiated at an appropriate time after the death of Ayatollah Khomeini, a relationship might have developed such that Iran would have been less inclined to support Hezbollah and its attacks against Israel in July 2006. Instead, left to its own devices, Iran has provided credence in the minds of many that it is a 'state' supporting terrorism.

Barrages of rockets, supplied from Iran and launched into Israel by Hezbollah, a group with strong ties to Iran, and attacks with radar-guided anti-ship missiles against an Israeli navy vessel and a

Cambodian vessel, have fuelled these beliefs. The timing of the attack on Israel, coinciding with the start of the G–8 Summit in St Petersburg, provides further food for thought. In 2005 Islamist terrorist chose the opening day of the G–8 Summit to carry out suicide attacks in London. 12 July 2006 was the day on which Iran was required to respond to demands made by the UN with respect to Iran's curtailment of its uranium enrichment activities. Again we see a situation in which Iran, feeling the pressures of the international community over its uranium enrichment programme, finds a way to cock a snook at the US, believing that, militarily, it is quite stretched. Vested interests of key players are also likely to cloud the issue, an aspect that Tehran is adept at exploiting, notably the reluctance on the part of Russia and China to impose sanctions on Iran. Meanwhile, Iran played for time over its response to the EU-led proposals and using the time to foment the situation surrounding Israel. Timing is always of the essence, especially in delicate political situations, but so too is speed of response a political necessity for many political leaders. Often it is allowed to cloud the issues, especially when dealing with terrorism. And just as the threat is so often not fully appreciated, so too is the terrorists' attitude to time. As Usama bin Laden and his other spokesmen have stated on numerous occasions, they have all the time in the world to achieve their ultimate aim of a great Caliphate. If they do not achieve their aim in this generation, they will achieve it in the next or some time later – but achieve it they will, or so they and their followers believe!

5

Terrorism: An Enduring Threat

Many national leaders, government officials, journalists and experts in the field of terrorism refer to 9/11 as a 'watershed'. For many around the world, not just in the United States of America, 9/11 should have been a wake-up call. However, the comprehensive and collaborative response that was required to reduce the threat, following the attacks on New York's World Trade Center and the Pentagon in Washington, has not materialized. The initial surge of sympathy and support in the immediate aftermath of those horrific events, which had been projected live round the world as they took place, has been short-lived. The original expectations of improved international cooperation, of the exchange of intelligence, evidence and information, and cracking down on the terrorists and terrorist groups have, in reality, not been fulfilled. Much has been made by politicians of the successes achieved against the terrorists, in particular against al-Qaida and its many associates, that now comprise the transnational network.

More than 4,000 individuals have been arrested in well over 100 countries in connection with the al-Qaida network, but Usama bin Laden and the *éminence grise* of al-Qaida, the Egyptian Dr Ayman al-Zawahiri, remain at large. Some terrorist-related finances have been frozen, but the network never seems to be short of sufficient funds every time it carries out attacks. 'Sleeper' and support cells have been broken up and impending attacks nipped in the bud. But cells have been reconstituted. New groups, linked to al-Qaida only by the ideology espoused by Usama bin Laden, have been spawned and attacks have continued: Djerba, Bali, Mombasa, Riyadh, Casablanca, Moscow, Baghdad, Jakarta, Mindanao, Istanbul, Madrid, Beslan,

London, Dehli, Amman, Mumbai and many more. Iraq has suffered more than its fair share of assassinations, bombings, hostage takings and the killing and maiming of thousands. The atrocities executed in the name of God and Islam, which many describe as a peaceful religion, have sunk to appalling depths of human savagery, by any norms, defying the imagination. The crimes of the terrorists have become more and more heinous. Tragically, the international response, strong as the rhetoric has been in the wake of each successive atrocity, has failed to keep pace with what is proving to be an extremely adaptable, cunning, ruthless and determined foe. The 'watershed of 2001' has become little more than a trickle in the sand.

Terrorism and terrorist groups have been with us for decades, even if they have at times been cloaked by some with a mantle of political acceptability, being referred to as insurgents, militants, guerrillas or freedom fighters. At the end of the day they have invariably used 'terror' as a tactic and often the attacks and atrocities they have committed in the furtherance of their cause have, in many cases, been crimes against humanity. Thus, even the most 'laudable' of causes have, to all intents and purposes, been prosecuted by groups whose members are nothing more than terrorists. Over the years, armed forces, security services and the forces of law and order have achieved a variety of results in tackling terrorist groups and dealing with insurgencies. Some of these have been brought to a successful conclusion, for example in Malaya (1958) and Oman (1975). Others linger on, year after year, bringing only death, dismemberment, displacement and destruction. Often the only beneficiaries would appear to be those who manufacture or traffic in arms and ammunition – the 'merchants of death' of this world.

Until 9/11 countries, for the most part, dealt with the terrorist threats with which they were faced either on their own or with some help from their friends and neighbours. But the scale of these attacks was unprecedented. The fact that they had struck at the heartland of the very nation that, for so long, had been seen by many peoples as the 'champion of the Free World' was itself a message from the terrorist organization responsible. As the dust cleared and the world woke up on 12 September 2001 the enormity of the threat with which it was faced was overwhelming. Although al-Qaida, as a known terrorist organization, had been around for some considerable time and had already been accused of the 1998 attacks against the US embassies in

Nairobi and Dar-es-Salaam, somehow it had always been seen as being at arm's length – operating against US interests in parts of the world where it was more at home, where its operators and supporters blended naturally into the local scenery: in Arab states, in the Middle East, East Africa and Asia. Suddenly the ground rules had changed, and changed dramatically. The attacks in New York and Washington were aimed at the very values that underpinned the free world. Democracy, justice, the rule of law, freedom of speech and expression, and an individual's freedom to observe the religion of one's choice – these were all being challenged on that fateful day. This terrorist organization, it was soon realized, transcended national boundaries. It was the first 'transnational terrorist organization' of the twenty-first century and, tragically, even when it has been dealt its death blow – as it surely will over time – it may not be the last. This was the challenge that now faced the international community; a monstrous challenge for which it was ill prepared and ill-equipped, despite the fact that terrorism and terrorists had been around in some form or other for decades.

EARLY DAYS

Terrorists and terrorist groups have featured in the daily lives of many peoples from many countries since the end of the Second World War (some even beforehand). The difference is that they have often been defined, correctly or incorrectly, as guerrilla movements or even 'freedom fighters'. True, there have been, and continue to be, genuine uprisings of minority groups suffering acute oppression under cruel dictators and autocratic regimes. This latter aspect does sometimes cloud the issue and provide the necessary excuse for those sympathetic to a cause to abrogate their international responsibilities. But those who call themselves 'freedom fighters' violate the very things that they claim they are fighting for, namely freedom, values, human dignity and human rights. Their means need to be delegitimized, even when their end might be justified – in some cases.

No matter how fancy or provocative the names, their intention has been to change, by armed force, the political, religious and/or social fabric of the country or the people they subject to their terror tactics. Such groups invariably had, and in a number of cases still have, a local agenda. Some of the earlier insurgencies, which were often Communist-inspired, were dealt with successfully. Most of the groups involved rode in on the back of post-colonial or post-Second World War vacuums. Two such examples were the Communist insurgency in Malaya and the attempt by the People's Front for the Liberation of the Occupied Arabian Gulf (PFLOAG), inciting the *jebalis*, the local tribespeople from Oman's southern Dhofar region, to seize the country's southern oilfields. These two particular campaigns were defeated in 1953 and 1975 respectively by, importantly, a successful 'hearts and minds' campaign aimed at the local population, combined with intensive internal security operations directed concurrently against the belligerents, leading to political negotiations and an acceptable, lasting settlement. These were useful lessons from which much has been learnt, but often all too quickly forgotten.

OF HEARTS AND MINDS . . .

The campaign in Malaya is often cited as one of the classic ways of successfully dealing with a terrorist insurgency. It had to confront both civil unrest in the urban areas and the infiltration and domination of rural areas, rich in natural resources – in this case rubber plantations and rich deposits of tin – by an ethnic group backed from outside by another state, in this case Communist China. This attempt to change the administration and its political structures required a variety of measures to be developed that both dealt with the day-to-day criminality of the terrorists and the instigators of the urban strikes, while developing and implementing ways of winning over the population to reject the insurgents and that which they represented. It required winning the 'hearts and minds' of the majority population for the short and medium term, as well as seeking an effective long-term political solution.

The Dhofar Campaign, as it came to be known, is another classic example of a successful 'hearts and minds' campaign against an insurgent or 'terrorist' movement. In its efforts to capture the southern oilfields of the Sultanate of Oman, the PFLOAG initially evoked support from the indigenous tribespeople of the Dhofar region. The *dhofaris*, a semi-nomadic people whose livelihood was based on camels, cattle and frankincense, inhabit the hilly region in southwest Oman that surrounds the seaport of Salalah, the country's second city. Initially, soldiers from Oman's relatively small armed forces were deployed to contain the uprising. These were later augmented by small teams of special forces from the British Army's Special Air Service (SAS) regiment, which were deployed into the *jebel* to establish contact with the *dhofaris*. Having identified the basic needs of individual groups of the tribespeople, the work of the special forces teams were then augmented by specialists from the Royal Engineers, who drilled wells, built clinics and provided other basic civic infrastructure. This effort was not without its risks from the PFLOAG elements and their sympathizers on the *jebel*. But concurrently with the efforts of the special forces 'training teams', a much expanded Omani Armed Forces engaged in a major campaign in the west of the *jebel* to disrupt, deter and eventually destroy the PFLOAG guerrilla forces.[1] The latter were eventually pushed back behind a formidable defensive line along the Oman/Yemen border at Sarfait. Jordan and Iran, then still under the Shah, also sent sizeable units to assist the Omani Armed Forces against PFLOAG. Although there is no connection between these events and today's Islamic terrorism inspired by Usama bin Laden, it is interesting to note that both his family and many of the PFLOAG guerrillas originated in the Hadramaut region in the eastern parts of South Yemen. At the time, the Cold War was still in full spate and the political leanings of South Yemen were toward the Soviet bloc, which maintained a maritime air base on Socotra, an island off the eastern tip of the Horn of Africa, from which the Soviets mounted maritime air patrols over the area and off the coast of Oman.

A similar politically motivated 'enterprise' against a new indigenous government took place from 1963 to 1968 in northeast Kenya, ostensibly as a result of Somali expansionism. On 12 December 1963, two weeks before Kenya achieved independence within the British Commonwealth, indigenous Somali tribesmen from Kenya's Northern Frontier District (NFD) carried out a series of attacks against Kenyan government targets.[2] These 'insurgents' were usually referred to by Kenya government forces and officials as *shifta*, a term that dates back before the Second World War to marauding bandits or cross-border cattle raiders who were commonplace in the area at that time. The stated reason in 1963 for their terrorist activities was that, as Muslims, they did not wish to be ruled by what they saw as a 'pagan' government in Nairobi. The fact that Kenya could boast the widespread existence of both the Anglican and Catholic churches, including having a cathedral each in Nairobi, did not enter into the equation. In reality it was the Communist-inspired government in Somalia that was instigating the insurgency with the intent of annexing a substantial portion of northeast Kenya, in which there was believed to be oil. At that time, British Petroleum (BP) was carrying out exploratory drilling in an area southeast of Garissa and quite near the Somali border, although nothing came of the exploration. Initially, with surprise on the side of the *shifta*, government forces suffered a number of early setbacks.[3] However, once the combined efforts of the nascent Kenya Army, the paramilitary police General Service Units (GSU) and units of the Kenya Police had achieved a number of successes against the *shifta*, the latter turned to preying on the nomadic Kenyan Somalis. Partly to protect these nomadic tribespeople and partly to deny the *shifta* support from possible sympathizers, whether or not it was coerced, the nomads were moved into secured camps, adjacent to the main government administrative centres, such as Wajir and Garba Tula. Although a low-intensity campaign by current criteria, it was still a form of guerrilla warfare in which terrorism was one of the tactics or weapons used by the insurgents. The conflict was eventually resolved in early 1968 with the intervention of Tanzania's President Julius Nyerere. Under his chairmanship dialogue prevailed and Kenya retained full control of its sovereign territory.[4]

There are some important lessons that can still be learned from these earlier conflicts, all of which involved Muslim entities in conflict with communities of other religious or political beliefs. First of all they demonstrate that it is possible, given the political will and the right approach, to find effective long-term solutions to what appear at the time to be intractable problems. True it is that in each of these examples there were elements, from within the protagonists, with whom it became possible to establish a dialogue. Such a situation does not pertain to al-Qaida or many of the emerging transnational Islamic terrorists or terrorist groups.[5] In this context the 'hearts and minds' approach, a significant factor that contributed to the successful conclusion of these earlier conflicts involving social, economic and political violence, must be developed. But it is an approach that has to be applied firmly as well as fairly. Working in conjunction with the majority Muslim populations, ways must be found, collectively, to reject the ways and thinking of the extremist minorities and provide long-term, sustainable solutions to today's problems.

Countering Terrorism

PERCEPTION, NOT A DEFINITION!

By today's standards all of these campaigns can be viewed as terrorist activities, even though at the time they were usually classified as an insurrection, insurgency or guerrilla war. All too often countries, because of vested interests or an underlying sympathy for the cause being invoked, regard insurgents as different from terrorists. This ambivalence, as we shall see later, has a direct and often quite serious impact on how such states approach their individual commitments to tackling terrorism. Furthermore, those terrorists who openly state that civilian casualties are acceptable in the furtherance of their beliefs are terrorists of the worst kind. Guerrilla fighters and terrorists are notorious for using elements of the civilian population as shields, behind which to hide or from inside of which to operate against security forces. In the July–August '34-day war' in Lebanon, Hezbollah not only fired missiles into Israel from villages but had built bunkers and tunnel complexes close to camps and observations posts (OP) of the UN's mission, UNIFIL.[6] Indiscriminate attacks against civilians – men, women and children going about their daily business – count as terrorism, and must be treated as such. Activities that support such acts are therefore by definition terrorism-related. However, the bottom line is that there are no circumstances and no causes that merit attacks on unarmed and defenceless civilians. Terrorism must therefore be outlawed under all circumstances and in all its forms.

Over the past 30–40 years, political and ideological discontent leading to insurrection and terrorism has become more commonplace and much more widespread, even affecting a number of European countries. France learnt to tackle the Armed Islamic (Resistance) Group of Algeria (GIA), Germany its Rote Armee Fraktion (RAF) or 'Red Army Faction', Italy the Brigato Rosso or 'Red Brigade', Spain the Euskadi ta Askatasuna (ETA)[7] and the United Kingdom the Irish Republican Army (IRA) and its many hardline splinter groups, such as the Provisional IRA, the Irish National Liberation Army (INLA) and the 'Real IRA'. In South America the ongoing cocaine wars still deny many people a safe and secure environment and a peaceful future. In Nepal and Sri Lanka government security forces, despite differing and somewhat sinusoidal ceasefire arrangements, are engaged with, respectively, Maoist rebels and the Tamil Tigers. Meanwhile, the two longest-running conflicts remain unresolved: Kashmir and the areas

Terrorism: An Enduring Threat

disputed by India and Pakistan, and the one that continues to generate so much emotion and sentiment internationally, namely between Israel and the Palestinians. Most of the conflicts mentioned above, for the most part, had been contained within national boundaries. However, once conflicts had spilled over into other states and started impacting nations not involved in the conflict, then and usually only then have there been reactions from the international community.

The initial evidence of this transformation comes from examining the tactics used and the targets selected by the local groups. For instance, Jemmah Islamiyah, a group aiming to establish an Islamic state in Southeast Asia, did not attack Western targets before 9/11. After this event, however, the group conducted coordinated simultaneous suicide attacks against nightclubs in Bali (October 2002), the J. W. Marriott Hotel in Jakarta (August 2003), the Australian Embassy in Jakarta (September 2004) and two restaurants in Bali (October 2005). Collectively, these attacks accounted for the lives of well over 200 people, with many more injured – a large proportion of whom were indigenous Indonesians. Similarly, the Moroccan Islamic Combatant Group (GICM), also seeking to create an Islamic state, conducted coordinated simultaneous suicide attacks against five targets in Casablanca in May 2003.[8] The targets were a hotel frequented by Israelis, a Jewish cemetery, a Spanish cultural centre and a Jewish-owned Italian restaurant; a total of 42 people died. Another entity associated with al-Qaida in Pakistan, Lashkar-e-Toiba, which usually operates against Indian targets, mounted an operation to target Australian interests in Sydney in 2004. The disrupted operation aimed to destroy high-profile multiple targets, a classic al-Qaida *modus operandi*. Unlike al-Qaida, most of its associates have a limited geographic reach, but with the help of the politicized and radicalized segments of their migrant and diaspora communities, these local groups are able and willing to plan, prepare and execute attacks in operational theatres far from their 'home' base. Although the local or indigenous groups are not as well resourced as al-Qaida, the financial support networks, established by bin Laden, continue to provide them with funds. Despite suffering the loss of its training camps in Afghanistan, al-Qaida's dispersed trainers, combat tacticians and explosives experts have been imparting the specialist knowledge required by the local groups to conduct al-Qaida-style attacks.

How can the transformation of local groups into al-Qaida look-alikes be prevented? The evolution of al-Qaida from a tightly struc-tured hierarchal organization into a global movement has not been adequately assessed by the security and intelligence community working on terrorism. While much of the threat posed by al-Qaida is known and manageable, the multiple threats posed by its associates and affiliated entities have not been fully studied and assessed. Even within the US intelligence community, the largest counter-terrorism intelligence community in the world, there are very few specialists who know and understand the Islamist terrorist groups associated or affiliated with al-Qaida. The real threat to the West comes from the politicized and radicalized migrant and diaspora communities. It is within these communities that terrorist groups originating in the 'global south' establish their logistic support and operational cells. Canada, Australia, New Zealand and many European countries remain safe havens for a dozen terrorist groups including Ansar al-Islam, Egyptian Islamic Jihad and Le Groupe Salafiste pour la Prédition et le Combat (GSPC). Millions of dollars raised in the West have strengthened multiple jihad and other terrorist groups. Although the terrorist support networks disseminated propaganda, recruited members and supporters, raised funds and procured supplies, they refrained from mounting terrorist attacks in most Western countries. As a result, the enforcement and intelligence authorities did not per-ceive the groups that operated in the West as presenting an immediate threat (to themselves!). Traditionally, Western politicians and bureau-crats either failed to understand or preferred to ignore the threat. Although the law enforcement and security and intelligence services of the West have a much better appreciation of the post-9/11 situa-tion, they need the legislation better to monitor, disrupt and break up the cells. Having hosted prominent individuals such as Sheikh Omar Abdel Rahman (in the US) and Mullah Krekar (in Norway), the founder leaders of the Islamic Group of Egypt and Ansar al-Islam respectively, the time is now ripe for many governments to be more responsible and accountable. Political leadership must take the initia-tive in reviewing and developing appropriate legislation that empow-ers their security and intelligence services and law enforcement authorities actively to prevent the operation of terrorist support and execution networks on their soil. But more importantly they must ensure that, when they do enact legislation, it is and can be enforced, and that includes the necessary resources. Otherwise, the West, the primary target of the Islamists, will continue to suffer from terrorism in the coming months and years.

THE FUTURE OF TERRORISM

In the future al-Qaida, the most hunted terrorist group in our history, will pose a lesser threat compared to its associated groups. Among such groups, that formed by Abu Musab al-Zarqawi's Tawhid wal Jihad (renamed 'al-Qaida of the Two Rivers'), with an expanding network in the Middle East and the West, already presents a much bigger threat to the US, its allies and friends. In place of one al-Qaida, the core group built and led by Usama bin Laden, we are now confronted by many 'al-Qaidas'. Al-Qaida's biggest success has been its ability and willingness to inspire and instigate a global family of jihadist groups. It achieved this singular success by attacking America's iconic landmarks in September 2001 and by disseminating frequent messages emphasizing the importance of waging a global jihad. These successes were reinforced by the protracted conflict in Iraq.

To respond better to terrorism, the international community must develop a deeper understanding of the global terrorism map, the drivers and the linkages, and further develop its capacities to respond to terrorism. Today the world faces sustained political violence in the geographic zones of the 'global south'. The regional conflicts in the Middle East, Asia, Africa, the Caucasus and Latin America produce both the perpetrators and the victims of violence. The political conditions in the Middle East, notably in Iraq, Israel and its Occupied Territories, Lebanon and Egypt, either suffer from or produce significant violence. Away from the glare of the media, Africa, particularly East Africa (and primarily Somalia and Sudan), produces significant violence. Although terrorist and guerrilla groups exist in Africa, most of the violence stems from tribal conflict. Both the Maghreb, notably Algeria, and to a lesser extent the Sub-Saharan African states provide a comfort zone for several existing and emerging groups.

Although the world has largely focused on the Middle East, Asia is the new theatre of violence, with active and new groups in Central, South and Southeast Asia. Southeast Asia presents an arch of instability caused by sustained violence in Indonesia, the Philippines and southern Thailand. Similarly, in the South-Central Asian interface –

Afghanistan, Pakistan, Uzbekistan, India and Bangladesh – tensions remain that rapidly fan the flames of religious extremism. The violence in the Caucasus, especially in Chechnya and Dagestan, has presented a threat beyond this region, and beyond Russia. In Latin America Colombia presents the greatest threat, but there are other areas ripe for violence, such as the Tri-Border Area (TBA) where Paraguay, Brazil and Argentina meet.[9]

What is important to understand is that Islamist groups have built robust networks worldwide. They are able to establish a presence wherever Muslims live, irrespective of nationality or social status. The only region where al-Qaida was weak was Latin America, but even here the group appears to have made progress and the visits of Khalid Sheikh Muhammad, the mastermind of 9/11, to Brazil in 1996 and of Adnan G. El Shukrijumah to the Tri-Border Area after 9/11 are causes for concern.[10] Shukrijumah (also known as Adnan G. El Shukri Jumah, Abu Arif, Ja'far al-Tayar, Jaffar al-Tayyar, Jafar Tayar and Jaafar al-Tayyar) was identified by the FBI and the CIA as a pilot and a colleague of Khalid Sheikh Muhammad. Known to travel on Guyanese, Saudi, Canadian or Trinidad passports, Shukrijumah, a Saudi national, is designated as an individual about whom the organization is 'seeking information'.[11] Although several known terrorists or their associates were targeted during the last decade in the Tri-Border Area, compared to the scale of activity of these groups the law enforcement successes have been limited. Al-Said Mokhles was extradited from Uruguay to Egypt; Ali Nizar Dahroug was convicted in Paraguay of tax evasion and sentenced to six-and-a-half years in prison; and Assad Ahmad Barakat, the Hezbollah financial kingpin in the Tri-Border Area, was extradited from Brazil to Paraguay, also to face tax evasion charges. Nonetheless, these developments demonstrate that al-Qaida, along with some of its associates, has established a small but important presence in Latin America. Traditionally, it was the Lebanese Hezbollah that operated in Latin America but, in the post-9/11 environment, even Sunni groups have made inroads to a region new to them.[12]

EARLY GLOBALIZATION

Back in the 1960s Palestinian terrorists extended their offensive operations into aircraft hijackings, attacks on passenger terminals at international airports and kidnappings. In response to these indiscriminate and barbaric attacks the international community did react. Under the auspices of the United Nations international conventions were adopted, aimed at suppressing these and other aspects of terrorism. The first of these instruments, resulting from threats to civilian passenger aircraft, airline passengers and crews, was signed in Tokyo on 14 September 1963 and is deposited with the International Civil Aviation Authority. However, some considerable time passed before it was adopted by many members of the international community. For many states there was little incentive if they did not feel directly affected, an attitude that, over time, we shall see as common to many aspects of the international response to terrorism. Nonetheless, in some countries the reality in day-to-day life, whether or not aviation security-related conventions were adopted, has been tighter and more stringent checks on passengers, their carry-on baggage and hold luggage. These measures increased still more for travellers, particularly in Europe, after the Lockerbie bombing of Pan-Am flight 103 in December 1988. Thus, to a large extent air travel had become generally safer and more secure until the events of 11 September 2001. As a result terrorist groups had turned to other forms of attack to publicize their cause and try to achieve their nefarious aims, that is until the alleged plot to blow up airliners transiting the Atlantic from the UK to the US, which was foiled by British police and security services on 10 August 2006. As a result of the ensuing arrests and investigations, passenger aircraft were once more on the terrorists' 'attack-menu'.

The significant increase in acts of terrorism during the closing years of the twentieth century was matched by their ferocity. Technological developments and the killing power of the weapons available were not lost on terrorist groups. Nor were they lost on dictatorial leaders who sponsored terrorism, such as Iran, Iraq and Libya, and those who committed acts of terrorism against their own peoples, notably Saddam Hussein's gassing of the people of Halabja. Coupled with rapid advances in satellite television and other communications systems, terrorists were quick to harness the power of the media and to publicize their grievances and ideologies on the world stage. The resulting publicity, with all its lurid details, is as abhorrent to some as it is lauded by others, polarizing communities and populations at the expense of greater understanding and tolerance.

Although not condoned, there is a significant difference in attacking a government's forces of security or law and order as opposed to its civilian population and civil infrastructure. Even if there are those who might consider that there is legitimacy when contesting political control over an area, there are few circumstances, if any, under which such activity might be condoned. It is a very different situation when the protagonists, whether a movement for independence or of just another political or 'economic' persuasion (as has been observed, for example, more recently in Kosovo), resort to attacking men, women and children going about their daily business. Ambushing the convoys or attacking the posts of security forces who are trained and armed to deal with such insurgencies and terrorists is very different from detonating improvised explosive devices in bus stations or morning rush hour trains. Such forms of attack against unarmed civilians are the height of cowardice and should be condemned universally. This, regrettably, has been the more common approach adopted by most terrorist organizations in the last 30 to 35 years, culminating in significant numbers of deaths and injuries, the destruction of property and damage to local and regional economies.

Against this backdrop of terrorist groups with a variety of agendas, operating in many parts of the world, one might have expected to see a more comprehensive and cohesive approach taken, collectively, by members of the international community. Twelve key conventions or instruments on the suppression of different acts of terrorism, comprising the United Nations Treaty Collection, were adopted between 1963 and 1999.[13] Four are deposited with the Secretary-General to the United Nations and eight with other depositories, such as the International Civil Aviation Organization (ICAO), the International Atomic Energy Agency (IAEA) and the International Maritime Organization (IMO). These are the twelve overarching international instruments. There are a further seven regional conventions held by their appropriate Secretary-Generals, for example the Arab League or League of Arab States (LAS), the Organization of the Islamic Conference (IOC) and the South Asian Association for Regional Cooperation (SAARC).

Besides different aspects of aviation safety, the conventions cover a variety of other subjects related to terrorism, including the criminalization of hostage taking, the marking of explosives, the suppression of terrorist bombings and the financing of terrorism. The response to these instruments, just as with the first one highlighted above, has varied significantly from state to state, region to region. The key factor is that the conventions, particularly the first twelve mentioned above, did when introduced, and still do, provide a framework on which individual states are able to base their counter-terrorism policies and strategies. These instruments are also intended to provide nation states with the basic framework to deal with terrorism as a whole. It is also important to note that they all pre-date the more specific UN Security Council resolutions directed at the international response to terrorism, such as UNSCR 1267 or 1373. When ratified and properly implemented, the conventions provide the means by which states can signal their commitment to combating crucial aspects of terrorism. The conventions are also a reminder of the legitimacy of the United Nations as the ultimate, multi-lateral forum with the authority to ensure global security.

6

The United Nations: Rising to the Challenge

The world has a love–hate relationship with the UN. States turn to the organization when it suits their individual agendas, calling for its intervention. Others, conversely, either veto or ignore its authority or shun its involvement. Such attitudes are not confined to terrorism related matters but permeate many aspects of the work of the Security Council. During the 1990s, while the good works and achievements of other component parts of the United Nations were often overlooked or ignored, the organization came in for serious and, tragically, often well-founded criticism. In particular, the appalling events surrounding the genocide in Rwanda in 1994 and the Srebrenica massacres in Bosnia in 1995 have left their scars on 'un.org' and its credibility. In the case of Rwanda, the political will did not exist and the intervention eventually sanctioned by the Security Council was far too little and far too late. Rwanda will remain a very black mark on the UN's record for many years, a point that was highlighted in the UN Secretary-General's commemorative speech in 2004. As for Srebrenica, this was to a large extent the result of too soft a line being taken with the belligerents over too long a period. The break-up of the former Yugoslavia in the summer of 1991, unleashing as it did pent-up nationalist agendas, was further aggravated by fierce and often brutal inter-ethnic fighting. Initially, fighting took place, for only a couple of weeks, between Slovenes and Serbs. The cession of Slovenia was not a major impediment to Slobodan Milošević's aspirations of a 'Greater Serbia', but Croatia was a very different matter. Croats seeking independence from Belgrade were taking action against 'minority' Serbs in four key areas of Croatia, who in turn were backed up by units of the Yugoslav National Army (JNA). Later, in April 1992, fighting erupted in Bosnia and Hercegovina between Serbs, Croats and Muslims, following a failed referendum (held on 28 February and 1 March 1992) on the future independence of that former Yugoslav republic.

The United Nations Protection Force (UNPROFOR) was originally established to keep the peace in the four minority Serb enclaves in Croatia; the Krajina (split North and South for UN administrative convenience) and East and West Slavonia.[1] These Serb-majority populated areas had been settled in the sixteenth century by the Habsburgs to provide a military frontier (*vojna krajina*) or defensive belt between them and the Ottoman Turks. In the old Serbo-Croat language the word *krajina* actually means 'border regions'.[2] Cyrus Vance, on behalf of the United Nations, brokered a rather shaky ceasefire between Belgrade and Zagreb at the end of December 1991 in what was then still a 'neutral' Sarajevo (hence the 'Sarajevo Accord'). Under a subsequent Security Council resolution, these parts of Croatia were designated UN 'protected areas' (UNPA). This particular resolution provided for a military strength of 10,400 infantry, 2,740 support personnel (i.e. logistics units) and 100 military observers (UNMO).[3] Then, after Sarajevo and much of Bosnia had gone to hell in a handcart in the spring of 1992, the Security Council decided to extend the mandate of UNPROFOR into Bosnia. The initial intention was to provide a security zone around Sarajevo and its airport.[4] Unfortunately, the situation on the ground throughout large swaths of Bosnia and Hercegovina continued to deteriorate, in some instances very rapidly. Almost daily there were more and more killings of civilians and the wholesale expulsion of ethnic minority populations from towns and villages, hence the coining of the phrase 'ethnic cleansing' – the empty houses being torched or razed to the ground. If the populations were not expelled, then the village or town in which they had sought sanctuary came under siege from the dominant ethnicity trying to control the area. Although significant numbers of people from all three ethnicities were subjected to this type of inhumane treatment, it was the Muslims who undoubtedly faired the worst. In short, it was because of an appeal to the UN from those under siege in Srebrenica, through the commander of UN troops in Bosnia at the time, the French general Philippe Morrillon, that the Security Council designated it a UN-Safe Area on 6 May 1993, along with areas centred on Bihać, Goražde, Tuzla and Žepa.[5] These five Bosnian Muslim (later Bosniak) enclaves, however, surrounded as they were by troops of the Bosnian Serb Army (BSA), were in reality very 'un-safe' areas.

As is too often the case, resolutions adopted in the Security Council, for all their apparent good intentions, end up as little more than political statements. The resolutions designating the 'safe areas' and many others relating at that time to the situation in the former Yugoslavia were no exception. Although Security Council resolution 844 (1993) authorized an additional 5,600 infantry and 2,000 support personnel to the troop strength of UNPROFOR, specifically as reinforcements for the 'safe areas', many of the troop contributions were either late in coming, ill-equipped for the task in hand or fell well short of the numbers and capabilities required for the tasks. Other contingents, despite being trained, equipped and fully capable, had their deployments restricted by their governments to specific assignments rather than conforming to the operational priorities of the UN mission's Force Commander. Those that did deploy to protect the 'safe areas' were subjected to continual harassment and obstruction, particularly by troops of the Bosnian Serb Army under the command of General Ratko Mladić, who was later indicted for war crimes. There were many occasions when this obstructionism was widespread – and it could be practised at any time by any of the three ethnicities. How, when and where usually depended on the mood of the local commanders, the weather or the early morning intake of rakia or slivovic by those manning the road blocks through which UNPROFOR or the humanitarian convoys had to pass.[6]

Nonetheless, there were some interesting examples of elements of UNPROFOR deciding that enough was enough and, after a fair warning, giving the belligerents a taste of their own medicine. One particular instance, worthy of note, was in the spring of 1994, when 'OP Tango 21', an observation post on the confrontation line between the Bosnian Serbs and the Muslims in the 'Sapna Thumb' area of northeast Bosnia, was being continually hit by Serb mortar fire. The commander of the Swedish infantry from NORBAT2, manning 'Tango 21', became rather bored with the Bosnian Serb mortar crews that kept dropping mortar bombs close to or inside his position.[7] He visited the Serb commander and warned him that if the mortaring did not stop then the UN troops would be obliged to respond. Despite this very fair warning, the mortaring continued. True to their word, the Swedes called up the Danish tank squadron, who deployed a troop of their

Leopard tanks and gave the Serbs a taste of their own medicine. Using the tanks' main armament, they shelled the mortar baseplate position, killing one Serb and injuring fourteen. History does not relate whether the Serb commander had difficulty controlling his men or whether he decided to call the UN's bluff – probably the latter. Either way it solved the problem. The incoming mortar rounds stopped and the incident was not followed by retaliation, as had often been feared by many in the UN mission if too tough a line was taken with any of the belligerents. Force, as was later proven, was the only deal that the Serbs respected, but even that was not without its tribulations for the peacekeepers.

The Danish squadron had originally deployed to the mission area, by rail, through the UN's logistic facility at Pančevo, courtesy of the JNA near Belgrade. However, the Bosnian Serbs, with the assistance of the authorities in Belgrade, used a variety of 'technical and procedural' reasons to stop the deployment; in the end UNPROFOR was obliged to remove the tanks, by rail via Hungary and Croatia, to Trieste in Italy. From there they were taken, courtesy of RFA *Sir Geraint*, a British Royal Fleet Auxiliary Landing Ship Logistic, to the Dalmatian port of Split and then taken by road to Tuzla. The engagement in Sapna in spring 1994 perhaps emphasized why the Serbs had gone to such lengths to stop the deployment of the tanks into Bosnia, especially since their armour and firepower was superior to that of the Bosnian Serbs.

Unlike the Nordic Battle Group (NORBAT-2), the Dutch contingent responsible for Srebrenica had no heavy armour. Equipped only with armoured personnel carriers armed with a single 0.5-inch (12.7-mm) heavy machine gun, it was under-gunned when compared to the Serbs, who had T54/55 tanks, mortars, artillery and multiple rocket launchers. Even the massacre of some 7,000 men and boys, systematically separated from their womenfolk and the rest of their families, was not enough for an immediate response, despite the international outcry. It did, however, 'shorten the international community's fuse', causing NATO and UNPROFOR to ratchet up their preparations to respond given the right circumstances – as if more were needed. The opportunity came when the BSA shelled a market in downtown Sarajevo on 28 August 1995, killing 30 and wounding 80 people. The response when it came was formidable, even if it was long overdue. Operation 'Deliberate Force' commenced on 30 August.[8] Over the next three weeks NATO aircraft, operating in support of the UN mission, struck at BSA targets in Eastern Bosnia and around Sarajevo. Cruise missiles struck at targets near Banja Luka. In addition, an Anglo-French Rapid Reaction Force (RRF), which had deployed into the theatre in summer 1995, fired more than 3,300 artillery and mortar rounds, every one of them observed shots, at the Serb targets.[9] This bombardment, coupled with the Muslim/Croat Federation assaults on Serb-held territory in Central and Western Bosnia, convinced the Bosnian Serbs that perhaps they would be wise to accept a cessation of hostilities agreement (COHA). They had lost huge swaths of territory and, with Federation troops and tanks poised only 30 kilometres south of Banja Luka, the Bosnian Serbs' 'western capital', they opted to stop fighting. The COHA was signed on 12 October 1995. The proximity talks that followed in Dayton, Ohio, produced the 'Dayton Peace Accord', which came into effect in December 1995.[10] Since March 1992 a substantial UN peacekeeping mission and numerous humanitarian organizations (NGOs) had been present in much of the former Yugoslavia. Their collective efforts undoubtedly reduced the loss of life during the inter-ethnic strife. Despite this significant international presence, the eventual end to the armed conflict was achieved only with military muscle to back tough diplomacy. But the muscle was provided by NATO – not the United Nations mission itself.

Previous attempts to threaten the belligerents with air strikes, under a dual-key (UN/NATO) release system, codenamed 'Blue Sword', had proved ineffective.[11] There had been two occasions when NATO fighters had been downed by Serb anti-aircraft missiles. The pilot of a US F-16 lost over northeast Bosnia was rescued by a daring US heliborne recovery operation mounted from a carrier in the Adriatic. The second occurred near Goražde, when a British Sea Harrier was downed while in the process of bombing a Bosnian Serb tank. However, when punitive air strikes were made on 25 May 1995 against BSA ammunition dumps near Pale in Eastern Bosnia, in response to Serb outrages, the latter responded by heavy shelling of the safe areas. The next day the Serbs responded to further NATO air strikes by detaining UN personnel for the third time as hostages. More UN hostages were seized over the next two days and there was also a bloody engagement between the Bosnian Serb Army and French 'Blue Helmets' at the UN's Vrbanje Bridge position in the centre of Sarajevo. Air power had not been a great success and had not achieved the required results. For the last big joint operation, however, all UN and NGO staff operating in Serb-held areas, predominantly around Sarajevo, were quietly and discreetly withdrawn to safer locations before attacks began against the Serb targets.

Once again an effective response, deeds not words, from the 'world body' (or at least some of its members) had come far too late. Yet again, this inability or unwillingness by the international community to make a timely and effective response boiled down to a lack of political will. Among the states responsible are those with the military, economic and diplomatic capabilities to ensure global peace and security. Early on in the conflict in the former Yugoslavia, James Baker, the US Secretary of State at the time, reportedly remarked: 'The US doesn't have a dog in this fight!' This was a classic example of how vested interests can influence the response of individual states, internationally, to events that threaten peace and security. Many Balkan commentators and interlocutors have suggested that what he really meant, however cynical it may appear, was that the US had no economic or political interest in the Balkans. Certainly, there is no oil in Bosnia, which might otherwise have energized the United States, sooner rather than later, into taking a more significant role in the debacle. Some of the European states involved considered that Yugoslavia was part of their backyard and resented US 'interference', which may well have prompted the US agreeing to back off and leave them to sort out the problem on their own. But ignoring the situation as it was in 1991 and 1992 may, in the long term, have proved a mistake for US interests.

FROM BOĆINA TO BERLIN

An earlier engagement in the efforts to resolve the conflict in Bosnia might have negated the need for the fledgling government of Bosnia, headed by President Alija Izetbegović, to accept assistance from Iran and the presence in his country of the *mujāhidīn*. Many of these so-called holy warriors, who came to fight alongside the Bosniaks in their struggle against the Bosnian Croats and Serbs, had been trained in al-Qaida camps in Afghanistan. Some had already won their spurs fighting against the Soviet occupation of Afghanistan or alongside Islamic militants in the disputed areas of Kashmir. With the departure from Afghanistan of the Soviet occupation forces, budding jihadists needed a new battleground on which to wage their jihad. Bosnia provided such an opportunity.

Jihadists from a number of predominantly Arab countries came to Bosnia, where they reportedly formed the *mujāhidīn* battalion. In the Bosnian language they were referred to as *el-Mudzahidin*. Referring to this ragtag grouping as a 'brigade' or 'battalion' may be over-gilding the lily somewhat, but they certainly worked, lived and trained together near Ribnica, west of Tuzla. Estimates vary, but it is known that a hard core of at least 300 'foreign fighters' came to support their 'Muslim brothers' in Bosnia. Other estimates put the figure much higher, even as high as 5,000;[12] this latter figure, however, may refer to the total of the more itinerant members who came and went between 1992 and 1995. The fact that they have been described as being under the command of one of the Bosnian Muslim commanders, General Rasim Delić, testifies to their involvement and their way of fighting. General Delić has been tried for war crimes by the UN's Hague Tribunal – the International Criminal Tribunal for Yugoslavia (ICTY) – on the basis of the atrocities committed by these *mudzahidin* against Croats and Serbs. The regard by the latter for the Geneva Conventions may at times have been remarkably thin, but that of the *mudzahidin* was non-existent. Few of the peacekeepers, or their civil affairs counterparts working in Bosnia at that time, were aware of the significance of these Muslim fanatics and their connection to al-Qaida. But in retrospect one does have to ask whether it was just chance or a coincidence that this group of foreign Islamist fighters was 'deployed' or accommodated in that part of UNPROFOR's area of responsibility (AOR) assigned to the UN Pakistani contingent (PAKBDE).[13] Members of the UN having to travel in the area were often instructed to use a special route avoiding the area near Ribnica, on the grounds that the road there was often shelled by the Serbs. Perhaps they had good reason to shell the area, especially after some of the atrocities committed against them by the *mujāhidīn* on behalf of the Bosniaks, represented by a video of *el-Mudzahidin* kicking the severed heads of their Serb victims around like footballs. The 'visiting fighters' were also credited with another attack on a Bosnian Serb field HQ in the Mount Igman area, in which all the incumbents had their throats slit, including the female nurses. Some of these 'foreigners' were to remain a major nuisance factor in the post-Dayton peace-building efforts and featured in allegations of support for al-Qaida, both before and after 9/11.

A number of these former *mujāhidīn* were given Bosnian citizenship, ostensibly on the grounds that they had married Bosnian women. After the Dayton Accord, some were allocated houses in two specific villages, Guči Gora (near Travnik) and Bočina (near Zenica), from which Croats and Bosnian Serbs had been expelled or 'cleansed' during the 1995 autumn offensive. Bočina proved to be a distinct thorn in the side of S-FOR's Multi-National Division (MND) North,[14] and staff at the HQ in Tuzla indicated early in 1998 that the Bočina valley was a virtual 'no-go-area'. This was certainly the case for US troops and US members of the United Nations International Police Task Force (UNIPTF). Even the Task Force's officers from countries such as Egypt and Jordan found the occupants of the Bočina valley extremely difficult, if not impossible, to deal with. It was not until the Danish S-FOR battalion assumed responsibility for the area that the international community in Bosnia began to get real visibility over these former *mujāhidīn*. Whenever the Danes patrolled the area they were constantly being shadowed by members of the group, using unregistered or incorrectly registered vehicles and carrying hand-held radios – presumably to call up reinforcements. The *mujāhidīn* certainly behaved as if they were a law unto themselves. Even the local Bosniak police from Maglaj were extremely reluctant to intervene in any way when requested so to do by either the UN or NATO.

The local police's reticence to demonstrate their authority effectively with the inhabitants of Bočina was very obvious on the occasion of the first 'graveyard visit' for Bosnian Serbs hoping to return. Enabling Serbs to return to their villages in the Ozren area, which can be dominated from the Bočina valley, was crucial to the overall scheme of maintaining the momentum of the return of displaced persons and refugees (DPR) in this sector of central Bosnia. Aware of the extremely hostile attitude exhibited by these former *mujāhidīn* to any outsiders, except perhaps to representatives of the Saudi High Commission for Refugees in Bosnia, the joint UN/NATO team organizing the visit had insisted on a strong civilian police presence to ensure security for the event. These were backed up by civilian police members from the UNIPTF, UN civil affairs officers and troops from the S-FOR Danish Battalion. Throughout the visit the 'temporary occupants' of Bočina were extremely threatening. Besides waving knives and axes at the visiting Serbs, the vast majority of whom were quite elderly people, the *mujāhidīn* spat on the bus and made throat-cutting signs. They jostled some Task Force officers and, just to show their utter contempt, made a point of chopping the heads off live chickens right in front of one the Danes' armoured personnel carriers. The hatred in their eyes towards all concerned was very clear to see. In the end it took the concerted and combined efforts of staff from NATO's Nordic Polish Brigade, representatives of the UN mission in Bosnia (UNMIBH) and the UN High Commissioner for Refugees (UNHCR) to persuade the Office of the High Representative to pressurize the Bosniak leadership to resettle their 'acquired citizens' elsewhere. During a number of visits to Boćina by UN civil affairs staff during 1998 the presence of Saudi humanitarian agencies was also noted. At this time the links between such organizations and al-Qaida, which were to surface later, were not common knowledge. The *mujāhidīn* from Boćina were subsequently dispersed around Bosnia. Some of them left the country, most probably taking their nefarious skills elsewhere, possibly to Chechnya. A key figure from the Boćina group, Reda Seyam, eventually ended up living on social welfare in Germany, possibly in Berlin for a while, before moving to other locations favoured by some of the more extreme elements of the Muslim diaspora. Reda Seyam had previously acquired German citizenship by marrying a German woman. Apparently his travels to Berlin had taken him via Saudi Arabia and Indonesia, where he had been imprisoned for a few months on immigration charges. Others of the group were subsequently deported from Bosnia, but some, along with their extremist sympathizers, remain. Even to this day one can often see women in the central Bosnian town of Zenica covered from head to toe in a full black Bedouin-style *abaya* with the face completely masked – a form of dress totally alien to Bosniak women and Bosnia's longstanding Muslim culture, with its Ottoman origins.

FROM AN UNHOLY ALLIANCE TO THE DAYTON ACCORD

Back in 1991 it had been left to the Europeans to resolve the conflict in the former Yugoslavia. The Balkans was considered their backyard, anyway, and there were many in Europe that actually resented any US interference to resolve this conflict. For some considerable time into the fighting Britain and France were reluctant to 'sanction' their old Second World War ally, the Serbs, particularly against the Croats, whom many still remembered for their wartime fascist tendencies and support of Hitler and the Nazi regime. The word *ustasha*, the Serbs' old term for their erstwhile Croat enemies, was heard all too often when national fervours were aroused and 'debated'. The Russians, for their part, remained even more supportive of the regime in Belgrade throughout the Yugoslav conflict; long-established ties to their 'Slav cousins' and a former Communist regime were, perhaps understandably, difficult to sever. When America did eventually start participating in the process it was on the side of the Croats and the Bosnian Muslims (later redefined as Bosniaks). To simplify the US way of thinking, the Clinton Administration worked hard, diplomatically, to develop the Federation between the Bosniaks and the Croats. Although this was something of an 'unholy alliance', the two ethnicities, despite their many differences, did coordinate their military efforts for a time. Certainly this initial collaboration lasted long enough in the autumn of 1995 for nascent 'Federation forces' to roll back the Serbs from huge swaths of territory in Western, Central and Eastern Bosnia and Hercegovina, leading to an eventual cessation of hostilities. The fact that this new-found Federation, enshrined as one of the two 'entities' in the constitution in the Dayton Agreement, continues to exist is due as much to the efforts of the international community as to the presence of the NATO-led Stabilization Force (S-FOR).[15] The presence of the latter was, until its departure in late 2004, a sufficient threat to restrain any serious outbreaks of inter-ethnic violence, despite the continuing attitudes of hardline elements within all three ethnicities throughout the country.

The basic problem with sending UN peacekeepers into Bosnia in 1992 was that there had been no peace to keep. The initial deployment of mechanized infantry units from NATO countries during the autumn of 1992, in addition to those deployed earlier in June to the Sarajevo area, including its airport, was intended to ensure the passage of humanitarian assistance into Central Bosnia and to Sarajevo.[16] Despite these units being quite well equipped, for example the British battalion had Warrior armoured infantry fighting vehicles, their rules of engagement were very restricted. They provided tough escorts but were not expected to fight their way through any opposition from the warring factions, only return fire in self-defence. That being said, there were one or two instances of the local belligerents finding that they had bitten off more than they could chew. Receiving a few well-aimed explosive rounds from a 30-mm Rarden cannon is not an experience that one often has the opportunity to repeat. After Dayton there was an agreed settlement, albeit one that has and continues to have a bumpy ride to progress. But progress, however slow, has been made. As then, and as regrettably continues to be the case, it is all a matter of political will, not only of the belligerents in a conflict, but also of the international community to resolve the conflict and support the post-conflict peace-building process. The latter situation is invariably much more difficult to manage and requires remarkable patience and in-depth understanding of all aspects of the situation, tempered with real firmness. Prior to its arrival, many within NATO military circles had been singularly critical of the UN efforts in Bosnia. However, despite all its bluster and having maintained significant troop levels for almost nine years, until handing over to a European Force on 30 November 2004, NATO failed to apprehend the two most wanted war criminals, Radovan Karadžić and his military commander, General Ratko Mladić. Why not? Perhaps one should ask the politicians. This 'collective reticence' by the international community to take the bull by the horns has, despite the horrors described above, continued with events in other parts of the world. Even though populations have been subjected to appalling atrocities and major displacement, as was the case in Afghanistan in the late 1990s and in the Darfur region of Sudan in summer 2004, the UN has been slow to react. Tragically, the closing paragraphs of the UN Secretary-General's very detailed and thorough inquiry report into the catastrophic events at Srebrenica have either been ignored or too quickly and too often forgotten:

> 504. In the end, the only meaningful and lasting amends we can make to the citizens of Bosnia and Herzegovina . . . is to do our utmost not to allow such horrors to recur.

> 505. To ensure that we have fully learned the lessons of the tragic history detailed in this report, I wish to encourage Member States to engage in a process of reflection and analysis . . . The aim of this process would be to clarify and improve the capacity of the United Nations to respond to various forms of conflict. I have in mind addressing such issues as . . . the inadequacy of symbolic deterrence in the face of a systematic campaign of violence; the pervasive ambivalence within United Nations regarding the role of force in the pursuit of peace . . . and a range of doctrinal

and institutional issues that go to the very heart of the United Nations' ability to keep the peace and help protect civilian populations from armed conflict. The Secretariat is ready to join in such a process.[17]

These words and the sentiments they express are as true today as they were then, not only with regard to the ability of the United Nations to respond effectively to cases of civil strife and political violence, but also in its ability and willingness to respond effectively to transnational terrorism.

Before leaving Bosnia it is important to record that, despite the horrors, shame and tragedy associated with the Srebrenica massacres, a great deal was achieved by a number of different UN agencies. Despite few routes suitable for large trucks, atrocious road conditions, particularly in the Balkan winters, and the vagaries of the warring factions, the UN High Commissioner for Refugees (UNHCR) and the World Food Programme (WFP), working with a plethora of NGOs, provided shelter and sustenance to thousands and thousands of the displaced and besieged, averting further deaths and alleviating some of the suffering. UNPROFOR also built up a comprehensive joint UN-civilian/military logistics organization, essential for operations throughout the former Yugoslavia since so few support troops mandated by the Security Council materialized. This equivalent of a 'logistics brigade' fielded around 1,300 UN civilian logistics personnel. Besides supply, movements and transportation officers there were rations and petroleum specialists, truck drivers and mechanics. These were required to manage and operate more than 300 prime movers, including buses, trucks, tankers, recovery vehicles, helicopters and a small air transport fleet that included three large Il-76 freighters. Overshadowed by the horrors of the ethnic cleansing and other crimes against humanity, successes such as these, attributable solely to a relatively small number of courageous and committed United Nations staff members, invariably go unrecognized.

BRAHIMI REPORT

As a result of the problems that had been faced by peace missions, particularly in Haiti, Rwanda, Somalia and Yugoslavia, some international soul-searching did take place. The UN Secretary-General commissioned a panel of specialists, with experience in various aspects of peacekeeping, under the chairmanship of Lakhdar Brahimi, a former Foreign Minister of Algeria, to undertake a thorough review of the organization's peace and security activities. A number of the recommendations contained in the 'Brahimi Report',[18] which was presented in summer 2000, have subsequently been introduced into the Secretariat's Department of Peace Keeping Operations (DPKO). The thrust of the report is directed at what the Secretariat needed to do better, but it does not touch upon one of the underlying problems, namely the commitment of member states to fulfilling resolutions and, in many cases, to put it bluntly, not 'putting their money where their mouth is!'

It is responses by the Security Council and the 'membership' of the organization to its demands that are the key to tackling situations involving threats to peace, security and to civilian populations. Wholesale attacks by the Sudanese Muslim militia, the *janjaweed*, against the African population of the western Sudanese province of Darfur, with all the signs, once again, of crimes against humanity and apparent efforts to drive an ethnicity from their homes, bring to mind the words of Kofi Annan, the UN Secretary-General, cited above, 'that go to the very heart of the United Nations ability to . . . protect civilian populations from armed conflict'. When at last the Security Council got round to discussing the Darfur situation seriously in summer 2004, attempts by some Council members to impose or even threaten sanctions against Sudan, which would undoubtedly impact on the Sudanese oil industry, were not supported by Algeria, China, Pakistan and Russia.[19] So instead the Council changed tack slightly and the 'mountain moved to Muhammad'. In November 2004 the Security Council met in Nairobi; this was only the fourth time in its history that it had convened outside New York. Unfortunately, the emphasis was on the long-running civil war in southern Sudan, not Darfur.

The session was attended by representatives of the Sudanese government and the Sudanese People's Liberation Movement and its military wing, the Sudanese People's Liberation Army, from southern Sudan, along with other interested parties, such as the Arab League and the African Union. The Council witnessed the signing of a Memorandum of Understanding (MOU) between the two factions, by which they undertook to reach a final agreement that would end the

'North–South' civil war that had plagued the country for more than two decades. Given the fact that both sides had been close to an agreement for almost a year, the Council's supporting statement lacked any bite and there was only a brief mention of the other conflict. The two sides in the dispute were promised aid and assistance if they fulfilled the MOU, ending the civil war and concluding a Comprehensive Peace Agreement by 31 December 2004.[20] Regrettably, the Council put no particular pressure on the Sudanese government, despite reports of continuing attacks against the African civilians in the Darfur region. Although the resolution made certain demands on the Government of Sudan, the Sudanese Liberation Army and the Justice and Equality Movement concerning the ongoing situation in Darfur, it did not apply real pressure on the Sudanese government to cease the atrocities. Yet again, the Council had missed a trick, highlighting again the lack of political will that is forthcoming when there is a need to crack down on terrorism. The US Government had already accused the Sudanese government of 'genocide';[21] like it or not, rape, pillage and driving whole communities from their homes and villages, which are then systematically torched, is nothing less than a form of terrorism. Systematically forcing an ethnic group, which may be at odds with the government of a country because of religious or political beliefs, to flee their tribal homes and lands in such a way as to change the demographics of a country was, when it happened in Bosnia, called 'ethnic cleansing'. That is what was, by all accounts, happening in Darfur. If proven, states would be obliged under the Genocide Convention to intervene in the Sudan crisis. The report by the International Commission of Inquiry (ICI) appointed by the Secretary-General in October 2004 to investigate the charges fell just short of using the actual term 'genocide': 'The Commission concluded that the Government of the Sudan has not pursued a policy of genocide', although it did go on to state 'that in some instances individuals, including government officials, may commit acts with genocidal intent'.[22] However, the Commission qualified this statement by stating: 'Whether this was the case in Darfur . . . is a determination that only a competent court can make'. It concluded this part of its findings by indicating clearly that 'International offences such as the crimes against humanity and war crimes that have been committed in Darfur may be no less serious and heinous than genocide.' Is this yet another example of the hand of political correctness diluting the truth just enough to avoid the ultimate embarrassment for an individual member state or the international community being forced to act?

A British House of Commons committee of Members of Parliament was, however, less generous with its findings on Darfur. In their report of 30 March 2005, *Darfur, Sudan: The Responsibility to Protect*, the MPs challenged the World Health Organization's figure of 70,000 dead, their estimate being much higher and closer to 300,000.[23] They went on to criticize the ineffective response of the international community and the UN Security Council, stating that

> The UN Security Council has failed to fulfil its responsibility to protect the people of Darfur, and to maintain international peace and security. Driven by national interests, the Security Council has been divided, weak and ineffective. There should be a referral of Darfur to the International Criminal Court, targeted sanctions and an extension of the arms embargo to cover the Government of the Sudan.

The Committee also considered that the priority given to the outstanding peace between the north and south had been misguided and had deadly consequences for the people of Darfur. At last a respected and influential member of the Security Council was saying what needed to be said, even if it was uncomfortable for some on the Council. One cannot overlook the fact that the Sudanese government had, to all intents and purposes, sub-contracted much of the 'counter-insurgency' work against those in Darfur to the *janjaweed* militias. It is tantamount to being 'state-sponsored' terrorism, even if it is directed against its own people.

Despite the 'peace agreement' that was reached on 5 May 2006, the Sudanese government should still be called to account since the main perpetrators of the 'crimes', the *janjaweed*, continue to rape and pillage. An even more worrying aspect of the *janjaweed*, and one that the international community has found it politically convenient to ignore, concerns their possible links with transnational Islamist terrorists – perhaps even al-Qaida. Although he denies the suggestions, a certain Musa Hilal, who has been accused of being the leader of the *janjaweed*, has reportedly 'said his fighters are engaged in a jihad, or holy war, and will not disarm even if the government demands it'.[24]

On 10 July 2006 an article by Douglas Farah appeared on the Counter-terrorism Blog website, in which he states that: 'A recent international intelligence document says there are credible reports that a cadre of about 15 al Qaeda operatives in Sudan is providing training to troops . . . of [the] Janjaweed leader Musa Hilal'.[25] By putting together such reports and statements, one can see how conflict situations, if not addressed adroitly, robustly and with alacrity by the international community, can quickly degenerate into circumstances that al-Qaida-related groups are able to exploit. Taken also with the exhortations attributed to Usama bin Laden it is easy to see how quickly the extreme Islamists try and exploit conflict situations to their advantage. In a taped message aired by al-Jazeera Television on 23 April 2006, bin Laden called the peace agreement between Khartoum and the southern Sudan 'unjust', because it

> permits south Sudan to gain independence from the north within six years . . . this agreement is not worth the ink by which it was written, and we do not accord the least concern to it. Nobody, whoever he was, has the right to accede an inch of the land of Islam and the south will remain an inseparable part of the land of Islam, God willing, even if the war continued for decades.[26]

Finally, bin Laden 'urge[s] the *mujāhidīn* to get acquainted with Darfur state tribes and land and its surroundings, keeping in mind that the region is about to face the rainy season that hampers means of transport'. In the same vein, classifying them as Crusader/Zionist attacks against Muslims, bin Laden calls into question the previous conflicts in Bosnia and East Timor, and the role of the UN.

It was therefore encouraging to see that at least one of the recommendations made both by the UN's International Commission of Inquiry and the UK's International Development Committee were reflected in the Security Council decision 'to refer the situation in Darfur since 1 July 2002 to the Prosecutor of the International Criminal Court'.[27] The decision was duly reflected on 5 April 2005 when the UN Secretary-General formally handed sealed files to the Prosecutor of the International Criminal Court in The Hague. These files, which had been prepared by the International Commission, contained the names of 51 individuals suspected of crimes against humanity in Darfur. However, resolution 1593 falls short of the Security Council recognizing its 'responsibility to protect' or of imposing any form of sanctions on the Sudanese government.

This 'responsibility to protect' was a recommendation of a committee, set up in 2001 by the UN Secretary-General Kofi Annan, to study the competing claims of state sovereignty and individuals' rights. According to an article in the *Economist*, the idea of the international community having 'not simply the right, but a responsibility to act to protect the people of a country when [the government of] that country abdicated that responsibility', which was quietly gaining momentum, was apparently derailed by one of the *post facto* justifications for the invasion of Iraq: 'that the invasion was justified on humanitarian grounds'.[28] (It remains to be seen how effective will be the outcome once a UN peace mission has been established to take over from the African Union mission in Darfur – as requested by the Security Council on 24 March 2006.)[29]

The reality is that individual states are prepared to get involved and discuss UN resolutions if they have economic or political interests. National interests will always play a prominent role in how nations respond to Security Council resolutions. Sometimes they will support them. Sometimes, for the same sort of reasons, they will not. Sometimes public opinion forces politicians to respond to crisis situations around the world, but often only after the media have played a significant part exposing the facts. Even then it is shameful to see the way in which politicians or their spokespersons can deny the facts so blatantly. In the end it is often the extent of the humanitarian crisis, the suffering and the atrocities, beamed in daily images around the world by the media, that provokes a response. It was scenes from Sarajevo and many other parts of Bosnia that eventually determined US involvement and that of many other nations. In particular, the 'Belsen-like' pictures of emaciated Muslims being held as 'prisoners of war' in a Bosnian Serb detention facility at Omarska, near Prijedor in northwestern Bosnia, had a major impact on world public opinion. But that involvement was still neither comprehensive nor tough enough to stop the Srebrenica massacres. Then, and only then, as we have seen, was there a strong reaction – but once again after the event and too late.

Similarly, it was a combination of media coverage, exasperated UN officials and humanitarian NGOs that had to publicize the human catastrophe that had been unfolding in Darfur since February 2003. The fact that it was fallout from the civil war in Sudan, which had been running for two decades, only made the situation worse. For years before the Darfur crisis, the world was aware of the suffering and strife that existed between the Arab and Islamic north of the country and the black Africans in the southern half. Perhaps it should come as no surprise, then, that in 1989 Usama bin Laden should have been invited by Hassan al Turbi, the then leader of the National Islamic Front of Sudan and a member of the Muslim Brotherhood, to assist in this conflict. In return bin Laden was able to set up significant training facilities and make considerable business investments in the country until the Sudanese government was forced, under substantial international pressure, to expel him in 1996. Contrary to previous assertions, it is now believed that when he left the Sudan for Afghanistan he did not have much wealth to take.[30] Over the next few years, however, he was able to give money to the Taliban, thanks to his access to a number of wealthy and sympathetic donors with deep pockets. Whether the payments were as 'rent' for his safe havens, or out of philanthropic support for the efforts of the Taliban against the Northern Alliance, is debatable.

7

Afghanistan: The Taliban and the Threat Beyond

In October 2001, when the US-led coalition intervened, the Islamic Emirate of Afghanistan ruled by the Islamic Movement of the Taliban was host to more than a hundred combat bases for housing, supplying, training and staging camps. Owned, managed and sponsored by al-Qaida and other jihadist groups, the training camps were the mainstay of Usama bin Laden's jihad movement. Before they returned to their home countries to participate in the local jihad, or travelled to target countries to wage the global jihad, a generation of Afghan alumni was provided with varying degrees of ideological indoctrination, and physical and weapons training. A wide range of theoretical and practical instruction was provided to generate the required expertise and the skills for guerrilla warfare. Would-be *jihadis* were trained to fight in the front line against combatants and in urban operations. Instruction was given in how to conduct terrorism against civilian targets. The indoctrination and training given to the recruits engendered an *esprit* among the core of followers, preparing them for future al-Qaida operations. The camps created the bonds – the institutional and interpersonal linkages – putting in place a far-flung network of support cells and operation cadres that continues to pose an enduring threat to governments and societies worldwide.

The training imparted at the camps ranged from very basic and quite general skills to advanced and specialist levels of expertise and knowledge: for front-line fighters, planners, document forgers, communications specialists, scouts, technicians, bomb-makers and hijackers. Ranging from two weeks to six months, the courses imparted the knowledge required to fight in different environments, on diverse missions and in a variety of roles. Al-Qaida, the Taliban and their associated groups worldwide provided 'scholarships' for training in Afghanistan to several tens of thousands of recruits from Bosnia, Chechnya, Indonesia, Iraq, Jordan, Lebanon, Myanmar, Pakistan, Somalia, Tajikistan, Turkey, Turkmenistan, Uzbekistan and other countries. In the network of camps in Afghanistan the 'culture of jihad' unified the recruits, creating a robust multinational network. The concept of the Muslim Brotherhood was witnessed at first hand, with Uighurs from Xingjian Province in Western China clutching a Chinese–Arabic dictionary while attempting to converse with a group of American Muslims in Arabic, the lingua franca of al-Qaida. Irrespective of nationality and continent, from Asia's Moroland in the southern Philippines to Canada, the Muslims met, discussed to their hearts' content, and planned to Islamize the world. Without fear or favour, the cradle Muslims from Asia, Africa and the Middle East welcomed those from the diaspora and the migrants, as well as the convert Muslims from Australia, Europe and North America.

There were two categories of Muslims that entered Afghanistan. When they arrived in Afghanistan, most recruits did not belong to any group: it was only after they had been trained that they joined the group of their choice. The second category of recruits comprised those who had already visited a group's recruitment centre or held membership of a group before entering Afghanistan to receive training. The camps, off-limits to all but the recruits and designated members of the Taliban and al-Qaida, contained classrooms, prayer halls, bunkers, testing fields and firing ranges. Some were even equipped with underground tunnels and concrete storage facilities where weapons and chemicals were stored. Only a handful of sprawling complexes that provided basic weapons and explosives training were visible from the sky. Most camps were in clandestine houses, training only a few dozen members in specialist skills and techniques. While the large, open training camps had heavily armed guards, the small and closed facilities had no visible security.

A Palestinian-Jordanian ideologue, Dr Abdullah Azzam, was the theoretician of the multinational *mujāhidīn* campaign against the Soviet occupation of Afghanistan. Azzam was also the author of *Join the Caravan* (1987). The attraction of the journey to Afghanistan for education, training, fighting and martyrdom was poignantly articulated for the first time by Azzam. No one contributed more than Azzam in defining in operational terms a politico-religious ideology of jihad on a global scale. Through his seminal works, which were compulsory reading for the *mujāhidīn* fighting in Afghanistan, Azzam articulated jihad as the most important mandatory obligation in Islam and martyrdom as a miracle. The ideological father of both al-Qaida and the Palestinian Hamas, Azzam created a fire that will burn beyond his lifetime. The culture of the *mujāhidīn* during the Soviet period gave way to an even more strident culture of jihadists during the Taliban period (1996–2001). After the demise of the Soviet empire, the US, together with its allies in the West and friends in the Middle East, had become the principal enemy of the jihadists or Islamist fundamentalists. Driven by a politico-religious ideology, they provided alms, trained, fought and finally sacrificed their lives. The obligation to serve God, Islam, the Muslim community and their Muslim brothers, spelled out in religious texts as well as poignantly articulated by the preachers, made it the right thing to do for a young Muslim. Most Muslims did not see anything wrong in travelling to Afghanistan to participate in the jihad, especially since their own governments and the West itself had initially financed and provided weapons to fight the Soviets. The ideologues of jihad articulated and inculcated in Muslim youth the belief that a good Muslim has four levels of obligations to fulfil towards fellow Muslims.[1] The vulnerable pious were led towards believing that it was a mandatory obligation to provide alms to fellow Muslims in need; to receive training in the use of arms, when Islam is under threat; to participate in combat in support of fellow Muslims when they are under attack; and, finally, to sacrifice one's life. Al-Qaida leadership and other ideologues presented the pinnacle of Islam as a martyrdom operation.

The international neglect of Afghanistan culminated in the 9/11 attacks and led directly to the state of insecurity that the world is witnessing today. Governments blamed the UN for inaction but, at the end of the day, the UN is only as good as its members make it or want it to be. Long before 9/11, before the threat reached a transnational level, the international community, through the auspices of the United Nations, had been playing a modest role against terrorism. Although not binding, the General Assembly had passed resolutions in 1994, 1995, 1996 and 1998 urging states to adopt measures to eliminate international terrorism.[2] Then, more specifically, during 1998 three separate Security Council resolutions had been adopted that were directed at the Taliban regime.[3] These resolutions arose from the civil war in Afghanistan and the atrocities being committed by the Taliban. They were also directed against the Taliban since they were harbouring Usama bin Laden, who was wanted in connection with the August 1998 bombings of the US embassies in East Africa. All these resolutions demanded that the Taliban cease its prosecution of such a horrendous civil war and the provision of sanctuary for Usama bin Laden. The demands were all ignored. Thus, in October 1999 the Council adopted another resolution that reinforced the demands already made on the Taliban and imposed sanctions against the regime.[4] Iran and Pakistan were already facing a huge refugee crisis. Large numbers of Afghans, over a considerable period of time, had fled the fighting in Afghanistan. These migrations had resulted initially from the Soviet invasion and occupation, then from the inter-factional fighting that followed the Soviet withdrawal, and lastly because of the Taliban's medieval barbarism and puritanical prosecution of Islam.

The presence of the refugees on their territory provided Pakistan with an ideal excuse to challenge the sanctions, supporting the Taliban's claim that it was the sanctions imposed by the international community, rather than the Taliban, that were causing much of the hardship to the population. This was in addition to the catastrophic effect of three years of drought-related famine, which had hit the country over the same period. Pakistan had been the main conduit of money and weapons, provided by the United States, other Western countries and Saudi Arabia, to the *mujāhidīn* who had been fighting, and ultimately responsible for ending, the Soviet occupation of Afghanistan. After the Taliban came to the fore in 1994, it was Pakistan, through its Inter-Service Intelligence (ISI) department, that assured political respectability and supplies of weapons and ammunition to the Taliban. This approach guaranteed the security of the bases and training facilities being used and run by al-Qaida inside southern and eastern Afghanistan. These camps were being used to train 'Afghan-Arabs' to fight alongside the Taliban against the Northern Alliance under Ahmed Shah Masood, with the 'militants' in Kashmir, and also al-Qaida operatives for the global jihad. Pakistan had a vested interest, particularly at that time, in ensuring it had 'strategic depth' in the event that India might invade. Securing that military advantage meant having good relations with whichever government or regime was in Kabul or Kandahar.

In addition, the feelings of the Sunni Muslims in Pakistan towards the Taliban and their fellow Pashtun tribesfolk, particularly those who inhabit the border regions, played and still play significantly into this equation. The border between Afghanistan and Pakistan, known as the Durand Line and a relic of the pre-independence British Raj, has never been formally accepted and agreed. It bisects a wild, rugged, mountainous area inhabited by fiercely independent feudal clans of the Pashtun tribe. They have historically moved back and forth, owing little or no allegiance to the governments on either side of the demarcation. The British resolved the ungovernable nature of these tribes by establishing Federally Administered Tribal Areas (FATA) on what is now the Pakistan side of the Durand Line. Inside these autonomous regions, the tribal or clan elders are the authority, their link with Islamabad being through a 'government agent'. The tribes-people and their region have been inextricably linked to the progress of the *mujāhidīn* as they fought with the Soviets, and then moved towards their support for the Taliban from the mid-1990s and, later, for al-Qaida. More recently, they have seen the resurgence of the Taliban, from late 2002, and its involvement in offensive operations against US-led coalition forces in Afghanistan and their Afghan Army allies from 2003 into 2006 – at least when the snows melt each year in the mountain passes. This latter-day presence of the Taliban, and some non-Afghan fighters connected to al-Qaida, has been challenged by Pakistani Government Forces with some notable success, but not without Pakistani losses in the exchanges of fire that have ensued. However, the presence of Government troops in the FATA, for the first time since Pakistan achieved independence, has caused some resentment among the tribal groups. During the Taliban era it was through these autonomous areas that goods obtained through abuse of the Afghan Transit Trade Agreement (ATTA) were smuggled. At a meeting in Peshawar with Frontier Corps officers and customs officials in April 2001, it was stated that the smuggling of high-value goods from Afghanistan into Pakistan was worth 15 billion rupees annually in lost revenues to Pakistan.[5] Under the ATTA these goods were allowed to be imported, duty and tax-free, into land-locked Afghanistan, usually through the Pakistan port of Karachi and then by road into southern Afghanistan. One might ask why such large quantities of modern television sets, video recorders and air-conditioning units were being imported into Taliban-controlled Afghanistan in the first place, since there was little or no electricity and, besides, watching TV and videos was banned under the Taliban regime.[6]

The Taliban used the Afghan Transit Trade Agreement and the opium and heroin trade to help finance their side of the war. Although the Taliban imposed a ban on the cultivation of opium poppies in 2000, it did little to reduce the trade in opiates, there being significant stockpiles in Afghanistan. It is important to remember that around 80 per cent of the world's heroin emanates from Afghanistan and, however cynical this may appear, the effect of the 'Tali's ban' was a marked increase in the price of heroin in 2001 and 2002. Needless to say, the December 1999 resolution, UN SCR 1267, had little or no effect on the Taliban; the al-Qaida camps continued to operate and Mullah Omar, the Taliban's one-eyed, reclusive leader, clearly had no intention of handing over their Muslim brother Usama bin Laden, least of all to the Americans. Such an idea offended their rules of hospitality, despite indications coming to light later of significant areas of discontent between the Taliban and the Afghan-Arabs. In December 2000 it was a somewhat frustrated Security Council that adopted yet another resolution, UN SCR 1333, tightening further the sanctions regime directed against the Taliban. However, it was generally agreed that the sanctions that had already been imposed in the previous resolutions were having no effect. Therefore, in addition to the sanctions measures, the Council also requested the UN Secretary-General to establish a panel of experts, tasked to recommend a mechanism by which the sanctions could be effectively monitored. This panel was given 60 days in which to fulfil the task and report to the Council. Despite the apparent urgency of the matter, it was three months before the panel came together and got underway. Once again vested interests appear to have entered the equation. Bangladesh, then a member of the Security Council, was concerned that there was no Asian representation on the panel. The problem was eventually resolved with the addition to the panel of a former Philippines ambassador to the UN Office in Vienna (UNOV) and the International Atomic Energy Agency (IAEA). At the time this objection, annoying as it was, as well as the delays it caused, did not appear to have an ulterior motive.

In order to accomplish its task this panel travelled to the peripheral states – Iran, Pakistan, Tajikistan, Turkmenistan and Uzbekistan – to hear at first hand from the governments concerned the situation along their borders with Afghanistan. Having completed its task in the required 60 days, the panel proposed a mechanism that would provide the Council with an effective oversight of the workings of the sanctions regime.[7] The report was presented to the Council on 5 June 2001 at an open session in the main Security Council Chamber. This procedure provided the opportunity for non-Council members to speak. Afghanistan's Permanent Representative (i.e. ambassador) to the UN, who represented the 'still recognized government', used the occasion to highlight the barbarity and illegality of the (Taliban) regime 'occupying' the bulk of his country.[8] Pakistan's Ambassador to the United Nations then launched a formidable attack on the panel's report and its recommendations, which included proposals to station border control, customs and counter-terrorism specialists in the peripheral states. Citing the refugee crisis and the adverse impact that the sanctions were having, forcing even more Afghans to flee their drought-stricken and war-torn country, he berated the very notion of the sanctions themselves and the idea that they should be monitored. This attitude was in stark contrast to the open and frank approach of all the meetings, briefings and discussions the panel had enjoyed during its visit to Pakistan, apart from one with officials of the ISI. The mood of this latter meeting had been singularly hostile, with the members of the panel sensing a strong underlying sympathy for the Taliban, a portent perhaps of the reaction to the panel's report that was to come and which surfaced in the Council chamber on 5 June 2001.

Despite Pakistan's concerns, the following month the Council unanimously adopted a resolution that established an independent mechanism to monitor the sanctions that had been imposed against the Taliban regime.[9] Sanctions-monitoring mechanisms were not a new adjunct to the work of the Security Council. Ad hoc panels had previously been mandated to monitor sanctions against Angola, Sierra Leone and Liberia (conflict diamonds for weapons), and to inquire into the rape of natural resources in the Democratic Republic of Congo. Each of these panels usually consisted of five or six expert members working in a variety of ways – but the work of all of them involved visits to the countries concerned and, ultimately, reports to the Security Council. None of these ad hoc panels was directly related to terrorism. However, the mechanism established by resolution 1363 for monitoring the sanctions against the Taliban was different.

In its original form the mechanism was intended to be in two parts. A 'Monitoring Group' was to work out of UN New York, which would direct, coordinate and support the work in the field of Sanctions Enforcement Support Teams (SEST). The SEST were to comprise up to fifteen members with expertise in areas such as customs, border security and counter-terrorism. These fifteen specialists were to be located in the countries bordering Afghanistan. The resolution envisioned them working alongside the senior government officials overseeing the actual implementation on the ground of the sanctions measures imposed against the Taliban regime. Notwithstanding the importance attached to this resolution and the urgency of the situation in Afghanistan, unnecessary delays also occurred in getting the mechanism up and running. Coincidently, it was Bangladesh that, once again, raised the objections. This time ostensibly it was on grounds of procedural precedent concerning the composition of the Monitoring Group. If any other non-permanent member of the Council had raised this sort of objection it might have been looked at in a different light: but for the same member to cause such an important process to be delayed, for a second time on procedural grounds, is difficult to regard as purely a coincidence. On one hand it is important for the non-permanent members of the Security Council to be able to exercise their rights and role on behalf of the 'block of nations' they represent. But, in matters of such international importance, it brings into question the ability of the Council, and with it the credibility of the UN, to carry out effectively its key functions relating to global peace and security. In the end a solution was found, although it had not been publicized, that would satisfy the Bangladesh objections just a couple of days before 11 September 2001. The events of that day were sufficient to inject a new impetus into getting the Monitoring Group off the ground and for resolution 1363 to come to life. This resolution has on occasion been referred to as the Monitoring Group's 'birth certificate'. From the point of view of what the UN has or has not been doing about countering terrorism, it is important to note that it pre-dates 9/11.

It had been a Security Council initiative, albeit subject to posturing and bureaucratically engineered delays, that was intended to

Countering Terrorism

bring pressure to bear on the Taliban owing to their support for terrorism and al-Qaida. Outwardly, the establishment of such a monitoring mechanism also sent a message to those states supporting the Taliban in contravention of the wishes of the international community. In the end the mechanism's effectiveness, in this particular context, was never put to the test. The events of 9/11 and the subsequent US-led coalition activity, resulting in the demise of the Taliban, precluded the deployment of the SEST. It was to be a new mandate and a new focus, namely Usama bin Laden and the al-Qaida network, that was to prove the real test for the Monitoring Group and the political will to support the Group's work. However, before that test was to begin other significant actions, initiated by the United Nations, would also have an impact on the response of the international community to terrorism and on the work of the Monitoring Group.

8

Initial Reactions to 9/11

The events of 9/11 were a direct assault against not only the United States of America and everything for which that country stands, including its economic strength, but also international peace and security. In the immediate aftermath of those horrendous terrorist attacks, which took place on such a bright sunny September morning in 2001 and resulted in impacts by aircraft into the World Trade Center in New York, the Pentagon in Washington, DC, and a field in Pennsylvania, the vocal response was swift and unequivocal. Many countries pledged their solidarity with the United States of America and their commitment to the actions that needed to be taken against terrorism. The very next day the North Atlantic Treaty Organisation (NATO) reaffirmed its commitment, invoking Article 5 of the Washington Treaty for the first time ever. Collectively, the NATO members pledged 'to undertake all efforts to combat the scourge of terrorism . . . We stand united in our belief that the ideals of partnership and cooperation will prevail.'[1]

On the same day, the United Nations Security Council unanimously adopted a similar resolution, which also called for greater cooperation between all states to work together urgently to bring to justice all those concerned with the attacks of 9/11. This particular resolution also called for the full implementation of the relevant anti-terrorist conventions and Security Council resolutions[2] – a clear indicator, if one was needed, of the fact that a significant number of states had done little or nothing to meet their obligations in this regard. When considering how long many of the conventions had been in existence this was a poor indictment of international response and political will.

Elsewhere, following the events of 9/11 and particularly as a result of the magnitude of the attacks, regional organizations were taking stock of their position and deciding upon the appropriate collective action. For instance, at its meeting on 21 September 2001 the European Council adopted a 'Plan of Action to Combat Terrorism'. This contained measures intended to speed up and improve the Union's collective ability to combat terrorism. The measures included extradition between states based on a European Arrest Warrant, establishing a Counter Terrorism Task Force within Europol and improving commonality in judicial systems (Eurojust), to mention but a few. Sadly, some of these measures were not afforded the priority they deserved and it took another major terrorist atrocity two-and-a-half years later – during Madrid's morning rush hour on 11 March 2004 – to re-energize the collective will of the Union.

At the UN headquarters in New York, actions swiftly followed the words. On Friday, 28 September 2001 the Security Council adopted resolution 1373. This established the UN's Counter Terrorism Committee (CTC) and was directed at all member states, calling on them to adopt legislation and administrative procedures that would suppress and prevent terrorist acts. The composition of the CTC is a mirror image of the Security Council. The following month the Secretary-General established the UN's own in-house Policy Working Group on the United Nations and Terrorism: 'Each of these steps served to underline the depth of shared international commitment to an effective, sustained and multi-lateral response to the problem of terrorism.'[3] At the turn of the year there was a third important initiative in the contribution of the United Nations towards the global efforts to combat terrorism with the adoption by the Security Council of a resolution directing sanctions against the al-Qaida network. It is important to assess the impact of each of these three initiatives in order to have a good understanding of the response of the international community to the threat posed by transnational terrorism.

RESOLUTION 1373 AND THE CTC

The requirements placed on member states by resolution 1373 were extensive and, if fully implemented, quite demanding. The resolution was intended to ensure that all states could prevent and suppress the financing of terrorist acts. The specifics, laid down in the operative paragraphs, are sufficiently comprehensive to cover not only those directly involved in terrorist acts but those who support and/or assist terrorists. The resolution also decides that, among other requirements, all states shall refrain from supporting terrorists or terrorist groups, including suppressing recruitment and eliminating the supply of weapons to terrorists; shall afford one another the greatest assistance in connection with criminal investigations 'including assistance in obtaining [relevant] evidence in their possession'; and prevent the movement of terrorists. This last requirement is to be effected by a combination of border controls and the effective control and issuance of travel and identity documents. In addition, states are called upon to cooperate in a variety of ways concerning the exchange of information, through bilateral and multilateral agreements, and, reiterating the words of the UN Secretary-General in his statement of 12 September 2001, to become parties to all the relevant international conventions and protocols.[4]

For many states, whether or not they were faced with a direct threat from terrorism, this resolution was a tall order. Understandably, many of them had never felt the need to place anti-terrorism legislation on their statute books. It presented them with significant challenges. There were of course other states, known at the time to support terrorist groups, that were likely to find a way round this resolution, its demands being contrary to their allegiances and the views and sympathies held by a number of such states. All member states of the United Nations are required to report to the CTC on the steps they either have taken or will take to implement the resolution. In order to expedite the reporting procedure, a set of guidelines was issued to all states by the CTC. A panel of experts was also established, at UN Headquarters in New York, to assist the Committee with its review of the reports from states.

By any standards the management of resolution 1373, ensuring that it became an effective vehicle for a truly international response to terrorism, was a daunting task. For such a course of action to be undertaken by the United Nations was not only unprecedented, but a formidable challenge. This is a resolution that impacts on the sovereign requirements of member states. Within the United Nations, national sovereignty is a very sensitive matter, a subject that has on numerous occasions drawn an adverse response to tackling terrorism internationally. Despite the challenge, the work of the CTC and the

Countering Terrorism

initial response by states to the resolution derived significant impetus from the widespread abhorrence of the 9/11 attacks. Many states, despite the shortcomings of their own legal, judicial and executive systems, particularly in respect of counter-terrorism measures, felt that it was important to respond to the requirements of resolution 1373.

Wary of the individual concerns of states to fulfilling the requirements placed upon them, the CTC adopted an approach designed to encourage states to comply. The aim was not to threaten them in the event of non-compliance, even though '1373' is a Chapter VII resolution, but to win their willingness to *cooperate* with the Committee, in achieving a common goal to suppress any form of terrorism and the activities of terrorist groups.[5] In this context, emphasis was placed on exploring the capacity of states to meet their obligations, combined with identifying sources of assistance and training from states and international organizations possessing the appropriate skills and know-how.

IMPLEMENTATION OF 1373

The response to this approach by the Committee and the will of member states to comply with the overall requirement were demonstrated by the fact that some 58 states had replied, despite the relatively short time available, by the initial deadline laid down in the submission guidelines (27 December 2001). Another 67 countries had reported by the end of January 2002, which, allowing for Christmas and New Year holidays and a variety of national administrative reasons, was probably an acceptable over-run. These late entries brought the total to 125, around 60 per cent of the membership, bringing a response that Kofi Annan described as, by UN standards, 'unprecedented and exemplary'.[6] It was certainly a marked improvement in the quality and quantity of reports when compared with previous reporting by states on the steps taken to implement earlier resolutions concerning terrorism, albeit sanctions resolutions. However, as time went by and states were asked by the CTC, by way of confidential questionnaires, to furnish further information, a tailing-off of the initial euphoria emerges. In January 2003 the Security Council stressed, yet again, the need for states to fulfil their obligations, calling on those states that had not submitted their first report (13 of them) and second reports (56 of them) to do so by 31 March 2003.[7] Nonetheless, by the middle of 2003, less than two years after first being approved, resolution 1373 was to all intents and purposes dead in the water.

On such a sensitive matter few states are likely to admit to their shortcomings in a public document. There are a number of possible reasons for the apparent reluctance of some states to comply fully with the resolution, including the lack of the appropriate legislation that would enable them to take the required measures. Many states at the time, for example, did not even have anti-money laundering (AML) laws. This was important because some states have been able to use AML measures as the basis for legislation to counter terrorist financing. Combined with this is the lack of ability and/or resources to draft and enforce the necessary legislation. Similar 'capability gaps' extended to other aspects of the implementation process, such as improving border controls.

Effective control of a nation's borders requires considerable resources: human, financial, physical and technical. In many cases states lack the necessary funds, properly trained manpower and/or appropriate equipment. This is especially true of the many countries where transnational Islamic terrorists have freedom of mobility and movement that needs to be interdicted effectively. Other states will openly, and sometimes resignedly, admit that they have very porous borders that are difficult to control. Some ask for assistance with training, equipment and exchange programmes. But sometimes there are political reasons behind the rather dilatory pace of compliance exhibited by a number of states. One of the underlying obstacles to fuller and more effective compliance is the lack of a comprehensive definition of terrorism within the United Nations.

A number of countries still try to differentiate between terrorists and 'freedom fighters', even when the latter deploy suicide bombers and car bombs against women, children and civilians going about their daily business. Terrorism is terrorism and under all circumstances must be seen for what it is. At no time should terror tactics be given a cloak of political respectability, just because the terrorists consider they are fighting an occupation. Nor does the use of such definitions as 'insurgent' or 'militant' alter the severity of the crimes being perpetrated by terrorist groups. Although the General Assembly has been asked to define terrorism, the jury is still out. (In its report dated 1 December 2004, the High-Level Panel on Threats, Challenges and Change, set up by the UN Secretary-General, makes proposals for a definition of terrorism that may clear this political log-jam, including reference to UN Security Council resolution 1566, dated 8 October 2004. These and other related issues raised by the High-Level Panel will be discussed in chapters Twelve and Thirteen.) Despite its significance, this ambivalence towards certain terrorist groups is not the only reason for the quality of reporting by member states. Thus, one has to look more deeply into why the process slowed down and why the CTC itself recognized the need for it to be 'revitalized'.[8]

The way in which the invasion of Iraq has been prosecuted has had an impact on the attitude of many countries towards requests for collective action emanating from the Security Council. Despite arguments to the contrary, many states consider that the invasion was illegal. As a result, the credibility of the Security Council has been challenged and its subsidiary organs have experienced obstacles in their work. Many states took to questioning, even if unofficially, the need for them to fulfil obligations to UN Security Council resolutions in the light of how the Council was split and its authority was brushed aside by those in favour of invading Iraq. Again, as is so often the case, vested or national interests played into the decision-making process and clouded the issue, providing a convenient excuse, if one was needed, for less than complete compliance. This reluctance to cooperate fully with international requirements, known to be led by the USA, even if they are cloaked in the 'multilaterality' of the United Nations, also spilled over to the sanctions regimes directed against the al-Qaida network.[9]

Although the CTC continued to engage with states during 2003, requesting further information or clarification of that already provided, the nature of the resolution is such that the ways in which states actually implement it is a little-known quantity. It is important to note that resolution 1373 is not a sanctions resolution. There is no provision in it, even if it is a Chapter VII resolution, for on-the-ground monitoring of the steps states have reportedly taken. Rather by accident than intention, it was the work of the Group that had originally been established, under resolution 1363, to monitor the implementation of sanctions against the Taliban that uncovered discrepancies in the implementation of resolution 1373. When the Group was reassigned in January 2002 to monitor sanctions against the al-Qaida network, following the rout of the Taliban, it discovered numerous differences in the interpretation of the resolution and those it was mandated to monitor.

AL–QAIDA SANCTIONED

On 7 October 2001 a coalition of US forces and the (Afghan) Northern Alliance, plus a little help from some of their friends, had begun an offensive against the Taliban in Afghanistan and their al-Qaida 'guests'. This action was in direct response to the attacks of 9/11 and was intended to 'punish' the Taliban for failing to hand over Usama bin Laden and for not closing the al-Qaida training camps. It was also intended to destroy the camps, to catch or kill bin Laden and his entourage, and to deny the latter their safe haven in Afghanistan. With the fall of Kabul, reported to the world by the BBC's John Simpson as he walked into the ravaged city with a camera crew on 13 November 2001, the Taliban regime collapsed and the Northern Alliance was in control of the Afghan capital. Kandahar, where the Taliban first came to prominence and the southern Afghan stronghold of Mullah Omar, 'the leader of the faithful', was also in the hands of coalition forces. Hundreds of Taliban fighters and their Afghan-Arab colleagues were detained, particularly in the northern half of the country. Others were arrested entering Pakistan. Many, who have subsequently resurfaced, slipped into cities like Quetta. Others, perhaps more fortunate, either just melted away to their homes and villages or, along with their Afghan-Arab guests, literally took to the hills and went into hiding in the rugged mountainous areas, the Tora Bora, bordering Pakistan. Many of these mountains are honeycombed with caves, a significant number of which had been improved during the era of the Soviet occupation and used by the *mujāhidīn* as hiding places and major logistics facilities. It was cave complexes such as these that bin Laden and his entourage used, initially, to elude the coalition forces that were attempting to seek and destroy them – 'dead or alive'. Since early 2002 bin Laden and his companion, and so-called deputy, Ayman al-Zawahiri appear to have vanished into the mountainous terrain, allegedly hiding in the more remote Afghan-Pakistan border regions.

With the ousting of the Taliban regime the circumstances in Afghanistan changed dramatically. In December 2001 plans were drawn up at an international conference at Bonn/Petersburg, Germany, for a phased return of democratic government of a type that suited

Afghanistan's tribal system. Agreement was reached for security, for Kabul at least, to be put in the hands of a multinational force, drawn from members of the NATO alliance and their 'partners for peace' (PfP), the International Security Assistance Force (ISAF). The deployment of ISAF was to be followed by a new UN assistance mission to Afghanistan (UNAMA),[10] the latter working with an Interim Afghan Authority to establish the foundations for the new democratic processes and eventually an elected government. Meanwhile, the same coalition forces that had led the rout of the Taliban were continuing their efforts to catch bin Laden, members of the al-Qaida leadership and key Taliban figures who remained at large. In support of this effort and, more generally, the disruption and defeat globally of al-Qaida and its associated groups, the Security Council adopted a new resolution on 16 January 2002, targeting sanctions against bin Laden and the al-Qaida network.[11]

Under resolution 1390, the Council decided that all states should undertake a freezing of financial and economic assets, a travel ban and an arms embargo. These 'targeted' sanctions were directed against individuals and entities that were designated on a list, the Consolidated List, managed by the UN's Sanctions Committee concerning al-Qaida and the Taliban.[12] The list is actually maintained and published on behalf of the 1267 Committee by the UN Secretariat. Under '1390' member states were required to report to the Council, within 90 days of the resolution having been adopted, on the steps they had taken to implement the stipulated measures. The Security Council also requested that the same Group, originally established under resolution 1363 to monitor sanctions against the Taliban, should now be assigned 'to monitor, for a period of 12 months, the implementation of the measures' in this resolution. The Council also requested 'the Monitoring Group to report to the [1267] Committee' every four months.

This new UN Security Council resolution, adopted under Chapter VII of the Charter, placed certain obligations on all states. It differed markedly from the previous ones against the Taliban. Those resolutions had had a certain 'geographical visibility' about them. Much of the implementation, particularly with regard to the arms embargo and the ban on flights into and out of Afghan territory under the control of the Taliban, was the responsibility, primarily, of the states peripheral to Afghanistan and one or two in the general region known to be sympathetic to the Taliban. The new '1390' measures were now truly global.

Over the next twelve months the five members of the Monitoring Group travelled to many countries, where they were briefed by the government officials responsible for implementing the required measures. This provided states with the opportunity to describe the steps they were taking and the challenges they faced in meeting their obligations. As part of these visits the Group also reviewed a number of international border entry points and travelled in border areas, to see the situation on the ground at first hand: how local officials were actually implementing the resolution; how they were using the information provided by the UN in its Consolidated List; and any problems that they encountered in the process. Based primarily on these visits and much detailed research of open-source material, the Group was able to provide the Security Council with a realistic analysis of the effect of these particular sanctions against al-Qaida, its associates and associated entities; the individual responses of states to the collective requirement placed on them; and an overall impression of the response internationally to the evolving threat from transnational terrorism. As a result of its monitoring of the sanctions regime during 2002 and the reports submitted to the Security Council, the Group was reappointed for a second year when resolution 1390 came up for review in January 2003. In addition to its established monitoring tasks the Group, under its new mandate, was requested also 'to follow up on relevant leads relating to any incomplete implementation of the measures'.[13] This authority to dig a little deeper, at least in its quest for the truth, fell short of much stronger 'investigative powers' that the Group had sought for its second term, monitoring the implementation of sanctions against the al-Qaida network. Nonetheless, the Group made good use of this extra clause in its work, as well as building on the knowledge and experience it had acquired during the previous fifteen months.

9

Towards Tougher Sanctions

Anumber of key ingredients are required for a sanctions regime to have any chance of success. There needs to be a clear mandate that defines the measures that have to be taken and against whom. The means by which the measures may be fully and effectively implemented have to be in place or put quickly into place: this involves clearly defined national policies; appropriate and enforceable legislation; a capable and experienced judiciary; and well-trained and effective law enforcement, security and supporting government agencies, such as customs, immigration and treasury. It also involves an effective partnership with elements of the private sector, particularly when dealing with the financing of terrorism. The implementation process needs to be monitored to ensure both the effectiveness of the measures and compliance by all member states. Sitting in the peace and tranquillity of their debating chambers in New York, it is relatively easy for the Security Council to draft and adopt resolutions, albeit 'on instructions from their capitals', deciding what actions states are to take, individually, towards collective goals of international peace and security. The reality on the ground is often a very different kettle of fish. Notwithstanding the fact that official documents of the United Nations, resolutions included, are issued in the six official languages of the organization, their interpretation, implementation and the results achieved vary immensely from state to state. Consequently, an effective system of oversight is extremely important if a sanctions resolution is to have any meaning and to contribute in the fight against terrorism – in this case against the al-Qaida network and all those individuals and entities associated with it. Such a monitoring system has to be independent of the pressures and politicking associated with the

Security Council and the organization's membership, to avoid its findings being compromised or suppressed. The mandate of such a monitoring mechanism needs to be sufficiently robust so that it is empowered fully to investigate relevant leads relating to any incomplete implementation of the stipulated measures. As more than one member of the 1267 Committee said, when referring to the work of the UN Monitoring Group: 'It is important that the [Security] Council hears what it needs to hear and not just what the member states would like it to hear!'

'NO LIST, NO SANCTIONS!'

The 1390 sanctions are based on the United Nations Consolidated List ('the List'), which had originally been set up under resolutions 1267 and 1333 to provide the necessary focus for the sanctions against the Taliban. It was then expanded in the wake of 9/11 and thereafter, as more became known about members of al-Qaida and the greater network. Given its structure, the effectiveness of this particular sanctions regime stands or falls by the detail and quality of the information contained in this List, and by how comprehensively it covers the terrorist network. The measures that states must take are directed only at those individuals and entities that have been designated on the List. In early versions of the List many of the designated individuals lacked the minimum identifiers required for them to be accurately recognized. Three years into the sanctions regime, there is still a significant number of individuals who do not have all the necessary identifiers recorded against them. This makes it extremely difficult for banks and other financial institutions to identify assets associated with those on the List. Too many names were rushed onto the List in the immediate aftermath of 9/11 without due regard for the longer-term consequences. There were also problems with both the quality of the 'transliteration' and the 'cultural construction' of the names themselves. These discrepancies had usually arisen from people in the 'information-chain' lacking the necessary qualifications to read, write and speak Arabic and not possessing a real understanding of Arabic/ Muslim culture.

There were numerous occasions when government officials informed members of the Monitoring Group that banks were having to freeze hundreds of accounts because of a commonality of a particular name of account holder – the oft-quoted example being 'Muhammad Ali' or 'Ali Muhammad'. It is commonplace in many parts of the Arab world, and in many countries where Arabs like to bank, to find people having these two forenames in their full name. However, without all the elements of an individual's name being recorded on the List, incorporating the names of the father and/or the grandfather (equivalent to the 'family name' in English), it is virtually impossible to differentiate between them. It is therefore crucial to have other accurate identifiers concerning age, nationality, addresses and/or identity papers. These are also essential for the travel ban and the implementation of the arms embargo. Without these minimum identifiers it is extremely difficult even to start on implementing the sanctions. In attempts to comply with the resolution, banks in a number of countries froze the accounts of anyone with a name similar to those on the List, causing innocent bank customers to become agitated and inconvenienced when they were denied access to their funds without due explanation. As a result much time was wasted in the earlier months of the implementation of 1390 by banks and financial institutions. Similar concerns and problems, caused by the lack of identifiers, were raised by states' border and consular officials. These deficiencies and the consequent usefulness of the Consolidated List were some of the first complaints raised by states both in their '90-day' reports (if they took the trouble to submit one) and when receiving the Monitoring Group. In the latter case, some states were quite vehement in their criticism, one or two going as far as to say that the List was useless. The deficiencies of the List brought into question the credibility of the UN and the whole sanctions process. It also provided convenient excuses, if any were needed, for many states to be tardy in their implementation of the resolution. For example, by the '90-day' reporting date (16 April 2002), only 43 states had submitted the report called for in resolution 1390. This was less than a quarter of the UN membership and contrasted poorly with the earlier response by states in reporting to the UN's CTC under resolution 1373.

Besides bringing this problem to the attention of the Committee, the Group initiated a major review of the format and contents of the List. In this initiative it was assisted by the Secretariat. But the final decision to make any changes rests with the 1267 Committee, and the inordinate amount of time invariably taken to agree on such straightforward amendments brings into question the commitment of the Committee, and hence the Security Council, to implement its own resolutions rapidly and effectively. At the recommendation of the Group, the Chairman of the 1267 Committee wrote to member states requesting that they provide any additional information concerning persons or entities already designated. This approach produced mixed results. Some states did proffer information to identify better some of their nationals, a process that has continued over time. However, other states have preferred to ignore such requests, highlighting an ambivalence that undermines the UN's realistic efforts in combating terrorism.

One particular example is that of Yasin al-Qadi and the Saudi authorities. The only pieces of information proffered are his first and last (family) names and, under 'other information', 'Jeddah, Saudi Arabia'. This is a perfect example of the lack of cooperation demonstrated by certain member states. In this instance it is the responsibility of the member state to furnish as many of the identifiers as possible, such as date and place of birth, national passport and/or ID number, place of residence and permanent address. None of these identifiers has been sent to the 1267 Committee by the Saudi authorities. On one hand, the Saudis are at pains to point out that they are victims of terrorism – al-Qaida terrorism. On the other hand, they are not prepared to face up fully to their obligations to the United Nations and comply with Chapter VII resolutions. The Group's detailed work in revising the List did eventually result in an improved version, not only from the point of view of the quality of the information, but also from its usability. In 2003 the Taliban section of the List was also significantly improved, following meetings in Kabul between representatives of the Monitoring Group, the UN Secretariat and the Interim Afghan Administration (the government of the Transitional Islamic State of Afghanistan), and with the assistance of staff of UNAMA.

However, despite all the improvements in the format, presentation and usability of the List, it still suffers from a major drawback. Notwithstanding the amount of intelligence and other information that has come to light concerning al-Qaida and its associates, the designation of individuals and entities has not kept pace with this rising tide of information about the terrorist network. Since 9/11 more than 4,000 people have been arrested or detained in more than 100 countries on the basis of their links with al-Qaida,[1] but only 212 individuals and 122 entities associated with al-Qaida (not including the Taliban) had been designated on the UN List by 25 April 2006. This lacuna, as it was so aptly named by Vic Comras, the US member of the Monitoring Group, severely limits the application of the sanctions measures and the impact that they might otherwise have in combating and disrupting the al-Qaida network. In the four or five years before 9/11, hundreds of budding young jihadists had undergone training in al-Qaida-run or sponsored camps and specialist facilities in Afghanistan and Southeast Asia. US intelligence estimates put the total number of fighters who underwent such training at between 10,000 and 20,000.[2] These estimates are in line with the often quoted figure of 'around 15,000'. From the point of view of the List, many of these would-be *mujāhidīn* returned either to their country of origin or to one whose citizenship they had acquired (or were attempting to acquire). In many cases these al-Qaida members, associates or supporters are known to the authorities of the country to which they travelled, but the countries concerned either will not or cannot legally list them. In many countries it is still not a crime for an individual to have travelled to Afghanistan (or anywhere else for that matter) and undergone training in terrorist techniques. In many states associating or having associated with known terrorists is still not a criminal offence, despite the requirements of resolution 1373. There are still countries that require a crime to be committed before those suspected of being involved can be detained or arrested. In the case of an assault or theft, for example, this is understandable. However, the main problem with this approach is that, if one waits for a series of explosions on commuter trains in the morning rush hour before apprehending those suspected of planning an attack, it is going to be too late. The terrorists have struck and won. Therefore when it comes to taking pre-emptive action against a terrorist attack in the making, a more proactive approach is necessary, albeit one that respects the Rule of Law. This will undoubtedly mean keeping tabs on terrorist suspects and their sympathizers.

Many of the 15,000 'or so' are often, rather dismissively, referred to by officials of some governments and some terrorism experts as being '*only* foot-soldiers of al-Qaida'. What exactly they mean is not always clear, particularly in the light of how al-Qaida and its associate groups operate. Perhaps it is a nice way of trying to dilute the extent of the threat. But all 'armies' need foot-soldiers, even ones that wage a global terrorist campaign. These so-called foot-soldiers are more than capable of setting up cells and providing logistic support for the movement of other operatives, as well as being good recruiters for the bin Laden-inspired global jihad, themselves having been well indoctrinated with the ideology. Despite law enforcement successes against 'sleeper' cells in many jurisdictions, some of these foot-soldiers have still been able to form cadres that have gone on to support subsequent al-Qaida or al-Qaida-like operations. In December 2003 the Saudi authorities published a list of its 26 most wanted 'terrorists', most of whom have been subsequently killed, who were allegedly connected with a number of attacks inside the kingdom, particularly the suicide bombings of the accommodation compounds in May and November 2003. According to the information available, at least 7 of the 26 had reportedly been to Afghanistan and trained in al-Qaida camps. But none of the 26 was ever proposed to the 1267 Committee for designation on the List. Then there are some more specific cases of people who certainly cannot be described as foot-soldiers but have not been listed. This brings into question, yet again, the will of those concerned to make the List and the sanctions regime against al-Qaida more than just a political statement.

Abu Bakar Bashir (alias Ba'asir), the (spiritual) head of Jemmah Islamiyah (JI), is a particular case in point. Despite the continuing activities of his group in Indonesia and Bashir being charged with terrorist-related offences, two years after the Bali bombings he had still not been proposed for designation. It is difficult to understand such an approach by any government. Of greater concern should be the fact that Bashir was released after serving only 25 months of his sentence for conspiracy in connection with the Bali bombings in October 2002. The government of Indonesia was reluctant to admit, at least openly, the presence of Jemaah Islamiyah in the country and that it was part of the al-Qaida network, even though it had been unanimously condemned for the Bali atrocity and designated by the United Nations as an entity associated with al-Qaida on 25 October 2002. Indonesia, however, was not alone in this reluctance to acknowledge or admit to the presence of al-Qaida inside its borders, not by a long way, for many other states display a similar reticence.

'TO LIST OR NOT TO LIST – THAT IS THE QUESTION?'

Some security and law enforcement agencies consider that it is more productive not to alert the suspect or would-be terrorists to the fact

Countering Terrorism

that they are being watched, tracked or under surveillance. Once an individual is on the UN's List it is very public knowledge, which is why listing charitable foundations, and those responsible for running them, that are known to have funnelled funds to or provided a front for terrorists is a good way of attempting to disrupt their support for terrorists. However, if the priority is to pre-empt terrorist strikes then there would seem to be a strong case for not alerting individuals before they can effectively be caught red-handed in the process of the final (or almost final) preparations for an attack. This aspect of the coordinated efforts of intelligence, security and police services is crucial if terror attacks are to be nipped in the bud. It is extremely important for good intelligence to be converted, in good time, into actionable evidence – evidence that can stand up to full scrutiny in a court of law, and bring the miscreants to justice before the atrocity is committed. A number of security and law enforcement service officers have a strong preference for this approach, especially in countries where the legal systems can support bringing people to justice for intent to cause terrorist attacks.

Unfortunately, too many countries, even those with long-established judicial systems, still do not have all the legislation on their statute books that enables their law enforcement services to prosecute cases on the basis of intelligence, no matter how good it might be. If there is merit in this approach of not listing, at least until arrest or conviction, in order better to disrupt and interdict the terrorists' operations, then it is arguable that the whole basis of this type of sanctions regime requires to be reviewed. Certainly there has been a significant number of arrests, some of which have been mentioned above, of individuals suspected of supporting or planning terrorist-related activities, either connected with al-Qaida or following its ideology, who were not listed prior to being detained and have not been designated afterwards.

EVIDENTIARY STANDARDS

Some states, particularly in, but not confined to, Europe, experience great difficulty with the United Nations process of designating or 'listing' entities or individuals. The evidence provided to the fifteen members of the al-Qaida and Taliban sanctions committee, the 1267 Committee, for individuals and entities connected with the al-Qaida network is often derived or based upon intelligence sources. As such it is difficult to 'challenge' the evidence through 'due process' and, in the eyes of some states, that calls into question the evidentiary standards being applied. Some of the dissenting or just genuinely more concerned states consider that, as the very basis of the authority vested in the Security Council by the Charter of the United Nations is directed at states and not individuals, the legality of designating individuals and entities by a UN committee can be questioned. Together these concerns may well provide some of the underlying reasons why so few states have actually proposed entities or individuals for designation.

In a similar vein, there are states in which evidence presented in court by the prosecution must have been obtained as a result of a police investigation and, as such, may be subject to cross-examination by the defending counsel for those accused. Evidence based upon intelligence alone is, in such cases, considered inadmissible. One such example occurred in two separate trials in the Netherlands on 2 December 2002 and from 12 May to 5 June 2003. In both cases the judges were obliged to dismiss the accused. As a result, a total of sixteen individuals, allegedly with links to al-Qaida or having provided al-Qaida with logistic support in Europe, were free to continue with their terrorist-related activities. However, two of the acquitted suspects were subsequently charged on immigration charges and sentenced to prison for two and four months for possessing false travel documents. As a result of these acquittals and their impact on the Netherlands' ability to combat terrorism effectively, at home and in cooperation with its neighbours, new terrorist crimes legislation was enacted and entered into law in August 2004. A complementary law, concerning protected witnesses, will allow for the admissibility in court of evidence obtained from official reports of the domestic intelligence sources (AIVD). To achieve this, the evidence will be reviewed by a separate investigating judge who will be allowed to hear the AIVD official (as a 'protected witness'), after which he will write a *proces verbaal* for the sitting judge.

This is just one example of how these matters can be and are managed to overcome such obstacles of admissible evidence. Law enforcement methods will have to be adjusted in the light of the threat posed and the attitude of the terrorists and their supporters, as compared to common criminals. There are still many countries that face a dilemma concerning individuals who are known to be connected or have associated with terrorist groups, but who have not actually committed a terrorist act. Even though these individuals represent a danger, these states are reluctant to deal with them seriously. It is in this area of a state's overall response to countering terrorism that there needs to be a good working relationship between the legislators and law enforcement. Unfortunately, the criteria for taking a tough line with terrorists or terrorist suspects can, for some people, be seen at odds with the rights of the individual. The question is, when dealing with such cold-blooded killers as those spawned by al-Qaida and those who actively and knowingly support them, whose rights are more important? The 'right to life' of the innocent victims, who are blown to pieces by a suicide bomber, or beheaded with the act being filmed and posted on the Internet, or those who commit or assist in the committing of such heinous crimes? For many law-makers this does present a dilemma. Senior politicians and diplomats urging the energetic pursuit and prosecution of terrorist suspects invariably qualify their statements with words regarding the necessity of remaining within the international standards of law and justice, including humanitarian law, the law on refugees and human rights. It is very important that the prosecution of terrorists conforms to established judicial norms, with the right of counsel and the defendant's opportunity to challenge the case presented by the prosecution. But the laws themselves may need to take account of the fact that the terrorists of today are far removed from those of 20, 30 and 40 years ago. In most cases, they require different legal treatment from common criminals, especially concerning the length of periods of detention while investigations are undertaken. One of the reasons for this latter requirement, which is often not understood and thus overlooked, is the borderless nature of the terrorist networks – *terrorisme sans frontières* – involving time and effort on the part of the more diligent law enforcement agencies having to extend their enquiries into other countries.

At the same time, those states that consider that the sanctions measures are applicable only to individuals and entities on the List should re-examine their obligations under resolution 1373, the over-arching counter-terrorism resolution. Resolution 1373 refers to all terrorist groups and forms of terrorism. It is not 'al-Qaida specific'. Furthermore, it is a Chapter VII resolution, the implementation of which is (expected to be) obligatory. Operative 2 of resolution 1373 declares that *all States* shall 'Deny safe haven to those who finance, plan, support or commit terrorist acts', and prevent those who undertake any of these activities 'from using their respective territories for those purposes against other states or citizens'. Resolution 1373 also requires that those involved in such activities be 'brought to justice and ensure that, in addition to any other measures against them, such terrorist acts are established as serious criminal offences in domestic laws . . . and that the punishment duly reflects the seriousness of such terrorist acts'. Taken together, these operative sub-paragraphs require member states to ensure that they can deal with terrorists in general and do not need to wait for an individual, suspected of association with al-Qaida, to be designated by the 1267 Committee. Nonetheless, the Monitoring Group recorded many instances of states appearing reluctant to come to terms fully with the threat and to see it for what it is.

'NOT IN OUR BACKYARD!'

Such reticence or reluctance on the part of many countries, which can adversely impact the collective efforts in combating terrorism, stems from a number of possible reasons. First, there is a belief that admitting to the presence of al-Qaida inside a state's borders might discourage inward investment and/or frighten off would-be tourists. Secondly, there is a concern that, by admitting the presence of al-Qaida and/or those associated with the network, such states will give the impression of being incapable of dealing with the terrorists and their potential supporters. These two reasons have been seen as contributing to the stigma of a possible presence of al-Qaida inside a state's territory. Besides the reasons already suggested for the reluctance by some governments to accept or outwardly recognize the existence of a threat to their country from al-Qaida or one of its associates, it appears that a number of predominantly Muslim countries are concerned about alienating elements of the population. A similar situation pertains even in one or two Christian countries with large Muslim minorities, where sympathy exists towards some of the causes espoused by Usama bin Laden. Then there is the situation, best described as a 'lack of national confidence', that can in part be connected to the second of the reasons posed earlier, whereby some states are reluctant for it to become known that they have difficulty in implementing sanctions measures, be it for a lack of the appropriate legisla-

Countering Terrorism

tion, executive procedures, training, actual resources or other reasons. In other cases, communications on the subject between the Permanent Missions to the United Nations of a significant number of countries and their capitals on the subject of the al-Qaida and Taliban sanctions regime appeared to be poor or, in some cases, almost non-existent. At which end the fault lay was often not clear. Even when the Permanent Missions had performed with the required diligence, there were numerous occasions when the capitals did not respond with the necessary alacrity or level of interest. In other cases the information that had been sent to capitals was ignored, became lost in the 'machinery of state' or presented a significant challenge with regard to thorough and effective interdepartmental coordination. These failures by states to fulfil their obligations under international law may also have accounted for their somewhat dilatory response to the 1267 Committee. Reports were submitted late, often very late, or the reports submitted lacked much of the required information.[3] Such less than perfect responses are a mirror of the more general malaise exhibited by a number of states when analysing their attitudes and response to many other requirements mandated by the Security Council, for example Rwanda, Srebrenica (Bosnia) and, more recently, Darfur (Sudan). But these various reactions to the sanctions regime in general, and the whole process surrounding the UN List in particular, raise another very important issue as to why so many countries prefer not to, and do not, propose suspected members of al-Qaida, its associates or associated groups for designation on the UN's Consolidated List.

Under resolution 1455 states were provided with guidelines, containing a series of questions, on which to base their '90-day' reports to the 1267 Committee. These guidelines were a major improvement compared with the reporting requirements called for in the previous al-Qaida sanctions resolution – resolution 1390 (2002). The first question in the guidelines asked states to define the threat posed to them and their region by al-Qaida. Despite the importance of the answer to this particular question, in setting the scene for states' reports, nearly a fifth of states' reports to the 1267 Committee either ignored or dismissed the threat, despite there having been al-Qaida-related activities inside their borders. This seemingly 'head in the sand' approach was experienced by the Monitoring Group during visits to a number of countries, when the same question was posed to the appropriate government officials.

During an official meeting in Riyadh the Group requested to be briefed on the threat from al-Qaida to the kingdom and the region. The response from the Saudi official was a broad and comprehensive dissertation on al-Qaida in general, but any threat it posed or relevance to the kingdom seemed somehow to pass by the members of the Monitoring Group. Clearly al-Qaida was not a threat to Saudi Arabia! That meeting took place just three weeks prior to the three suicide bomb attacks, on 12 May 2003, against residential housing complexes occupied by Western expatriates. Even after these terrorist attacks, the impression presented by Saudi authorities was that it was non-Muslims who were being targeted, the aim being to rid the 'Land of the Holiest Sites of Islam' of 'infidels' (non-believers). It took another attack, in November 2003, against an accommodation compound at al-Muhayya, in another section of Riyadh, occupied by expatriates from Arab and Muslim countries, before the Saudi authorities started to admit, outwardly at least, that they really did have a threat to their internal security, and acknowledge how they are perceived by Usama bin Laden and many of his extremist, hardline followers.

During September and October 2003 requests by the Monitoring Group for a further visit were 'conveniently inconvenient' for the Saudi authorities. In both resolutions 1390 and 1455 the Security Council 'urge[s]' all states to '*cooperate* fully with the (1267) Committee and with the Monitoring Group'. In resolution 1456 the Council called upon all states 'to implement fully the sanctions against terrorists and their associates, in particular al-Qaida and the Taliban and their associates . . . and to *cooperate* fully with the Monitoring Group'.[4] Therefore, the Saudi government should not have been surprised, nor should some of its neighbours who had proved to be equally unforthcoming with requests for information, to find that the UN Al-Qaida Sanctions Monitoring Group had detailed these lacks of cooperation in their last report.[5] Coincidentally, shortly after the Group's report became public, albeit by being leaked to the press, the Saudi government did invite the Chairman of the 1267 Committee to Riyadh. This was either a remarkable coincidence or more likely it was the Saudi authorities trying to redress the balance between being accused by the 'independent' Monitoring Group of a lack of cooperation and demonstrating a willingness to be seen to be working with the 1267 Committee. This is a classic example of how a member state of the UN will try to manipulate the system. Knowing that the

Chairman of the 1267 Committee, himself a Permanent Representative of his country to the UN, has to observe the required 'political correctness' of one diplomatic official towards another state, the state in question feels comfortable with such a public liaison.

As has become so popular elsewhere – it is all a matter of spin! On one hand, the impression that should be presented to the world at large, especially the industrialized Western part, is of a nation, itself threatened by al-Qaida, denouncing the terrorists and taking them head-on. At the same time, the reality is that concurrently the Saudi regime is continuing its efforts to spread the more extremist, puritanical form of Islam, generally referred to as Wahhabist or Salafist, through its charitable organizations: building mosques, funding 'religious schools' and providing aid to the poor and to refugees. Just to 'top the spin', it was on or about the date of the visit of the Chairman of the 1267 Committee that the Saudis released the list of 'the 26 most wanted terrorists in Saudi Arabia'. As stated earlier, however, none of the 26 has ever been designated on the UN's List, either before or after their subsequent death or capture by Saudi security forces, despite their known connections with al-Qaida. At the expense of repetition, it is important to remember that at least seven of them had, allegedly, been trained in al-Qaida camps in Afghanistan. This is just another example of a member state of the United Nations not fulfilling its obligations under a Chapter VII resolution and trying to avoid admitting, on paper at least, that al-Qaida was present inside its borders. Some members of this Saudi-based group were reported as having taken part in attacks against US and other Coalition forces in Iraq. During the course of 2004 significant inroads were made into this group of terrorists by the Saudi authorities. A rather amateurish attack in December 2004 on the US Consulate in Jeddah by some of those still at large highlighted poor planning and execution, resulting in four of the assailants being killed in the resulting fire-fight and one captured alive. However, over three days (4–6 April 2005) Saudi security forces had a long running engagement with elements of this same 'al-Qaida in Saudi' group. The exchange of fire began in the town of Al-Rass, some 300 kilometres north of the capital, Riyadh, when the security forces attempted to raid a house suspected of being used by 'militants'. After the three-day engagement fourteen terrorists had been killed and one captured. Two of these were among the twenty-six originally listed in December 2003. Despite such successes, ongoing sympathy for the cause espoused by the militants continues to exist within certain sections of the Saudi population. It therefore remains to be seen how effective, in the long term, the security apparatus will be in eradicating these terrorist and anti-government elements.

The Monitoring Group had a similar experience in September 2003 with Moroccan government officials who were also reluctant to acknowledge an internal threat to their kingdom from al-Qaida. On 16 May 2003 suicide bombers simultaneously detonated five devices in Casablanca, just three days after the attacks in Riyadh. A total of 41 people were killed and many more injured when the bombs exploded in a luxury hotel, a Spanish club, a Jewish community centre, a Jewish cemetery and in a narrow street between an Italian restaurant and the Belgian Consulate. When this subject and those who might be responsible for the attacks were raised during the Group's visit, the response from the Moroccan authorities was that they had been unable to establish that these members of Salafia Jihadia, who conducted the attacks, were connected to al-Qaida. On a previous occasion, much to their credit, Morocco security services had successfully disbanded a 'sleeper' cell, including three Saudi citizens, that was planning to attack British and US ships in the Straits of Gibraltar. Despite both the latter plot and the suicide bombings in Casablanca having all the hallmarks of a 'classic' al-Qaida operation, its 1455 report to the 1267 Committee, dated 28 July 2003, states that 'At the present stage it is difficult to evaluate the threat posed by al-Qaida for our country . . . Furthermore . . . it is premature to speak of the involvement of al-Qaida in the attacks of 16 May 2003 in Casablanca.'[6]

A number of countries have enacted the necessary legislation so that they can fulfil their obligations. Other states achieve the required aim by using administrative or executive declarations, or even royal decrees. However, there are many others that have not introduced appropriate legislation. In some cases this is due to a genuine lack of know-how, capability or resources. In others it is due to the states concerned being at odds with the definition of terrorism and their tacit support for such causes, for example that of the Palestinian people. It is hardly a coincidence that of the Gulf Cooperation Council states Saudi Arabia has signed, but not ratified, the 1999 Convention on the Suppression of Terrorist Financing, and the United Arab Emirates did not ratify it until 23 September 2005. In addition, as of 31 August

2006, Iran, Lebanon, Malaysia, Oman, Pakistan and Qatar are not participants of this important counter-terrorism convention.[7] Nonetheless, well before ratification the United Arab Emirates had hosted two international *Hawala* conferences in 2002 and 2004.[8] Nowhere in the overall spectrum of the international response to terrorism is the requirement to enact the appropriate legislation more pertinent than when it comes to starving the terrorists of funds and denying them access to other fiscal assets.

10

Life-blood of Terrorism

Finance is the life-blood of terrorism. Consequently, it has received a great deal more attention than the other sanctions measures called by the international community in the fight against terrorism. It is the one set of measures over which some form of visibility is possible and which, if fully implemented, could yield tangible results. As more and more information has come to light, particularly since 9/11, so have the intricacies of funding the al-Qaida network. The *Oxford English Dictionary* defines 'intricate' as 'perplexingly entangled', 'obscure' or 'involved'. The methods of financing used by al-Qaida, its associates and associated entities fit into any or all of these definitions and, when viewed in detail, much more. They range from the use of the formal banking system, 'deep-pocket' donors and charitable foundations, through the drug trade, to the same, day-to-day methods utilized by common criminals. Bona fide businesses too are used both to raise funds and to provide a legitimate cover for support and 'sleeper' cells. The financing of terrorism has proved to be a subject about which those who need to know and understand most about it often do not realize how little they know. In order to understand the financial infrastructure of al-Qaida and its global network, it is necessary to review the history of its various phases. In particular, one needs to look at the sources and methods of finance utilized by the group during its evolution to the movement we know today.

PHASE I: PAKISTAN

Al-Qaida al-Sulbha ('The Solid Base') was conceptualized by Abdullah Azzam in early 1988,[1] and formally established by Usama bin Laden as an organization in Peshawar, Pakistan, on 10 September 1988. Prior to its inception, al-Qaida existed for four years, camouflaged within the auspices and framework of Maktab-il Khidmat (MAK), the Afghan Service Bureau. As the premier Arab group supporting Afghan groups in their struggle against the Soviet Union, MAK received substantial support from the Saudi government and from Muslims living worldwide. It trained foreign supporters to fight against the Soviet occupation, which in turn served to foster the concept of jihad as an operational role in the ideology against communism.

Abdullah Azzam, the Palestinian-Jordanian scholar, and his student and protégé Usama bin Laden had established the Afghan Service Bureau in 1984. Its purpose was to facilitate recruitment, training and fundraising for foreign *mujahidin*, as well as to chronicle the multinational jihad against the Soviet occupation of Afghanistan. Both Azzam and bin Laden managed the Bureau, while Azzam also oversaw *al-Jihād*, a weekly magazine. As bin Laden controlled the funds, he was the primary leader of operations while Azzam focused on ideology and popularizing the concept of jihad. Abdur Rasool Sayyaf and Gulbuddin Hekmatiyar (and his military commander, Jalaludin Haqqani) were the organizers of the anti-Soviet jihad. They received military and financial support from a multilateral coalition organized by the CIA that comprised the US, UK, Saudi Arabia and Pakistan. The three organizers were close to bin Laden, and a significant percentage of Arabs served in the individual groups they led. The MAK built an infrastructure of guest houses and training camps to support the flow of Arabs into Afghanistan to fight against the Soviets.

The MAK provided visiting *mujāhidīn* with funds and accommodation. Each *mujāhid* would receive a Kalashnikov rifle, two hand grenades, a canteen, webbing equipment and ammunition. There were numerous guest houses including those in and around Peshawar: Beit al Ansar, Abdara Road; Beit al Salam; and Beit al Quraba and Beit al Shehada (House of Martyrs), both in the district of Hyatabad. Others were located at Miram Shah, on the Afghanistan/Pakistan border en route to Khost, and in Torkhan on the Khyber Pass route between Pakistan and Afghanistan. Another guest house existed solely to house the wives of Arab *mujāhidīn*. Camps had also been established beginning in 1987. They included al-Masada (Lions) Camp at Jaji (established by bin Laden); Areen Camp, also in Jaji; and the more specialized camps Khaled Ibn Waled, earlier known as al-Faruq, in Khost.

Having played such a vital role in supporting the Afghan factions against the Soviets, Azzam and bin Laden began to focus on Israel and its steadfast supporters, especially after the first Palestinian uprising in 1987.[2] The broad outlines of what would become al-Qaida were formulated by Azzam in 1987–8. He envisaged it as an organization that would channel the energies of the *mujāhidīn* into fighting on behalf of oppressed Muslims worldwide, and play the role of a pioneering vanguard of the Islamic movement. Upon its creation, al-Qaida inherited a fully fledged infrastructure of trainers, camps, weapons and sources of finance. In addition to the Afghan training and operational infrastructure, al-Qaida benefited from the worldwide network created by its predecessor, with 30 offices overseas.

In 1989 bin Laden and Azzam split over disagreements regarding al-Qaida's priorities: bin Laden wanted to fund the Egyptians and Algerians, while Azzam wanted to focus on the Islamization of the Afghan government. Most followers joined bin Laden, despite Azzam's assurances that, following Afghanistan's Islamization, he would wage jihad starting with Chechnya, and with Tajikistan and Uzbekistan in Central Asia.[3] Azzam took control of MAK and a building that housed the Sabalil ('Strong Lion at Night') Mosque, and established Camp Khalden at Parachinar on the Afghanistan-Pakistan border. Azzam was assassinated by members of the Egyptian Islamic Jihad in November 1989 with bin Laden's acquiescence. After his death MAK failed to generate as much money, with some workers skimming off funds that were intended for the support of the Arab *mujāhidīn*.[4] With his rival eliminated, bin Laden became the backbone and principal driving force of al-Qaida.

In this first phase of its development, al-Qaida was primarily a commander–cadre organization. Its operations were run via a vertical leadership structure that provided strategic direction and tactical support to its horizontal network of compartmentalized cells or associated organizations. Separate operational committees – military (operations); finance and business; fatwa and Islamic studies; and media and publicity – were individually responsible for day-to-day operations.

Financing the activities of al-Qaida during its formative years was based primarily on contributions from wealthy Arab benefactors. Initially the movement had been supported by bin Laden's personal resources. However, subsequently al-Qaida fundraisers turned to wealthy financiers, charities and businesses.[5] One of the main reasons al-Qaida re-established a presence in Saudi Arabia was the vast potential for recruitment and fundraising. A chart recovered from a computer in the Benevolence International Foundation's Bosnia office on 19 March 2002 identified some of the respected individuals in Saudi Arabia, Kuwait, Qatar and the United Arab Emirates (UAE) who provided support. Wa'el Julaidan, alias Abu al Hassan al Madani, a Saudi who managed the Pakistan office of the International Islamic Relief Organization (IIRO),[6] provided funds to Asadallah al-Sindi, the treasurer. Abu Ibrahim al-Iraqi, a relative of an al-Qaida leader, managed the Peshawar office of the Kuwaiti Red Crescent Society, lectured about jihad and provided funds for the *mujāhidīn*. Another Iraqi, Mamdouh Salim, alias Abu Hajir al-Iraqi, managed guest houses in Pakistan and was appointed the first head of al-Qaida's finance and investment committee.[7] To facilitate such transactions, businesses and banks in the Gulf were used as fronts. Al-Qaida also siphoned funds from legitimate Islamic charities and NGOs that it infiltrated.[8]

As an indication of how keen al-Qaida was to monopolize the finances emanating from Saudi Arabia, bin Laden authorized the killing of Jamil Ur Rahman, an Afghan leader who reportedly had close ties to representatives of the Saudi Arabian government and 'had attempted to influence wealthy Saudis not to provide money to bin Laden and his al-Qaida network'.[9] He was killed by Abdullah al Roomi, an al-Qaida member, who was instructed by Mohammed Atef (alias Abu Hafs), usually referred to as the al-Qaida Chief of Operations, certainly during the latter part of 2001.[10]

PHASE II: SUDAN

Following the Soviet withdrawal from Afghanistan, bin Laden returned to Saudi Arabia. The presence of 'infidel' American troops on Saudi soil as part of Operation 'Desert Shield' in 1990, and their continuing presence after the first Gulf War, led bin Laden to campaign against the Saudi regime. He joined the ranks of dissidents claiming that the al-Saud regime was composed of false Muslims and needed to be replaced by a true Islamic state. Complaints that he was 'financing subversive activities' in Algeria, Egypt and Yemen, as well as criticism of Saudi policies, caused bin Laden to fall out of favour with the Saudi government. After being warned of his impending arrest, bin Laden fled to Sudan, where he set up the headquarters of al-Qaida from April 1991 to May 1996.

Even before al-Qaida moved its operations from Peshawar to Sudan, the group had established a small presence in Khartoum. Azzam and bin Laden had dispatched Battan al-Sudani, a trainer at the Khaled Ibn Waled Camp in Afghanistan, and Abdul Halim Mohamed Dosman to Khartoum in 1989.[11] Having established an office to recruit *mujāhidīn* and begin training of the Eritrean Islamic Jihad, al-Qaida established a small organizational presence in Khartoum beginning in 1989. When the National Islamic Front (NIF) led by Hasan al-Turabi came into office, al-Turabi invited bin Laden to relocate to Sudan. In response, bin Laden dispatched his representatives to study the political, financial and security environment. He was satisfied with their findings, and Abu Ibrahim and Abu Hajjir moved to Sudan to establish a series of companies owned by al-Qaida.

Bin Laden's inherited wealth, which has been grossly exaggerated, nonetheless provided a basis to establish businesses and diversify al-Qaida's finances while in Sudan. Its investments and economic ventures increased significantly and reportedly encompassed some thirty companies. These commercial ventures employed as many as 3,000 workers in Sudan in a diversity of fields, ranging from high-tech laboratories engaged in genetic research to civil engineering businesses. Al-Qaida trainer Bathan al-Sudani managed Taba Investments, one of bin Laden's main companies.[12] In particular, economic infrastructure and ambitious construction projects became key areas of investment. An al-Qaida camp builder, Abu Muath al-Urduni, built both the Tahadi ('Challenge') road linking Khartoum and Port Sudan, and another road linking Damazine and Koromuk.[13] Bin Laden's organization also cooperated directly with the Sudanese government, including co-investing in a business for constructing roads and bridges.[14] Bin Laden's stature and the influence of al-Qaida increased through his extensive business ties with the Sudanese political and military leadership. This was done to protect himself and his organization, rather than necessarily be a significant source of revenue.

Although al-Qaida appears to have focused on its business investments between 1992 and 1996, its terrorist and militant activities continued unabated, with the economic ventures providing opportunities to further its agenda. The Soba and Damazaine farms, agricultural facilities owned by al-Qaida, served by night as training facilities for jihadist groups. Similarly, al-Qaida transported camels from Sudan to Egypt for sale, but used the opportunity to smuggle weapons for the jihadists in Egypt. In addition to serving with al-Qaida's finance and investment committee, Abu Hajir al-Iraqi attempted to procure radioactive material for al-Qaida. While on a visit to Germany for such purchases in 1998, he was arrested and extradited to the United States.[15] But, because he refused to cooperate with German and US authorities, Western nations still lack a complete and detailed knowledge of al-Qaida's financial and economic empire. During this period, al-Qaida also furthered its links with Islamic groups engaged in guerrilla warfare and terrorism, providing them with funds, training and weapons.

In 1995, after the failed attempt to assassinate the Egyptian president Mubarak in Ethiopia had attracted the attention of the intentional community, the United States intensified pressure on Sudan to expel bin Laden, using the threat of sanctions. Although bin Laden had some success in investing his personal wealth in Sudan, his enterprises ultimately lost money because of the international sanctions. As his wealth evaporated, bin Laden's anger grew against both the West and the Arab regimes that were close to the United States, notably Saudi Arabia and Egypt. By 1994–5 Western and Israeli security and intelligence agencies had identified bin Laden as a key financier of terrorism. Sudan finally bowed to international pressure in 1996 and asked the 'Saudi businessman' and al-Qaida to leave.[16]

PHASE III: AFGHANISTAN

The relocation of al-Qaida from Sudan to Afghanistan in May 1996 hastened the transformation of bin Laden into a truly international terrorist. Afghanistan, a landlocked country where Western intelligence agencies had virtually no presence, enabled al-Qaida to revive, recoup and reorganize its training and operational infrastructure. With bin Laden's expulsion from Sudan, the Western intelligence community that had previously monitored his activities lost track of his operations entirely.

Within months of bin Laden moving to Afghanistan, the Taliban seized control of significant swaths of the country, including the capital, Kabul. Supported by Pakistan's Inter-Services Intelligence Department (the ISI or ISID), the Taliban's membership was initially drawn largely from Afghan youths, predominantly Pashtuns, who had grown up in Pakistan and from *mujāhidīn* leaders in Pakistan. Bin Laden quickly consolidated his links with the Taliban leadership by financing and materially assisting the regime. Specifically, al-Qaida formed a guerrilla unit to assist the Taliban. While functioning as a separate organization, this was integrated with Taliban troops for the purpose of fighting the Northern Alliance. The Taliban regime reciprocated al-Qaida's assistance by providing sanctuary, weapons, equipment and training facilities.[17]

Bin Laden was warmly welcomed in Afghanistan. As the most prominent Arab that had fought against the Soviets, he was the hero both of the Afghan and the Pakistani *mujāhidīn* groups, with a natural following from the several thousand Arabs who had remained in Afghanistan and Pakistan. Unwelcome and unwanted in their home countries after the Soviet withdrawal from Afghanistan, these individuals saw bin Laden as a new-found 'Salah al-Din'. To them he was the 'warrior leader' in their ideologized war against the enemies of Islam. After the first World Trade Center attack in February 1993, when the United States warned Pakistan to rid themselves of the *mujāhidīn* or be declared a 'terrorist state', Arab *mujāhidīn* located in Pakistan moved to Afghanistan.

When bin Laden himself relocated to Afghanistan from Sudan in 1996 it created the opportunity for him to build a truly global jihad network, consolidating old relationships and building new ones. Many of the North African and East African jihad groups that al-Qaida trained in Sudan established a presence in Afghanistan. Further, bin Laden deepened the traditional links to Middle Eastern terror groups, particularly those from the Persian Gulf, and developed closer ties with Asian groups. As an organization with a global membership, al-Qaida used Afghanistan as a location in which to train, finance and indoctrinate Islamist groups from Asia, Africa, the Middle East and the Caucasus. Almost all the Muslims who were recruited came from contemporary conflict zones: Bosnia and Hercegovina; China's Xingjiang Province; Dagestan; Kashmir; Mindanao in the Philippines; Maluku and Poso in Indonesia; Russian Chechnya and Tajikistan.

Countering Terrorism

Others found their way to the al-Qaida facilities in Afghanistan from Albania, Egypt, Jordan, Kosovo (in Serbia and Montenegro), from the Ogadan, Somalia, Nargono Karabakh, Rohingiya (Myanmar) and Yemen. The aim was to build a core group of fighters that al-Qaida claimed would alleviate the suffering of Muslims at the hands of the oppressive and repressive regimes and rulers supported by the United States, their allies and friends.

In addition to its own training camps in Afghanistan, al-Qaida dispatched trainers to establish or serve in the training camps of other groups in Asia, Africa, the Middle East and the Caucasus. For instance, beginning in 1988 and increasing after 1994, al-Qaida made efforts to embed its influence in Southeast Asia. This was first attempted by dispatching Muhammad Jamal Khalifa, the brother-in-law of Usama bin Laden. Khalifa established the Manila branch of the International Islamic Relief Organisation (IIRO), a respectable Saudi-based charity, allegedly to provide assistance to Islamist groups in the region. (Afternote: On 4 August 2006, the Philippines offices of IIRO were designated on the UN Consolidated List in connection with al-Qaida.[18]) Although not proven, evidence exists suggesting his association with Ramzi Yousef and the foiled Operation 'Bojinka'.[19] Together with the 1993 World Trade Center bomber Ramzi Ahmed Yousef, Khalid Sheikh Muhammad (the mastermind of 9/11) travelled to Southeast Asia in 1994 with plans to destroy US airliners over the Pacific. Similarly, within the MILF Camp Abu Bakar complex, al-Qaida's Kuwaiti trainer Omar al-Farooq established Camp Vietnam to train Southeast Asian groups in guerrilla warfare and terrorism. Al-Qaida replicated this model worldwide from the Caucasus to North Africa.

Financing 3,000 or 4,000 al-Qaida members in Afghanistan and clandestine agents overseas is estimated to have cost at least $36 million a year. In addition, the group's set-up costs – weapons, technology, infrastructure, camps, offices, vehicles, etc – are reckoned to have been close to $50 million. This estimate has been computed by examining the budgets of terrorist groups in relation to their sources of finance, geographic distribution, organizational sophistication, size and other factors.[20]

Immediately following the Soviet withdrawal from Afghanistan, and for the remainder of the century, the international community ignored and abandoned Afghanistan and, to some extent, Pakistan. As a result, Afghanistan and Pakistan developed throughout the 1990s as the centre for both ideological and physical training of Islamist guerrilla and terrorist groups. After the Oslo Accords in the early 1990s, Afghanistan replaced the Syrian-controlled Bekaa Valley as the principal hub of international terrorism. As the West looked the other way, Afghanistan evolved into a 'Terrorist Disneyland'. Al-Qaida and the Islamic Movement of the Taliban – the ruling party of the Islamic Emirate of Afghanistan – were collectively responsible for training upwards of 20,000 foreign *mujāhidīn* before the US-led coalition intervened in Afghanistan in October 2001.

PHASE IV: THE GLOBAL JIHAD MOVEMENT

With the loss of Afghanistan as an operational base, al-Qaida entered a new phase of its development. Since the 11 September 2001 attacks, al-Qaida's core strength has shrunk from about three or four thousand to a few hundred members, with nearly 80 per cent of its operational leadership and membership killed or captured. Even though al-Qaida maintains a presence in Afghanistan and Pakistan, it is significantly degraded and less capable of exercising direct control over its wide-ranging affiliated groups. Instead of providing operational guidance, al-Qaida's greatest success has been its ability to transfer its operational knowledge to other groups. The most hunted terrorist group in history has evolved into an ideological vanguard, working with and through associated groups, networks and cells, which collectively are referred to as the 'global jihad movement'.

Notwithstanding the loss of its territorial sanctuary, al-Qaida has successfully disseminated its ideological agenda of global jihad to its many followers. Through communications from bin Laden, al-Zawahiri, al-Zarqawi and others, delivered primarily via the Internet or the occasional audio or videotape via al-Jazeera TV, al-Qaida provides indirect but critical ideological and strategic direction. The overarching ideological goals of al-Qaida, to expel foreign forces from the Islamic world and ultimately create an Islamic caliphate, facilitate the organization of regional and local groups. The World Islamic Front for Jihad against the Jews and the Crusaders, al-Qaida's umbrella organization created in February 1998, attempts to unite its African, Asian, Caucasian and Middle Eastern groups and provide them with a common agenda. Several regional groups have developed alliances similar to al-Qaida's World Islamic Front. For instance, Hambali – both an al-Qaida and a Jemmah Islamiyah (JI) leader – convened a meeting of Southeast Asian groups in Malaysia in 1999 to form the Rabitat-ul-Mujahideen ('Legion of God's Warriors'). After 9/11 and, more significantly, after the 2003 invasion of Iraq, the international intelligence and security community reported unprecedented unity between these groups.

The attacks in Madrid and London point to the fact that Europe is a primary target for al-Qaida. As in Spain and Britain, the phenomenon of near-autonomous, home-grown terrorist cells carrying out attacks in Europe is a well-recognized model for contemporary al-Qaida operations. The invasion of Iraq spurred the radicalization of alienated Muslim diaspora in Europe, who were incited ideologically and received material support from radical preachers and networks associated with al-Qaida. In particular, some of the most significant al-Qaida-affiliated cells planning attacks in Europe have origins and links to North Africa. For example, the cell in Wood Green, north London, discovered by the authorities in January 2003 that was, initially, believed to be making ricin, was originally an Algerian support cell. Although the cell had obtained precursors to make ricin, none was ever detected.[21] Throughout Europe, Algerian terrorist support cells had generated propaganda, funds and supplies for their campaign to replace the military government in Algeria with an Islamic state. Likewise, many of the terrorists involved in the Madrid train bombings in March 2004 were from Morocco, or from the Moroccan immigrant community. While European governments initially responded slowly to this threat, the 2004 Madrid bombings and the 2005 London bombings jarred Europeans into the necessity for action against the wider al-Qaida network, not just individual cells in their countries.

Developments in Europe call into question counter-measures pursued after 9/11, especially those in the financial sector. A key component of the 'global war on terror' has been the effort to cut off financial support for terrorism. Since 11 September 2001, combating terrorist financing initiatives have gained greater prominence as part of the international counter-terrorism effort (described in detail in chapters Eight and Nine). But European Islamists that currently subscribe to al-Qaida ideology have learned rapidly from the past mistakes of the movement and its associated cells. Current dedicated operational cells of al-Qaida and its associated entities are now familiar with, and can easily circumvent, governmental measures, making the cells difficult to detect. Operating through front, cover and sympathetic organizations, al-Qaida and its entities established charities, human rights groups, humanitarian organizations, community centres and religious associations to raise funds and recruit new members, especially among impressionable youth.

Largely as a result of the measures national governments are taking to close down financial support, al-Qaida and its networks have been forced to change their financing methods still further. With most of the operations now at the local or regional level, individual cells have become increasingly self-financing, largely through criminal activities, as was demonstrated, for example, in the Madrid train bombings. Since 9/11 a significant number of subsequent terrorist attacks are believed to have been financed by individual terrorists or through local or regional cells, despite the CIA interrogation of Khalid Sheikh Muhammad revealing that immediately after these iconic events al-Qaida had no shortage of funds.

Phase IV or the post-9/11 al-Qaida infrastructure has been the most difficult to combat. As investigative, intelligence, enforcement and compliance agencies have worked to unravel and react to aspects of the funding, so the network has demonstrated its flexibility in countering the subsequent measures brought into play by the international community. It is generally considered that al-Qaida had anticipated that its financial systems would come under substantial scrutiny as a result of the 9/11 attacks and had 'aimed-off', in readiness for whatever international reaction transpired. This may be one of the reasons why, in the first weeks and months following 9/11, the sums of money reportedly frozen in bank accounts of individuals and entities associated with al-Qaida totalled little more than the equivalent of $75 million.[22]

Higher totals, as much as $130–200 million, have been bandied around by officials of certain governments, but because most states reporting freezing actions give few if any details of the breakdown and the account holders involved, it is difficult to reconcile the final figures. It is not inconceivable that, in an effort to exaggerate success in the general field of tackling terrorist financing, higher sums have been quoted that include assets of other terrorist groups, such as Hamas, Hezbollah and Islamic Jihad, that have also been frozen, particularly in the US. The most substantial figures within the reported

Evolutionary Phase	Source(s) of Finance	Organizational Structure
I. Pakistan (1984–91)	Solicitations of wealthy Middle Eastern benefactors, charities	MAK infrastructure under bin Laden and Azzam
II. Sudan (1991–6)	Business fronts, Usama bin Laden's personal wealth	Hierarchical structure in consultation with Sudanese government, plus extended network
III. Afghanistan (1996–2001)	State support (Taliban regime); abuse or diversion of charitable funds, smuggling, heroin trade and solicitations	Hierarchical structure with extensive training camps, networks and partnerships, including with the Taliban
IV. Post-9/11	Self-financing of cells through petty crime; cash card, cheque and bank fraud; wealthy benefactors; collections in mosques and some abuse of charities	A weakened al-Qaida hierarchy providing inspiration and ideological incitement to a loose affiliation of regional associates and individual cells – the transnational Islamist terror network

total of $75 million related to the al-Qaida network are those from five states: Pakistan ($10.6 million), Saudi Arabia ($5.7 million), Switzerland ($25.5 million), Turkey ($2.0 million) and the US ($29.9 million).[23] Compared with the pre-9/11 figure that the CIA had estimated al-Qaida needed to run its activities, namely $30 million per year, the denial of these sums to al-Qaida will have had little impact on the network's operational capability,[24] more so in the light of subsequent investigations.

Terrorists do not need large sums of money for the attacks that have taken place since 9/11: even that event's costs, according to most estimates, did not exceed $500,000. If anything, the overall costs of the operation may have been nearer $400,000.[25] There is considerable evidence to indicate that Mohammed Atta and his group used the formal banking system to support the planning, preparation and execution phases of this major atrocity. They used it both to move funds, albeit in relatively small sums so as not to attract attention, and to provide normal banking facilities for themselves throughout the planning, preparation and training period. In this way the attackers could lead normal lives with bank accounts and credit cards to support their daily living and travel needs and to give them 'social credibility'.

Subsequent attacks attributed to the al-Qaida network, however, have cost a lot less money. For example, the costs involved mounting attacks such as the Bali nightclub bombings, the Djerba Synagogue, the Jakarta Marriott Hotel and those in and around Mombasa (car-bombing the Kikambala hotel and the attempt to down an Israeli charter airliner with SA-7 missiles) range from about $15,000 to $50,000. The attacks on the morning commuter trains in Madrid in March 2004 (3/11) were mounted for even less. It has even been suggested that the attacks in London of 7 July 2005 cost barely £1,000. But a terror network on the scale of al-Qaida, no matter how loose the affiliations of the various constituent groups, does need money, significant sums of money.

It needs funds for its recruiting, proselytizing (religious and ideological indoctrination), travel, personal documents and all aspects of logistic support. Many of the investigations and arrests, both before and after 9/11 – and it should be remembered that al-Qaida was instrumental in a number of earlier attacks or attempted strikes – have indicated that al-Qaida operatives and their support cells have either used or been in possession of extremely high-quality travel documents. Some of these were original documents that had somehow 'slipped out of the back door of a consulate'. To ensure their freedom of movement and cover their tracks, al-Qaida is clearly prepared and able to pay premium rates. In other instances, extremely high-quality counterfeit documents have been found to have been used or were being used or prepared for use. Evidence to support this important aspect of al-Qaida's modus operandi has come to light in the wake of arrests and investigations connected with the planned bombing of the Strasbourg Christmas Market, of al-Qaida cells in Milan (Italy), in Belgium, the UK and a number of other European towns and cities.

On 12 December 2004 more than 700 police in Germany were involved in a major anti-terrorist operation. Fifty-seven dwelling places in the areas of Bonn, Düsseldorf, Frankfurt, Freiburg and Ulm were searched, resulting in eleven individuals originating from various Arab countries being detained. False identity documents and blank passports featured among material seized and one of those arrested was reported as having used eight false identities. This logistic network, allegedly connected to Ansar al-Islam and Tawhid wal Jihad, two of the terrorist groups operating in Iraq under the leadership of Abu Musab al-Zarqawi and associated with al-Qaida, was also recruiting jihadists to fight with these groups.

Investigations such as these have also shown that most of the cells, particularly in Europe and unlike their counterparts in many other parts of the world, are self-financing. Funds are raised from petty and street crime: selling drugs, ATM (cash) theft, credit card and cheque fraud. In Britain and France, investigators have found that the terrorists and their supporters do in fact raise significant sums of money. In France, according to Judge Jean-Louis Bruguière, by 'cloning' credit cards (using a small device hidden in the ATM that records the card details of a genuine customer while he or she is extracting cash), the terrorists can raise as much as €100,000 per month.[26] In Britain, terrorists, would-be terrorists or their supporters have raided ATMs and have also obtained significant sums of money.

Using the more lowly methods of common criminals, the cash thus raised is used to pay for day-to-day living expenses; travel to and reconnaissance of sites chosen or considered as possible targets; the provision of false travel documents; and the ingredients for making bombs or improvised incendiary devices (IED). It has been suggested that the perpetrators of the Madrid atrocities, which killed 191 people and wounded some 1,800, funded the attacks by selling stolen vehicles and hashish, the latter 'imported' from North Africa; the explosives were stolen from a quarry in northern Spain. One of the main suspects, Jamal Zougam, had been running a small mobile telephone business in Lavapiés, one of the older quarters of Madrid itself. This business, besides raising money legally, provided a useful cover for those concerned and equipment and expertise for the backpack bombs used in the attacks on the four commuter trains. These bombs were detonated using the wake-up alarms from mobile or cellular phones. In this way the bombers were able to board the trains, leave the packs and get off well before the devices exploded. These were not suicide attacks, for the attackers intended to make further strikes. Fortunately for the people of Madrid and the public at large, a number of suspects were apprehended, and by 16 November 2004 seventeen had been charged and awaited trial. One, a young Spaniard, who stood guard while the explosives were being stolen from the quarry and then acted as a courier, taking them with him on a bus to Madrid, was arrested on 14 June 2004. For this involvement with the terrorists, reportedly, he admitted to having been paid $1,200 – 'peanuts' in comparison to the costs of the damage and suffering caused on 3/11. Known only by the pseudonym El Gitanillo ('the Little Gypsy'), since being only sixteen he cannot be named, he was tried and found guilty on 16 November 2004. Other suspects died on 3 April 2004, detonating a device as Spanish anti-terror police were about to raid an apartment in the Madrid suburb of Leganes in which the cell was hiding out. A total of seven, suspects and supporters, died in that operation. One of the policemen was also killed and eleven injured in the blast.

In a later case, on 23 January 2005, the authorities in Germany arrested an Iraqi who, having taken out a sizeable life insurance policy, was intending to fake a fatal car accident in Egypt. Using the false 'death certificate', the plan was to claim on the policy. Part of the total sum payable, €830,000, was to go to his German 'wife', whom he had married towards the end of the previous year, and the rest was destined to go to al-Qaida associates operating in Iraq. The Iraqi was then going to take part in the jihad in Iraq with the apparent intention of carrying out a suicide bomb attack. In Germany they have a saying 'Kleinvieh macht auch Mist!', which literally translated means 'small animals also make manure!'

Further afield, post-9/11 investigations have revealed that entities associated with the al-Qaida network have benefited from a variety of other methods of funding. Groups in Bosnia, Chechnya, the Middle East, South and Southeast Asia and the United States have either received money through Islamic charities or been connected in some way with them, for example, in fundraising activities. Charities have provided al-Qaida with a useful international channel for soliciting, collecting, transferring and distributing the funds it needs for indoctrination, recruiting, logistics and operational support. These funds are often merged and hidden among donations used for quite legitimate, charitable and humanitarian purposes. But these particular humanitarian programmes also provided a means for indirectly promoting the stricter or Wahabist form of Islam, through support for religious schools or madrasas, building mosques, 'seconding' imams to the countries concerned and providing prayer mats and copies of the Qur'an, often in Arabic, to Muslims in non-Arabic-speaking lands. The process can be likened to a new type of missionary work or 'Islamist colonization', in support of which experts estimate that Saudi authorities have spent in excess of $75 billion over the past 20–30 years.[27] Most of the charities in question have their headquarters in Saudi Arabia, with offices in Jeddah, Riyadh or both these important cities.

Within Saudi Arabia and other parts of the Muslim world there is a long-established tradition of obligatory donating for charitable purposes, known as *zakat*. It is one of the five pillars of Islam. Who donates and how much is donated is treated with the utmost confidentiality. Consequently, there has been virtually no oversight, making it relatively straightforward for these Saudi-based charities to be abused 'downstream' by local officials – some of whom are al-Qaida supporters who have been able to infiltrate the field offices. The roots of these charitable networks stem from the days of the anti-Soviet jihad in Afghanistan during the late 1980s. During that campaign al-Qaida was able to draw on the support of a number of state-assisted charities and other deep-pocket donors that supported the anti-Soviet cause. However, subsequent investigations of such charitable foundations funnelling money, wittingly or unwittingly, to elements of the al-Qaida network have led to a number of them or some of their offices being designated, first by the United States and then by the United Nations. Investigations in the US into an Islamic charity called the Benevolence International Foundation (BIF) led investigators to other countries, thousands of miles away, highlighting the way in which the terrorists' financiers were exploiting legal means of globally conducting business to suit their nefarious ends.

In March 2002 Federal Police in Bosnia and Hercegovina raided the Sarajevo offices of the Benevolence International Foundation. This Islamic charity was suspected of being a conduit for funds to al-Qaida. Among the wealth of information seized in the raid was a document, generally referred to within al-Qaida as the 'Golden Chain', which contains the names of twenty 'deep-pocket' donors, all top Saudi bankers or businessmen who had been providing financial support to al-Qaida or elements of the terrorist network. This document has subsequently been cited in US court cases against an alleged financier of al-Qaida.[28] Two of those named in the document, in addition to Usama bin Laden, have also been designated on the UN List. However, subsequent analysis would suggest that others named in the 'chain' have not been presented for designation on the UN's Consolidated List as they represent individuals that withdrew their support for the organization around the time of Azzam's death due to the internal disputes that developed at that time.[29] Nonetheless, when one considers the reluctance of the US Government really to tackle the government of Saudi Arabia over the many and various allegations concerning the involvement of Saudi-based charities and other financial support that has found its way to al-Qaida, the fact that these personalities have not been put forward for listing should, perhaps, come as no surprise. All the time that the US, and for that matter other industrialized and developing countries, are so reliant on Saudi oil there is unlikely to be any significant movement in that particular direction. Similarly, while such 'religious philanthropists' are able to continue their support for terrorism unabated, the collective efforts of the international community to combat transnational terrorist activities are being continually diluted and are unlikely to succeed. It is also possible that concerns exist in these oil-dependent countries that, if too tough a line is taken with the Saudis, a significant proportion of the estimated $1.5 trillion wealth invested by Muslims in the US might be moved to centres of investment in other parts of the world. As it turns out these latter fears seem to have been unfounded and up to September 2004 it was reckoned that around 85 per cent of this wealth remained in the US.[30] Despite such concerns in some quarters, the pursuit of charities considered to have been implicit in their support for terrorism has continued.

On 13 March 2002 the offices of al-Haramain Islamic Foundation in Somalia and Bosnia and Herzegovina were designated by the UN Al-Qaida and Taliban sanctions Committee. Further investigations indicated that al-Haramain (or al-Haramayn) offices in other parts of the world had been supporting elements of the al-Qaida network. Accordingly, the foundation's offices were designated by the UN in Indonesia and Pakistan on 26 January 2004, followed by those in Afghanistan, Albania, Bangladesh, Ethiopia and the Netherlands on 6 July 2004 and finally those in the Comoros Islands and the United States on 28 September 2004. All these branches of al-Haramain were supposed to have ceased operating long before the dates they were listed. The cessation intention had been announced by the authorities in Saudi Arabia as far back as 15 May 2003, albeit qualified as a request for al-Haramain and all Saudi charities 'to suspend activities outside Saudi Arabia until mechanisms are in place to monitor and control funds in order to ensure they are not misdirected for illegal purposes'. As Saudi Arabia had not ratified or acceded to the 1999 Convention on the Suppression of Terrorist Financing, there was little inclination for those running offices of al-Haramain Foundation to respond to a call from the Saudi authorities to cease operation. Consequently, it did not happen, and even after the various offices were designated and the main office in Jeddah was eventually closed, in October 2004, Saleh ibn Abdul Aziz al-Sheikh, the Minister of Islamic Affairs, Endowments, Dawa and Guidance, reportedly stated that 'the closure of al-Haramain Foundation was not because of any suspicions surrounding its activities . . . The Ministry, he said, has not reported any misconduct from the part of the charity and did not receive any documented information to this effect from any side.'[31] This statement was made around 1 January 2005, at about the same time that the Saudis announced the establishment of a new body, namely the Saudi National Commission for Charitable Work Abroad. The operations and assets abroad of the dissolved charities were to be 'folded into the new body'. According to the Minister for Islamic Affairs, 'the commission would be very active abroad . . . [and] would be subject to strict financial legal oversight . . . to ensure that charitable funds . . . are not misused'.[32] Clearly, this statement would appear to be somewhat at odds with the fact that so many branches of al-Haramain had been closed and that it was the Saudi authorities themselves who had originally announced the closures in May 2003. The statement also tends to overlook certain events involving al-Haramain branches in Bosnia and Hercegovina.

WHAT'S IN A NAME . . . ?

Over a period of time, following the designation of the al-Haramain office in Bosnia, while elements of the charity were being targeted elsewhere, it was noted that the Bosnian office had changed its name to 'Vazir' (or Vezir) and was continuing operations from the same address in Travnik, a predominantly Muslim town in central Bosnia.[33] This situation was subsequently rectified on 26 December 2003 with 'Vazir' being designated by the UN 1267 Committee, alongside al-Haramain (Bosnia). In addition to this blatant disregard for the requirements of the international community, highlighting the ease with which charities can be abused, a foundation with a similar name was also observed operating in Bosnia during the same period. Known as al-Haramain al-Masjid al-Aqsa Charitable Foundation', one of its directors was, reportedly, Wa'el Julaidan (also spelt Jalaidan). Julaidan, an influential businessman living in Saudi Arabia, had himself had been on the UN List as an al-Qaida associate since 11 September 2002. However, despite the activities of al-Haramain al-Masjid al-Aqsa being known about and the matter being raised by the UN's Al-Qaida and Taliban Sanctions Monitoring Group in its second report in December 2003, the charity was not designated until 28 June 2004, some six months later. Apparent delays of this nature in cracking down on entities alleged to be involved in financing terrorism raise two questions, once again, concerning the whole process of the effective use of the List and the ways in which sanctions measures are perceived and pursued by some states.

The first question relates to the political will behind the process. These last two named charities had followed a practice that appears to be quite common – changing names and continuing to function. This practice was easy to effect due to the total lack of oversight of such foundations. Often, when an entity is designated, it promptly changes its name and continues operating: 'business as usual'. Nor has this practice been confined to 'humanitarian organizations'. One such example, which has received considerable publicity, involves one Youssef Mustafa Nada who, along with a number of his commercial interests, was designated on the UN List on 9 November 2001. Among the designated interests were two 'companies', Al Taqwa Trade, Property and Industry Company Ltd and Ba Taqwa for Commerce and Real Estate Company Ltd.

On 28 January 2003 Youssef Nada travelled through Switzerland from his home in the Italian enclave of Campione d'Italia to Vaduz, Liechtenstein. In doing so he was in violation of the travel ban imposed under resolution 1390 (and reinforced under resolution 1455).[34] In Vaduz he changed the names of two of his enterprises. Al-Taqwa Trade, Property and Industry Company Ltd and Ba Taqwa for Commerce and Real Estate Company Ltd became, respectively, Waldenberg AG and Hochberg AG. Both these changes, which had been missed, overlooked or ignored by the Liechtenstein authorities, were brought to the attention of the 1267 Committee by Nada himself. In spring 2003 he requested, under the terms of UNSC resolution 1452, the release of funds frozen in one of his bank accounts in Switzerland.[35] The release of the money, in the form of a bank guarantee, was requested 'in order to pay Italian taxes on the purchase of a building in Campione d'Italia, Italy, in 1985 of Euros 58,850 and Euros 7,168 to pay legal fees incurred in defending the interests of Waldenberg AG before the Italian tax authorities'.[36] In reviewing Nada's request it became clear that, not only had he been in breach of the travel ban, but he had been allowed formally to change the names of designated entities registered in Liechtenstein. Nada had then continued running them (albeit in liquidation) and also retain control of a property, an asset by definition under resolutions 1390 and 1455, that had not been subject to seizure by the Italian authorities. The UN List was subsequently amended to take account of the changes of company name, Waldenberg AG on 4 November 2003 and Hochberg AG on 26 December 2003. The inclusion of this case study in the Monitoring Group's second report for 2003 generated somewhat indignant reactions from the governments of Italy, Liechtenstein and Switzerland: not because of the facts, but because the states concerned had not had the opportunity to 'persuade' the Group to remove their names prior to the report being released. The statement to the Security Council by Switzerland in response to the report – that in view of their existing customs agreement no border controls existed between the three locations concerned – misses the point. The authorities should have made it their business to know where Nada was and inform him of the restrictions under which he had been placed at the time of his designation by the United Nations.[37] This particular case study had been undertaken by the Monitoring Group, primarily, as an example of how an important aspect of the financial sanctions was not being fully implemented. In their response to the Monitoring Group's report, the Italians did state that they were drafting ad hoc legislation to plug this legal lacuna, albeit somewhat after the event. (The case in Switzerland against Nada was dropped on 31 May 2005, although while careful to give Nada the presumption of innocence, a Swiss official stated at the time that 'the investigation is "suspended" but could be revived if new evidence arises'. Nonetheless Nada remains an individual designated on the UN Consolidated List.)

Such a response could in fact have emanated from any number of countries. This particular measure had been required of all states for more than two years. It is a decision of the Security Council that requires to be implemented and is contained in resolutions 1373, in general terms, and in resolutions 1390 and 1455, specifically in relation to al-Qaida and its associates. It is reflected in the European Council Regulation (EC) 881/2002 of 27 May 2002, which reiterates UN requirements and provides the common approach to which EU member states are required to adhere. Despite thirty states having reported the freezing of financial assets to the UN, by 30 July 2004 only three (Albania, Bosnia and Hercegovina, and Italy) had reported seizing any other types of assets. The items frozen were described as insurance policies and investment funds. No property or businesses appear to have been included. States seemed relatively comfortable with the demands placed upon them to freeze the bank accounts of entities and individuals, but tackling economic assets appears, in many cases, to end up in the 'all-too-difficult' tray, challenging once again the value and effectiveness of the sanctions measures or, more to the point, states' willingness fully to implement measures mandated by the Security Council. This case surrounding Youssef Nada brings us to the second question, namely the judicial processes involved to achieve effective implementation.

Seizing economic assets brings into the equation a whole raft of legal complications and practical implications that, perhaps understandably, have caused delays in the appropriate legislation being drafted in many countries. The evidentiary standards and the impact such a measure is likely to have on the rights of the individual also raise serious considerations. For example, property can be owned by a number of individuals, not all of whom may have links or be associated with terrorism. If the property is subject to seizure, then all could be affected. Who is responsible for the upkeep and maintenance of a property once it is seized? Commercial enterprises raise further questions that easily become obstacles. Who, for example, will be responsible for the jobs, livelihoods and the ongoing administration and management if a going concern is seized? Who will be responsible for any liabilities, especially financial ones that might exist in a company, if and when it is subject to seizure? Who will be responsible to any shareholders if the concern happens to be incorporated? In the case of a commercial entity, all those concerned with the 'management' of an enterprise should be aware of how the profits are being disbursed; if any are being used to support terrorist activities, then all the 'managers' should be subject to sanctions. That means not just the company for which they have a responsibility but their own assets, since they are an 'accessory to the fact' by concurring with the support of terrorist organizations.

It is within this context that those responsible for the management and operations of Islamic charitable foundations should be subject to much closer scrutiny and investigation. Instead, such ideas are readily dismissed, it being suggested that they are not necessarily aware of the downstream abuse of disbursed funds. Clearly these are problems that states face in meeting their commitments under international law. However, problems require solutions so that the problems do not become excuses for inactivity. Finding solutions to problems as difficult as these, particularly when national interests are involved, requires political will and determination to see the process through to a successful conclusion. That requires a tough yet even-handed approach being taken by all states concerned. There is no room for compromise in this matter. Compromise will lead only to concessions. Concessions will in turn lead only to the violators of the relevant sanctions being let off the hook. One of the biggest failings of the implementation process is that the penalties that it might be possible to award for breaches of the procedures, or in starker terms 'sanctions-busting', are far too lenient, if indeed the required legislation exists at all.

The 'Golden Chain' document, mentioned above, contains the names of individuals who, along with other business interests, are noted as being board members of the International Islamic Relief Organization (IIRO). The IIRO has been associated with activities related to groups connected with al-Qaida in Southeast Asia. Usama bin Laden's brother-in-law, Muhammad Jamal Khalifa, a regional director for the IIRO, was married to a Filippina from Mindanao, a predominantly Muslim area in the southern Philippines. Intelligence reports suggest that IIRO was acting as a conduit for funds to the Abu Sayyaf Group, a designated al-Qaida associated entity. Abu Sayyaf and the Moro Islamic Liberation Front (MILF), operating from remote jungle areas, have both been, and continue to be, responsible for a series of terrorist attacks on civilian and security service targets in the southern Philippines. Although the 'political' agenda of the MILF almost certainly has a strong local flavour, numerous reports exist of it running terrorist training camps or facilities. Invariably these are little more than a couple of *bashas* in remote jungle locations. However, the training provided in these facilities is not confined to 'militants' from Southeast Asia. Extremist elements from countries in the Middle East and Asia are reported to have been trained by the MILF.[38] The IIRO, established in 1978, has some eighty offices or branches throughout the world, in Africa, Asia, Europe and the Americas.[39] The charity has been implicated in providing support (re-9/11) for al-Qaida training camps in Afghanistan and linked to people involved in the bombings in 1998 of the US embassies in East Africa. Despite the existence of such suspicions the IIRO, unlike the BIF and al-Haramain, had survived designation by the United Nations 1267 Committee, that is until July 2006, when the charity's offices in the Philippines were listed. On a more positive note the IIRO is, according to reports to be found on the internet, active in many of the world's trouble spots. In late 2004, according to press reports, the foundation provided medical and other urgent aid to refugees from the conflict in the Darfur region of Sudan.[40] IIRO also joined other aid agencies in the Christmas 2004 Tsunami disaster relief operations in Indonesia. However, despite these good works, to what extent the foundation is being investigated and/or the appropriate checks and balances are being instigated to avoid further possible abuse is difficult to ascertain. The Saudi system, along with many others, lacks the required transparency. What is more important to the long-term solution of this global problem is to address the whole business of how a less tolerant form of Islam has spread to so much of the world.

One example of Saudi funding being used in an attempt to change the political and religious fabric of a country is in Bosnia and Hercegovina in the post-Dayton era. Working through the Saudi High Commission for Relief for Bosnia and Hercegovina, money has been donated to repair, rebuild or build anew some 550 mosques in the Muslim- or Bosniak-dominated parts of the country.[41] One of these, in particular, the King Fahd Mosque, is a very grand affair located in Nedjaricic, a main residential suburb towards the western end of Sarajevo. Its style and architecture are very similar to mosques that are to be found in the Gulf States. As such it is totally out of keeping with the Ottoman style of mosques normally seen in the towns and villages of Bosnia. Sarajevo's main mosque complex, which survived the recent conflict, is in the centre of the old city, in the downtown area of Bistrik. It therefore begs the question as to the necessity to build a new one so far from the offices of Bosnia's Grand Mufti. In a country with 36 to 40 per cent unemployment, it would seem more appropriate, if a donor country is feeling generous, to invest in the economy rather than in spreading a form of a religion that is not truly representative of the country, its peoples, history and culture. Funds could have been put to better use if they had been put at the disposal of the state through its central bank to benefit the new country as a whole. During such a post-conflict era substantial funding is invariably needed to assist with reconstruction and stabilization. Assistance to the state budget, when there is insufficient income to generate a viable amount of internal revenue from taxation, and investment in new industries would have been of much greater benefit to the peace process. Financial support just to religious aspects of one of the three ethnicities, estimated at a little over 40 per cent of the total population, only brings into question the motives of those providing the funds, especially as they are provided in such a way that it is difficult for them to be controlled and audited. Fortunately there is opposition to the stricter interpretation of Islam, as promoted by the Saudi approach, from among many of Bosnia's own Muslim or Bosniak population. This extremist form of the religion is alien to the way the Muslims in that part of the Balkans have followed Islam for hundreds of years.

But its presence only adds fuel to the latent fears of both the Croats and the Serbs. The latter in particular are quick to quote the emergence of an Islamic-based nationalism in the region to support their military opposition to the Bosniak regime founded by Alija Itzbegoviç and others in his hardline Muslim Party for Democratic Action (SDA). If ever there were a need to encourage the rekindling of the secularity that existed throughout most of Yugoslavia prior to its break-up in 1991, it is here in Bosnia. Over 40 per cent of all marriages in the former Yugoslavia were of mixed ethnicity. Jews were also an accepted part of Sarajevo's cosmopolitan fabric, which has been torn to threads by the conflict and, for long-term peace and stability in the Balkans, desperately needs being sewn back together again. Allowing any form of religious extremism to dominate in a country, to the extent that minority religious groups are either persecuted or victimized, is no longer acceptable in this day and age. The international community needs to put much more of its effort into ensuring that genuine secularity is a norm and not, as it is often now becoming, an exception. Just as many people want, in this new millennium, to express their political ambitions and aspirations with freedom of expression, speech and democracy, so too should there be freedom to follow an individual religious belief. No one religion has the right for its followers to want to ram it down the throats of those with other beliefs.

Saudi attempts to spread the Wahabist form of Islam in many parts of the world, riding in on the back of charitable foundations, have been causing concern in many other circles, particularly since 9/11. Earlier mention of the figures quoted by David Aufhauser (about $75 billion over the last 35 years or so) cannot be ignored.[42] Although Saudi officials continue to deny such association, understandably when considering that most of the Saudi charities have the patronage of the Saudi government, the fact remains that far too many instances have come to light in which people working for Saudi-based charities or foundations have been implicated in supporting terrorist groups. Such support has not only been for al-Qaida, but for terrorist groups opposed to the Israeli government and its so-called occupation of Palestinian lands. However, in order to see how the efforts to curb terrorist finances within the international community might bring the required scrutiny and transparency, one needs to look at the approach taken by the OECD's Financial Action Task Force (FATF).

This inter-governmental body was originally established in 1989 by the Heads of the G-7 countries at their Summit, when it met in Paris. These countries comprised the start-up membership of the Task Force, along with the European Commission and eight other states. It was originally set up to combat money laundering, particularly the proceeds of organized crime. In April 1990 the Task Force had drawn up a framework, composed of 40 recommendations, for countering money-laundering activities. Then, during 1991 and 1992, the FATF membership was expanded from the original sixteen members to twenty-eight. In October 2001, in the wake of the 11 September attacks, FATF met in extraordinary plenary session and decided to 'focus its energy and expertise on the world-wide effort to combat terrorist financing'. In order to achieve this goal, the FATF agreed upon eight (later a ninth was added) 'Special Recommendations'.[43] They cover the following aspects designed to counter the financing of terrorism: ratification and implementation of United Nations instruments, that is the twelve anti-terrorism conventions; criminalizing the financing of terrorism and associated money laundering; freezing and confiscating terrorist assets; reporting suspicious transactions related to terrorism; international cooperation; alternative remittance; wire transfers; non-profit organizations (humanitarian and charitable organizations); and cash couriers.

Agreement to these recommendations committed the members to a series of actions, some of which complemented the demands laid down in Security Council resolution 1373. In certain instances the FATF recommendations had more 'teeth' than the UN resolution. In the supporting FATF Action Plan, it was agreed that there would be a process of identifying 'jurisdictions' that lacked the appropriate measures to combat terrorist financing and the discussion of steps to be taken, 'including the possibility of counter-measures, for jurisdictions that do not counter terrorist financing'. Unlike the UN resolution 1373, FATF was threatening states that did not meet the required criteria with the possibility of being somehow subject to sanctions or even being 'named and shamed', the latter being a course of action with which the UN has proved to be extremely uncomfortable. The Security Council raises it as a possibility, but actually following through on such threats is extremely rare and, when it does occur, it usually provokes the fiercest indignation by those named, or worse still, it does not work. The FATF actively pursued its policy, inviting all countries around the world to participate on the same terms as the actual members.

One of the Special Recommendations on Terrorist Financing, referred to above, deals with 'Non-profit Organizations'. The recommendation, Number VIII, if fully implemented, provides the framework for effective and transparent oversight of charitable foundations, such as those operating with the blessing of the government of Saudi Arabia. However, for the recommendation to be fully and effectively implemented, it will require both the political will of the 'modernists' within the Saudi government and, in view of the concern these charities pose, an appropriate oversight mechanism, preferably from outside the kingdom to ensure the necessary credibility. Ideally, that oversight should come from an independent monitoring body, mandated by the Security Council, to which it would report directly. Its oversight functions should extend to any other charities, not just those that are Saudi-based, that have been suspected of supporting terrorist groups, including, for example, those operating in Chechnya, Kashmir and Southeast Asia. On reflection it is probably fair to say that the multilateral organization that has given the greatest impetus to tackling the financing of terrorism, expected of states, is the FATF. Unfortunately, as is proving so often to be the case, the necessary political will has not been forthcoming as the vested interests of countries are threatened. Therefore it remains to be seen to what extent the FATF recommendations will or will not continue to be fully implemented. Unfortunately, charities as such did not feature initially in the wording of UN resolutions dedicated to the suppression of terrorism and terrorist financing. The requirement for them to be dealt with, due to the concerns already discussed, were, however, raised regularly during 2002 and 2003 in the reports to the Security Council by the UN Monitoring Group overseeing the implementation of sanctions against the al-Qaida network.

As a result, the Security Council did eventually introduce wording that was more specific towards charities when, in January 2004, the al-Qaida sanctions resolution came up for review. Operative paragraph 4 of the resulting resolution (1526):

> *Calls upon* States to move vigorously and decisively to cut the flows of funds and other financial assets and economic resources to individuals and entities associated with the Al-

Qaida organization . . . taking into account . . . international
. . . standards for combating the financing of terrorism,
including those designed to *prevent the abuse of no-profit
organisations.*[44]

Just as the terrorists have adapted their ways of raising and moving money to support their various activities, so they have also learnt
to adapt to other key aspects of globalization. Like the rest of the
modern world, much of whose aspirations, ways of life and material-
ism they despise in their rhetoric, Islamist terrorists have learnt to
make great use of the media and the internet. The internet café boom,
especially in, but by no means confined to, countries lacking access to
comprehensive, modern telecommunications facilities, has been a
godsend for the terrorists and their supporters.

I I

Terrorism and Modern Communications

With the dawn of the twenty-first century, the tools of modern communications have become an indispensable component of the terrorist arsenal. Although the Islamist terrorists and extremist groups subscribe to puritanical ideologies, they are adept at harnessing modern instruments of globalization to advance their mission. Beginning in the 1970s, three generations of terrorists used and, by trial and error, perfected the use of cheap and inexpensive modern communications for a multiplicity of purposes. Ayatollah Khomeini used cassette tapes in the 1970s to further his rise to power;[1] bin Laden used videotapes in the 1980s and '90s to popularize his message that 'it is the duty of every good Muslim to wage jihad'; and Abu Musab al-Zarqawi used many forms of multimedia and the Internet to an unprecedented degree in the furtherance of his Satanic, but totally ill-defined, goals in Iraq.

For al-Qaida, its associated groups and its affiliated cells, the Internet has become the quintessential tool.[2] For 'home-grown' cells, the most formidable of the three classes of terrorist grouping that comprise the current transnational extremist threat, the Internet has been and continues to be used for propaganda, recruiting, indoctrination, fundraising, procurement and communication. As the technology has progressed, so the threat groups have kept pace with the development: they have moved with the times from the cassette tape era to that of the videotape, and to the sophisticated options available across the internet.

After the loss of Afghanistan (1989–2001), the crucible of postmodern terrorism, the internet has become the principal means for the terrorists to spread their propaganda and to communicate. The enduring dependence on the Internet by the modern jihadists cannot and should not be underestimated. Both for terrorists and for counter-terrorism practitioners the Internet has emerged as undoubtedly the single most important source of information.

DEVELOPMENT OF THE WWW.TERROR-THREAT

Today, without exception, all the major terrorist and extremist groups use the internet. The four main categories of terrorist and guerrilla groups – left and right wing, ethno-nationalist, politico-religious and single-issue groups – have a presence on the unregulated web. The internet, a dynamic information platform, is used for multiple purposes. It became the main platform for the ideologues of violent jihad and their facilitators to recruit, politicize, radicalize and mobilize new generations of terrorists and extremists. The protagonists themselves use the world wide web to discuss and debate the issues, to learn and to propagate their vision.

On the internet, the terrorists and extremists direct psychological operations (Psyops) against their own members, and conduct Psyops against their perceived enemy and towards the general public. In the first instance they direct their Psyops at their own followers and believers to boost their morale and provide direction: in many instances this can be as radical as preaching hatred towards, and total intolerance of, all beliefs and lifestyles other than that of the Islamist extremists. In 'enemy Psyops', their cyber-effort is directed at demoralizing, disinforming and misinforming those who are perceived to be the enemies of (their interpretation of) Islam. Psychological operations directed towards the general public are designed to recruit from, or instil fear in, the public at large or to shape international public opinion. Particularly after October 2001, following the loss of Afghanistan as a sanctuary and their expulsion or rapid departure, the terrorist and extremist groups reconnected and re-established contact through the Internet. Furthermore, al-Qaida and its associated groups created a virtual training camp on the Internet with the know-how to make explosives such as triacetone triperoxide (TATP) and hexamethylene triperoxide diamine (HMTD), to conduct surveillance and reconnaissance of future intended targets, and provide contact details for those seeking to travel to the lands of jihad. The multiple uses of the Internet include secure and secretive communication, communicating to a group of like-minded individuals and communicating in real-time. The reach, simplicity and effectiveness of the Web were exploited to the full by Khalid Sheikh Muhammad, alias 'Mokhtar' ('The Brain'), the mastermind of 9/11. Within al-Qaida he popularized both the use of encryption and the methodology of the electronic 'dead letter' box. His protégés, including Muhammad Naim Noor Khan, the al-Qaida communications coordinator, and Dhiren Barot, alias Esa al-Hindi, believed to be an al-Qaida leader in the UK, and others used the internet extensively.

UNDERSTANDING THE NET

Professor Gabriel Weimann, the leading academic specialist on the use of the Internet by terrorists, states that they are attracted to it because it provides

> easy access; little or no regulation, censorship, or other forms of government control; potentially huge audiences spread throughout the world; anonymity of communication; fast flow of information; inexpensive development and maintenance of a web presence; a multimedia environment (the ability to combine text, graphics, audio, and video and to allow users to download films, songs, books, posters, and so forth); and the ability to shape coverage in the traditional mass media, which increasingly use the Internet as a source for stories.[3]

The use of the internet by terrorists and extremists can be traced back to the mid-1990s. Initial users were the terrorist supporters of radicalized diaspora and migrant communities living in the United States, Canada and Europe. As a result, to this date, the vast majority of terrorist and extremist websites are hosted in the West. In the United States, one of the first groups to use the Internet was that of the supporters of the 'Blind Sheikh' – Sheikh Omar Abdel Rahman – the spiritual leader of the Islamic Group of Egypt. After the 'Blind Sheikh' was imprisoned, they used the Internet to disseminate anti-West propaganda and to raise funds in the United States and Canada. Gradually they spread their network into Europe, communicating with pockets of supporters in Austria (Vienna), France, Germany, Italy and the United Kingdom.

The widespread use of the web is not limited to jihadist groups: the Liberation Tigers of Tamil Eelam (LTTE, the 'Tamil Tigers') was one of the first terrorist groups both to use the internet to communicate and disseminate propaganda and to conduct an information infrastructure attack. An LTTE cell based at a university in the United States conducted coordinated simultaneous attacks on Sri Lankan diplomatic missions worldwide in the mid-1990s, disrupting the government communication system. In addition to ethno-nationalist groups, right-wing groups, such as Neo-Nazis and the Ku Klux Klan, and left-wing groups, including the New People's Army in the Philippines and the Maoists in Nepal, also use the internet. Just as a common ideology of violent jihad unites the jihadist groups, so groups bound by the communist ideology also use the Internet to work together. For instance, the Revolutionary International Movement (RIM) uses the Internet to coordinate worldwide activity by terrorist and extremist groups from Latin America to Southeast Asia. The spread of the Internet from the 'industrialized West' to the rest of the world witnessed terrorist and guerrilla groups, located in conflict zones from Latin America, through the Middle East to Asia and Africa, also taking to it.

EXTENT OF THE PROBLEM

While the security and intelligence communities monitored the use of the web, little was done by officials and politicians to regulate, let alone understand, its use. Interestingly enough, it was in the context of terrorist financing that the UN Monitoring Group on sanctions against al-Qaida and the Taliban first became concerned about usage of the Internet by al-Qaida-related terrorist groups. In the wake of 9/11, when the international community was placing so much emphasis on tracking and interdicting terrorist financing streams, it seemed a logical progression, in view of what was already known concerning the movement of their funds, for the terrorists to exploit this facet of modern technology. Internet banking was by then commonplace, even for those prepared to risk putting so much personal data on the internet. Why shouldn't the terrorists or their proxies and deep-pocket supporters follow the contemporary practice, especially since there was greater opportunity to conceal their real identity? As a result of research and discussions, at the time, it soon became clear that the terrorists were already exploiting another major aspect of 'globalization'. In its second report, released in May 2002, the Monitoring Group drew attention to this very important issue:

> 26. Another way in which criminals and terrorists move their money, to avoid detection, is by means of the Internet. The Group is particularly concerned about the use of the internet by al-Qa'idah and many of its associates, not only regarding financial transactions but also in support of their communications, command, control and logistics.[4]

Even ten years after the terrorists and extremists mastered the use of the internet, government policy and decision-makers have done little to address the problem. At the heart of the issue is the lack of understanding that terrorism is 90 per cent intent and 10 per cent capability. Instead of developing a robust ideological response to terrorism and to extremism, governments are targeting the physical infrastructure of the terrorist cells and groups. As long as the conceptual infrastructure is intact, as the Israeli-Palestinian case has demonstrated, the terrorists will develop the physical infrastructure and fight back. The internet hosts the terrorist conceptual infrastructure. In cyber space the terrorists and the extremists have won the battle. There are a few thousand terrorist and extremist websites but only a very small number of counter-terrorist and counter-extremist sites. Governments are many years away from catching up with the extensive use and exploitation of the internet by the terrorists and their supporters. As a result, every day several hundred youths are indoctrinated, to the point where some are prepared to plan, prepare and mount terrorist attacks. In the jihadist spectrum of groups, the phenomenon of self-radicalization by self-indoctrination will present a major threat in the coming years. It will require significant thinking by governments and other institutions that can influence governments to develop effective and enduring policies and operational responses to this significant and growing threat.

AL–QAIDA'S NERVE SYSTEM

Without exception, al-Qaida was the group that popularized the contemporary use of the web and other modern tools. Bin Laden himself was committed to using modern state-of-the-art equipment, and had no qualms about wearing a NATO-style combat jacket and carrying a Soviet AK-47 assault rifle. Similarly, he used an aircraft purchased in Arizona and a satellite phone obtained in New York. Although the jihadists condemn the West, they exploit many aspects of its modernity and technologies to fulfil their aims and advance their objectives: Usama bin Laden himself is a living example of this approach.

If finance is the 'life-blood of terrorism', then communications are its 'nerve system'. Just like today's armed forces with their 'hi-tech' and sophisticated weapons systems that rely on state-of-the-art communications and information technology, so too do the terrorists. For some years terrorist groups are known to have been making good use of the internet. Al-Qaida has been no exception. The evolution and developments in the growth of the 'global village' have provided the network with the means for its associates and cells, however loosely engaged, to stay in touch. Here was an important facet of day-to-day life, given the rapid advances in technology, that the terrorists could exploit and, by all accounts, already were exploiting.

Some of the major pronouncements to the Muslim world by Usama bin Laden have shown the world in general just how 'media-savvy' he has become, an aspect of his behaviour that has continued despite, we are given to believe, being on the run in the Afghan/Pakistan border regions. The discovery in Afghanistan in late 2001, by members of the US-led Coalition, of the 'CNN Tapes', which confirmed attempts by al-Qaida to develop crude chemical agents, highlighted yet again their penchant for keeping abreast of the times, in this case with video recordings of their experiments. During the same period, other videotapes had been made showing masked *mujāhidīn* undergoing training and lauding their warrior-like prowess. These were distributed by al-Qaida by various means, both physical and electronic, to rally budding jihadists to the cause. Subsequent research by a number of intelligence and security agencies, and by academic and private concerns, has highlighted the extent to which use or, better said, misuse of the internet by terrorist groups with hundreds of dedicated websites has become an everyday occurrence rather than a phenomenon.

In the case of Islamist extremist groups, the sites invariably contain colourful, lurid exhortations to participate in the jihad or demand support for it in a variety of other ways. Particularly since

9/11 a number of agencies, both governmental and private institutions, have been tracking al-Qaida-related sites. These terrorist sites have been used not only to spread its ill-informed and unfounded ideology, but to recruit, indoctrinate and even provide training for would-be terrorists. One site, the Arabic language 'Muʾaskar Al-Battar' ('The Training Camp'), was established specifically as a training magazine, providing instruction in a variety of weapons popular with terrorists.[5] The first issue of this bi-monthly internet periodical concentrates on the AKM and AK-47 assault rifles. Another explains the workings of the MP-5 sub-machine pistol and a third the infamous RPG-7 shoulder-fired anti-tank rocket launcher. By June 2006 there had been 22 editions. This site exists for anyone to access, unlike many other al-Qaida-related sites, which have vanished. Attempts to access one of the earlier mouthpieces of al-Qaida, a website at alneda.com, are now greeted with the phrase 'hacked, tracked and now owned by the USA!' Others appear to have suffered similar fates. Tracking the terrorists' websites is all the more difficult because of the international or global nature of the internet business. It is very simple for a user to pay to set up a site with a service provider on another continent thousands of miles away from where the 'cyber-terrorist' is based, thereby virtually concealing his or her identity. Despite this apparent anonymity, there have been successes against the terrorists whereby some internet service providers (ISPs) have shut down sites when they have become aware of its purpose.

Often, just as happens when one squeezes a balloon, as soon as the terrorists' sites are closed down in one place they pop up in another. Other sites, however, have maximized on the many and various techniques that have sprung up concerning general misuse of the internet. One such example featured in a recent SITE Institute Intel Update concerning a computer software programme called Steganography. According to the SITE report:

> Steganography, which allows users to embed files within
> the contents of another, such as a picture or video clip, was
> recently provided by a member of the password-protected
> jihadist forum, mohajroon, and explained with screen cap-
> tures of the program in action. Using such technology, a
> user may merge a document within a picture file, transmit
> it to another user, and feel secure that from the surface a

hacker or investigator would not perceive the existence of the secret communication.

Software such as this, and others that provide for anonymity, secret exchange, and security precautions, are common amongst the jihadist forums, and indicative of the degree of computer literacy and technical acumen amongst their membership.[6]

The SITE report then provides a translation and graphic display of the 'click-by-click' use of this program. As this example demonstrates, many of the 'cyber-tactics' invoked by members of the 'greater al-Qaida', their supporters and their messengers have not gone unnoticed. Many of these techniques are not specific to al-Qaida. They have been and continue to be used by most of the current terrorist groups. Hamas, Hezbollah and Islamic Jihad have all made the most of this global phenomenon that has come to such prominence in so many peoples' lives in the last few years. It is just as easy to spread Islamist extremist propaganda as it is to go internet shopping on eBay. But just as there have been a great many benefits from the internet boom, so too has there been the downside – hackers and those who manipulate the systems to their pecuniary advantage at the expense of legitimate owners and users.

Forced underground, to avoid detection while continuing to communicate between cells, associates and individuals, the Islamist extremists have taken to boring into other unsuspecting owners' websites and 'riding' unseen on the back of their systems. This practice has also been copied by others who have set up phoney 'call shops' in order to provide cut-price calls back home for immigrants, legal and illegal, and migrant workers in European countries. Hacking into such prominent global entities as Continental Airlines, 'call shop crooks' have been able to offer their immigrant customers international calls for the price of a local call in the location from which they operate.[7] The use of a telephone shop as an outwardly legitimate business has already been discussed in chapter Ten as providing the Madrid train bombers with cover and the technical know-how for the timing devices used to detonate the IEDs for those attacks.

Important as these aspects are in this communications kaleidoscope, the most pronounced misuse of the internet by the terrorists has been to raise the profile of their cause and to recruit new members for their misplaced and ill-defined 'unholy war'. Swords, scimitars and AK-47s adorn brightly coloured pages, often wreathed in flames and glorified with Qur'anic verses. In those worlds where young people exist without visible futures and devoid of hope, these electronic clarion calls provide a focus for their minds and a mythical opportunity to escape a life of survival in depressed surroundings. Al-Qaida's own website went even further in its exhortations about the rewards of martyrdom: the joys of spending the rest of one's eternal youth in the company of 72 (beautiful, it is to be hoped) virgins. As a means of enhancing the global 'glorification' of the cause espoused by Usama bin Laden and his cohorts, the logo of the al-Qaida site in 2003 depicted an Arab horseman, his scimitar or *saif* raised high above his head, in a manner clearly reminiscent of the Crusaders' renowned medieval adversary, Salah al-Din (or 'Saladin'). Just as Salah al-Din is revered even today in many Arab circles for his prowess in battle against the original medieval Crusaders, Usama bin Laden has been hailed by some as the new Salah al-Din. Even Abu Musab al-Zarqawi tried to assume such a mantle as the outright leader of 'al-Qaida in the Land of the Two Rivers' (i.e. Iraq). Nor are the sites directed only at adult males and Muslim youth. Besides calling on boys to revere this murderous way of life and follow Islam, women have also been a target.

At the end of August 2004 a new al-Qaida website appeared, directed specifically at women. *Al-Khansaa* magazine, published by 'al-Qaida's Arabian Peninsular Women's Information Bureau', called on women to follow jihad. It stated how they should stand shoulder-to-shoulder with their men: how their place in the family was so important to the faith and its correct (Sunni) interpretation.[8] Despite its war-like tones, *Al-Khansaa* nonetheless projected modern 'girl-appeal' with its pages adorned in shades of pink – hardly a warrior-like colour. Happily, the magazine's publishers did not have it all their own way. A few days later, a cross-section of Saudi women came out strongly against the launch of a new internet magazine targeting Saudi and other Arab women as well as children in the al-Qaida-inspired drive against 'infidels in the Arabian Peninsula'. By calling on women to join in or support preparations for jihad, the terrorists were, yet again, misinterpreting the Muslim faith. For the concerned women of Saudi Arabia, Islam stands for mercy, compassion, tolerance and justice. 'What do they want to achieve?', asked radio journalist and broadcaster Samar Fatany from Jeddah, 'What they are preaching is extremism and revenge which are totally un-Islamic.'[9] Although access to *Al-Khansaa* appears no longer to be available, the radicalization of women over the internet, particularly Western converts to Islam, has continued. One such example was Muriel Degauque, a 38-year-old Belgian woman who, although born into a white Christian family, converted to Islam. She was so radicalized that she followed the call of the Islamist chat-rooms to Iraq and, in November 2005, died as a suicide bomber in an attack on a US convoy. Nonetheless, for the terrorists, the internet can also be a two-edged weapon.

Despite the efforts of the terrorists to cover their tracks and hide the identities of some of their more important means of communication, using such means as password-protected access, security and intelligence services have found ways of tracking them. Using state-of-the-art technology and software, 'sigint' and 'elint' teams have found ways and means of tracking many of the terrorists' transmissions, leading to arrests and the foiling of attacks being planned. One recent case in point was the arrests in Toronto on 2–3 June 2006 of seventeen men of South Asian decent, all members of an Islamist terrorist cell suspected of planning attacks against a number of important sites in and around Toronto. On being questioned, they are alleged to have told police that the three tons of ammonium nitrate in their possession was for gardening! Security services in Canada were alerted to the suspects' activities as a result of monitoring internet chat sites.[10]

One of the most prolific and skilled 'hackers' who appeared to have a strong affiliation towards al-Qaida and is credited with postings on its behalf went under the nom de plume of 'Irhabioo7' ('terrorist 007'). His 'cyber-exploits' had been attracting the attention of intelligence and security services for about two years when he suddenly went off-air. On 21 October 2005, police arrested a 22-year-old man, Younis Tsouli, in west London. He was charged under the UK's Terrorism Act 2000 with 'conspiracy to murder, conspiracy to cause an explosion, conspiracy to obtain money by deception, fundraising and possession of articles for terrorist purposes'. The departure of Irhabioo7 from the cyber-scene appeared to coincide with the arrest of Younis Tsouli by the authorities in the UK when they were investigating another terrorism case. What they found at Younis Tsouli's premises was the information that eventually led them to believe they had arrested this particular cyber-terrorist.[11]

In addition to the exploits of such individuals as Irhabi 007 and the silent cut and thrust taking place across the internet, between the terrorists and their sympathizers and the intelligence services and private institutions trying to keep track of them, the role of the media must also be considered. Every time the terrorists detonate a roadside bomb or a suicide bomber explodes his or her device somewhere in Iraq, television channels across the globe provide free propaganda for the terrorist groups. Many sensible, sound-thinking people would argue that the horrors only harm the image of the terrorists and their 'cause'. But the fact is that in many parts of the world there are Muslims who see these events as justifiable retribution against those who have waged an unpopular invasion of Iraq or another unending conflict based on flawed intelligence. Fortunately, there are many Iraqis who would not agree with this view and are glad that Saddam Hussein and his regime no longer rule the country – not that many are happy with the current aftermath. The same can be said of suicide or rocket attacks by Islamists against civilian targets in Israel, be it Tel Aviv or Haifa.

Tragically, in the context of this particular subject, TV channels survive economically on their ratings, and undoubtedly blood, bangs and bodies make news. Thus one has to ask the question, why is it always the Qatar-based satellite TV company al-Jazeera, and only al-Jazeera, that appears to have exclusive rights to screening audio and visual pronouncements by Usama bin Laden and his deputy, Ayman al-Zawahiri? Doubtless, if al-Jazeera were to stop acting as the mouthpiece for the remnants of the original al-Qaida leadership, another broadcaster would be happy to scoop up the baton (and anyway the al-Qaida tapes would be broadcast over the world wide web). In fairness to al-Jazeera, on some occasions that is exactly what they report, namely repeating what has already been sent out on an al-Qaida website. Evan Kohlmann, in an investigation published on MSNBC television, provided a simple explanation of the process as to how videotapes featuring bin Laden and al-Zawahiri are recorded, 'polished' for presentation and then distributed.[12] The raw recordings of the now familiar videos of bin Laden and Zawahiri are taken from the 'secret' location where they were made, suggestedly by a locally recruited cameraman, to al-Qaida's PR component – As Saahab – who 'top n' tail' them into more polished productions, which includes, when appropriate, adding English sub-titles. As Saahab then passes the final product to internet outlets for global distribution. Kohlmann's article even includes a simple interactive presentation of the process. Reference to the article can also be found on the Counterterrorism Blog.

The exploitation by terrorists of the worldwide web notwithstanding, one can sometimes be left with the impression that al-Jazeera is promoting terrorism – and terrorism of a particularly heinous form on those occasions when it is the exclusive broadcaster of al-Qaida's messages. A more sinister aspect of this apparent media exclusivity that also demands an answer is how much money does the company pay to bin Laden or his 'nominated trustee'? Clearly, if any money is changing hands then al-Jazeera should be subject to UN sanctions, and the company should accordingly be designated on the 1267 Committee's Consolidated List as a financial or material supporter of al-Qaida. This aspect of how the international community or elements of it (and the media is a very important element) play their different roles in responding to the threat from transnational Islamist terrorism brings us full circle: from defining and understanding the threat, through the 'life-blood' to the 'nerve system' and the community's role in confronting it.

Although the role of the UN is to be addressed in greater detail in a subsequent chapter, a recommendation of the UN Analytical Support and Sanctions Monitoring Team (ASSMT), in its third report, once again drew the international community's attention to this very significant problem demanding effective action to curb its activities and effects.[13] In its fourth report it goes further in highlighting the extent of the problem. However, its quoted figures are at some variance with those of other institutions. The ASSMT quotes an OSCE study with giving al-Qaida credit for 'over 2600 [sites] today' on the internet. Professor Weimann of Haifa University, on the other hand, in his recent book on the subject, quotes an increase in the number of terrorist websites from 12 in 1998 to 4,300 today, albeit not just al-Qaida alone.[14] Although the ASSMT highlights the problems that are recognized and faced by members of the international body, sadly it offers no recommendations on how to move forward. Drawing readers' attention to the preamble in Security Council resolutions 1617 (2005) and 1624 (2005) with regard to cooperative action by states to prevent terrorists exploiting sophisticated technology in the furtherance of their aims will have little or no effect. Even when the Security Council states that 'States shall take' certain measures, often little happens unless there is a clear and distinct benefit for the state(s) concerned. This diplomatic and political inertia cannot be used as a reason for not sitting down and addressing the problem on as broad a scale as the web itself. Clever and constant exploitation of the internet by the terrorists and those who support them highlights yet again the reality of the threat from *terrorisme sans frontières*, a threat that will be countered effectively only by reciprocating cross-border measures, agreed and accepted by all concerned. Herein lies one of the most significant dilemmas for many people around the world and their elected governments, particularly those who take seriously genuine democracy and the rights of the individual.

DATA PROTECTION OR PHYSICAL PROTECTION

There is no doubt that the vast majority of citizens from the world's industrialized nations, and those who aspire to the same economic standards and lifestyle expectations, think carefully about the balance between their civil liberties and the intrusion(s) of the state(s) into their lives. Pillars of democratic societies include the right of individual citizens to privacy in the course of their day-to-day lives – provided that these activities are legal. Long before terrorism reached its current ascendancy, legal means existed in many countries for security and law enforcement services to intrude electronically into the lives of those suspected of criminal- or terrorism-related activities. But these intrusions can be viewed very differently from state to state and from country to country. Memories are still fresh in Europe of the roles played, first in Hitler's Germany, by the Gestapo and later by the Stasi[15] during the Cold War Soviet occupation of East Germany. Civil libertarians will, and perhaps quite correctly, demand that the rights of the individual to privacy are paramount and in fact they normally will be for the vast majority of law-abiding citizens. The conflicts arise when security and law enforcement find themselves confronted by the small percentage of criminals and terrorists who are intent on operating either outside the law or beneath it. Because the internet is global, solutions to the problem of intrusions and controls have to be international. Just as with measures that are proscribed under UN Security Council resolutions to tackle the financing of terrorism and supported by regional and international groupings such as the

European Union and FATF respectively, measures need to be developed that will effectively curb the misuse of the world wide web by terrorist groups. Such measures should demand the same levels of accountability from internet service providers (ISPs), and the governments in whose territory they are based and from where they operate, as those expected of financial institutions and governments.

REALISTIC COUNTER-MEASURES

In the final chapter of his book *Terror on the Internet*, Professor Weimann puts forward six approaches to 'achieve this balance between security and liberty within today's cyber-reality'. Perhaps the most significant of these refers to 'fostering international collaboration'. In the relevant section mention is made in some detail of a draft proposal for an 'International Convention to Enhance Protection from Cyber Crime and Terrorism', which would combine protective and reactive measures. This proposal, sponsored by a consortium led by The Hoover Institute, had already been made in August 2000.[16] Unfortunately, nothing has come of it, but it is the first and most logical step. Drafting and the adoption of an international convention on countering the use, abuse or misuse of the internet and media by terrorists and terrorist groups are fundamental to the international collaboration required. Thirteen international conventions already exist (see chapter Five), adopted under the aegis of the United Nations, which provide member states with a framework on which to base national legislation to combat a range of activities related to terrorism. Moving forward with a convention on this subject is all the more important because of the need for the international community to make tracks to overhaul the terrorists' current advantage. The absence of the long-awaited comprehensive convention on terrorism, which continues to wallow in the doldrums of international diplomacy for want of an internationally accepted definition of terrorism, should not be a reason for not advancing with a convention on the internet and cyber-terrorism. Clearly, the wording of such an instrument will need to take account of the borderless nature of the web. Legislation will need to reflect the seriousness of activities emanating inside a state's boundaries on the territory of other states. While freedom of speech and freedom of expression are always to be encouraged, especially in those countries where such liberties are not written into law or enshrined in constitutions, precedents do exist that outlaw the incitement to inter-ethnic hatred and the support and perpetration of terrorism or terrorist-related acts. In the United Kingdom, for example, provision now exists that 'makes it a criminal offence to directly or indirectly incite or encourage others to commit acts of terrorism . . . [including] the glorification of terrorism, where this may be understood as encouraging the emulation of terrorism'.[17] Thus, despite the perceived difficulties of adopting such a convention, the need now outweighs the complications. Just as was seen with the slow progress of states becoming party to the International Convention on the Suppression of the Financing of Terrorism, the response to a convention concerning terrorism and the web is likely to be equally pedantic; but it needs to be done and it needs to be done well.[18]

Once a convention exists, the very nature of its adoption through the UN General Assembly, though not binding, means that it has universal acceptance. A platform is therefore in place on which to base not only national legislation, but also other steps that can be taken and measured, and if necessary be the subject of sanctions. The important point to be registered is the need for accountability. Such measures can and should be effected through UN Security Council resolutions. Self-regulation, while being encouraged, often falls short of meeting a 'common global standard' due to other interests dominating the process. Therefore, while it is accepted that ISPs exist that can be encouraged to monitor, deter and shut down terrorist websites, a procedure is needed better to police those who are less responsible. Consideration may also be given to the establishment of a body, similar to the FATF, to provide regulatory guidance, provisions and monitoring of governments' performance in ensuring that the necessary standards are met and physically enforced.

If international requirements, including Security Council resolutions, are adopted to combat one of the greatest man-made threats to global peace and security of the twenty-first century, they must be more than just political statements; they have to be fully implemented. Otherwise there is no point in the Council wasting its time, or anyone else's, in drafting and discussing resolutions if they are going to be ignored. It thus follows that if member states of the United Nations do not abide by the Charter and meet their obligations, then they should expect to be sanctioned. But sanctions can be a two-edged weapon. Those who call for them and who wish to see them imposed and effectively monitored must ensure that they have the moral high ground. With that in mind, and recalling the value of lessons learned – even if there are those who would prefer to ignore the lessons when they do not suit a particular agenda – it is important to recall the impact of the invasion of Iraq on the international community's efforts, post-9/11, in combating terrorism (see chapter Two). Despite its impact, however, it is only one of the factors that have adversely influenced the international community's response to combating terrorism. As we have seen, there has been, and continues to be, a general malaise when it comes to taking firm and decisive action to deal with threats to peace and security. This inertia is not confined to the Security Council or the politically unwilling member states.

12

The Reluctant Leadership

ack in October 2001, while the work of the UN's Counter
Terrorism Committee (CTC) had been getting underway, the
Policy Working Group on the United Nations and Terrorism
(PWG) had been established at the behest of the Secretary-General. The
purpose of the PWG was 'to identify the longer-term implications and
broad policy dimensions of terrorism for the United Nations'. The
group's report to the Secretary-General in August 2002 contains some
interesting conclusions and no fewer than 31 recommendations. The
Policy Working Group 'considered that the United Nations should concentrate its direct role in counter-terrorism on the areas in which the
Organization has a comparative advantage . . . [it] should bolster and
reassert the leading principles and purposes of the . . . United Nations
Charter, the core of which are undermined and threatened by terrorism.' This approach was to be based on three principles: dissuasion,
denial and cooperation. Disaffected groups were to be *dissuaded* from
becoming terrorists. Terrorists or would-be terrorists were to be *denied*
the means to support terrorism or commit terrorist acts. International
cooperation was to be sustained in the efforts against terrorism.

The recommendations of the PWG reiterated once again the
importance of all states not only ratifying, but 'effectively implementing the 12 . . . counter-terrorism conventions' as part of the process
of *dissuasion*. Under the heading of *denial*, the report contains recommendations intended to enhance the work of the CTC and the capacity
of individual states to meet their obligations under resolution 1373.
The report stresses the need for better international *cooperation*, particularly among regional organizations and between them and the UN,
in order to promote the adoption of best practices. The PWG also

recommended that 'the Department of Political Affairs should be identified as the focal point of the United Nations system for political and strategic issues related to counter-terrorism'. Subsequent events would question the wisdom and sincerity of this decision. How, with time, has the recommendation been implemented – or not – and to what extent has effective acceptance and implementation of this stated responsibility actually been met? One of the most significant findings of the PWG, contained in its 'General Considerations', states that the organization [the United Nations] is not well placed 'to play an active operational role in efforts to suppress terrorist groups, to pre-empt specific strikes, or to develop dedicated intelligence-gathering capacities'. In the case of gathering intelligence and pre-empting strikes by terrorist groups the PWG is probably correct, or was at that time – these are not functions deemed appropriate to the United Nations by some, at least, of its member states. Playing a more active operational role in this overall context, by taking a lead in countering transnational terrorism, is a responsibility that the United Nations, and only the United Nations, is legitimately placed to assume. Regional and sub-regional organizations can, should and must play a significant part in the overall effort to combat transnational terrorism. However, the necessary leadership has to come from the top. It is clear that no one country on its own, no matter how strong, can defeat the threat that the transnational terrorism of today poses to global peace and security.

The more cynical might say that, in recommending that the UN should do what it is best at doing, it was recommending that it should carry on doing nothing! Regrettably, this attitude towards the UN is borne out by the fact that there was only the one report from the PWG, which is still to be found in pride of place in the centre of the UN's webpage under the title 'The UN and Terrorism'. The PWG does not appear to have met again; if it has, then no further reports have yet been made public. Also, in throwing its weight behind the work of the UN's CTC, the PWG (and probably the Secretariat with it) abrogated further any 'leadership' role in what was then and still is a very high-profile subject. It is a matter that continues to engage governments, regional bodies and such other international caucuses as the Club de Madrid. Although many of the participants of this latter body recognize and support the role of the United Nations in comprehensively tackling terrorism, there are others from a broad spectrum of international academia and expertise who have written off the UN in the fight against terrorism. Certainly, if one looks at its track record concerning Somalia, Rwanda, Bosnia (particularly Srebrenica) and later Darfur (Sudan), one can, perhaps, understand the basis for so many disparate bodies coming to the same conclusions.

RESOLUTE OR RESOLUTIONS?

Despite the strength and tone of the rhetoric emanating from the Security Council, concerning the revitalization of its own Counter Terrorism Committee (the CTC), it took from early 2004 to late 2005 before the new CT Executive Directorate (CTED) was properly established. Unnecessary but typical bureaucratic in-fighting and a lack of political will seriously delayed the appointment of the Directorate with its full complement of international experts, whose role is to support the work of the actual Committee. Former officials of the UN have blamed this situation on the fact that, unlike the original panel of experts who were employed as consultants, the members of the new directorate are to be UN staff members. Consequently, the rules of the organization for the recruitment of personnel had to be followed and these are bureaucratically cumbersome and long-winded. However, this argument tends to wear thin when comparing the time taken to recruit people for the CTED with that for hiring the eight experts, also as UN staff members, for the Analytical Support and Sanctions Monitoring Team (ASSMT),[1] which replaced the Al-Qaida Sanctions Monitoring Group. Seven of the eight experts were recruited and had started work within two to three months. As is so often the case: 'Where there's a will, there's a way!'

This Analytical Support Team, unlike its predecessor, is not operationally independent. It works with, to and at the direction of the Al-Qaida and Taliban Sanctions Committee, which was originally established under resolution 1267 (1999). Its history emphasizes, once again, the lack of political will and necessary resolve to countering terrorism on the part of the Security Council. On 13 November 2003 Chile's ambassador Muñoz, then Chairman of the 1267 Committee, was quoted in an interview with the US Fox News Channel as saying that 'UN sanctions against the Al-Qaida terror network and Afghanistan's ousted Taliban regime are often circumvented and need "more teeth".' Two months later, however, the same Chairman

Countering Terrorism

had changed his tune. Under his stewardship and with the support of the governments of the Russian Federation and the United States, the mandate of the Monitoring Group, whose last report had provided him the means with which to make such forthright and accurate statements to the media, was allowed to lapse – only to be replaced by the Analytical Support and Sanctions Monitoring Team (ASSMT). Regrettably, the establishment of an entity such as this demonstrates the reality of the UN approach, which provides the ammunition for the sceptics. Although the ASSMT was established for eight experts, one did not join the panel for almost nine months after the resolution had been approved, and that was the US government's nomination – so much for 'leadership' in the so-called 'war on terror'!

This perhaps is an indicator of another aspect that should be of concern, namely the level of interest and support that, in reality, the US placed on the UN's role in countering terrorism. On numerous occasions, during their travels to countries in 2002 and 2003, it was often crystal clear to the members of the Monitoring Group that information that should have been made available to them, but was not, had been passed to the US government. The governor of one state's central bank, when asked for specific information concerning frozen bank accounts, stated that it had already been given to the US: 'you can ask them for the information'. Needless to say the response from the Monitoring Group was very emphatically that 'we do not work for the US government – we work for the United Nations!' This bilateral approach of the United States proved, quite often, to be counter-productive to the monitoring of the al-Qaida sanctions regime. This, taken with the adverse responses of Italy, Liechtenstein and Switzerland to being mentioned in the 'Nada and Nasreddin Case Study' in the Monitoring Group's last report, demonstrates the ambivalence that so often prevails in the work of the UN Security Council. These 'national' reactions highlight, yet again, the attitudes of member states and, hence collectively, the weak response of the international community to countering terrorism.

Another example of the Security Council 'talking the talk' but in the end, once again, not 'walking the walk' was the 'Beslan Resolution'. On 1 September 2004 Chechen separatist rebels committed an appalling terrorist atrocity at School 'Number One' in Beslan, North Ossetia.[2] In response to this callous and cowardly act, the UN Security Council approved resolution 1566 on 8 October 2004. This resolution was initiated by the Russian Federation and was co-spon-sored by China, France, Germany, Romania, Spain, the United States and the United Kingdom. It reiterated once again the need for states, not already party to the twelve anti-terrorism conventions, to become so 'as a matter of urgency'. In Operative 8 of the resolution, the Council '*directs* the CTC, as a matter of priority and, when appropri-ate, in close cooperation with relevant international, regional and sub-regional organizations to start visits to States, with the consent of the States concerned, in order to enhance the monitoring of the imple-mentation of resolution 1373 (2001)'.

This operative is interesting in itself. To 'direct' is very strong language in UN Security Council terms, suggesting a frustration with a committee that is only a mirror of itself! For the CTC to undertake the visits means senior diplomats being away from New York. Ambassadors or their deputies who are members of the Council do sally forth from New York from time to time when making official vis-its to particular countries. However, such visits tend to happen only once or twice a year, usually to a location where there is major prob-lem requiring their attention. The very nature of their work tends to preclude them from travelling extensively and, if such visits are to be effective, that is what is necessary. If instead the council had mandat-ed a group composed of experts in the areas requiring to be moni-tored, then this approach would stand a chance of producing much more practical and effective results. Such a monitoring group could be more objective in reporting their findings, since they are able to distance themselves from the politicking and pressures to which members of the Council are subjected.

Then there is the point of undertaking this task 'in close coop-eration with . . . '. By the time that all the various bodies mentioned in resolution 1566 have been informed, liaised and consulted with, especially at the speed that such consultations often take, much valu-able time will have been lost. Furthermore, this is the seventh time that the word 'cooperate' or 'cooperation' appears in this resolution, never mind how often it has already appeared in previous resolutions on related matters. Although there are circumstances associated with these words that have improved since 11 September 2001, particular-ly in the field of countering terrorism, the words themselves have become rather threadbare. One senior academic, who would wish to remain anonymous, said in May 2004: 'If I had a dollar for every time

I have heard the word *cooperation* used in the context of countering terrorism, I would be a very rich man now!' The cooperation exists because certain states have an ulterior motive for wanting to cooperate. It is rarely for nothing. That being said, cooperation at peer level between certain states has been, and continues to be, excellent and has resulted in significant arrests of terrorist suspects and a number of terrorist plots being foiled or nipped in the bud. But, as has been indicated earlier, there are a variety of reasons why states cannot or will not always cooperate as readily as the Security Council's words would deem necessary.

This lack of cooperation has affected the al-Qaida and Taliban sanctions regime and the value of its associated list, the latter being but a sub-set of the total number of individuals who should be subject to the called-for restrictions. Consequently, the utility of establishing 'a working group . . . of all members of the Security Council to consider and submit recommendations to the Council [itself] on practical measures to be imposed upon individuals, groups or entities involved in or associated with terrorist activities, other than those designated [as al-Qaida or Taliban]' is questionable. In its last report, the Monitoring Group stated unequivocally that the al-Qaida sanctions required to be strengthened. In a number of its reports the Group had emphasized the need for the List to be extended to address the lacunae that existed with so few individuals and entities being designated. The Group had also pointed out the need to strengthen the sanctions regime, such that states were obliged to implement the measures.[3] If, as is the case, the sanctions regime targeting al-Qaida requires to be improved significantly if it is to be really effective, there seems little point in spending time and effort devising yet another anti-terrorist sanctions regime, before the first one has been made to work properly. Logically, it would seem more realistic to get one system working well, rather than chalking up yet another political statement, which may be politically correct but which is just another resolution that states interpret and respond to as it suits them. In addition, one has to weigh the impact of another list of designated individuals and entities that will have to be maintained, processed and promulgated, and against which actions will have to be taken. At a time when many states are calling for tighter evidentiary standards and a more transparent review process of those designated, which conforms better to recognized norms and the rule of law, consolidation of what is already in place would seem to be a more prudent approach, or one has to make dramatic changes to the present system. In view of the recommendations of the High-Level Panel on Threats, Challenges and Change in *A More Secure World: Our Shared Responsibility*, there was once again an opportunity for the UN to take the lead in the international community's efforts to combat terrorism, starting with that against the current transnational terrorist threat.[4]

13

Pathways Out of Violence

O ver the years the UN has worked with varying degrees of effectiveness and success to reduce threats to international security. Among the seminal documents produced by the UN was the report of the Secretary-General's High-Level Panel that was released on 2 December 2004. This report provided a comprehensive and far-reaching review that had been long overdue. By United Nations standards much of the language used is really quite strong. There are many people who actually believe in the organization, despite its shortcomings. Others, who have worked or still work in it, have striven to ensure that the standards to which they themselves aspire and maintain, and demand of others, are not the 'lowest common denominator'. For many of these people the criticism of the Panel could have been tougher. They want to see improvements and want to belong to an organization that, as a whole, can at all times be proud of its achievements. The recommendations of the Panel for confronting terrorism go well beyond the requirements laid down in resolutions 1267, 1373, 1526 and 1566.

The report sets out a bold new vision for collective security. It addresses underlying causes leading to insecurity. The Panel spells out the need to tackle the problems that give rise to the transnational terrorist phenomenon, as well as terrorism as a whole. It reminds the world community that acceptable and lasting solutions need to be found to some of the longest-running problems where terrorist groups have flourished; the Kashmir conflict and Israel and the Palestinians. This latter conflict has fuelled the hatred that has become the by-word of Islamic fundamentalists. In addition, scenes, broadcast round the world by Arabic satellite television channels such as al-Jazeera and al-

Arabiya, of Israeli troops bulldozing Palestinian homes, and of 'US occupation forces' in Iraq mistreating prisoners in the notorious Abu Ghraib and using sledge-hammer tactics against terrorist strongholds, have only added fuel to the same fires. When the Palestinians, however, despite the handover to them of Gaza, have continued to fire rockets into Israeli areas, and then Hezbollah has initiated totally unprovoked attacks into northern Israel, it is clear that it is the Arab world and Iran, respectively, that need to stand up and be counted. Tragically that has not happened. Instead of showing some initiative themselves they turn to the UN, despite the fact that many of them have systematically baulked efforts for the adoption of a universal definition of terrorism. On 15 July 2006, after an emergency session in Cairo, 'foreign ministers of eighteen Arab countries passed a unanimous resolution calling on the UN Security Council to intervene to stop escalating Mideast fighting'. Paraphrasing the words of Amr Moussa, the Secretary-General of the Arab League, the Middle East peace process had failed and it was time for the whole process to be sent back to the (UN) Security Council. They were unanimous in their decision to pursue this route with the problem. Tragically, there was no statement, unanimous or otherwise, from the Arab League or its members doing anything more positive or practical about the situation. Perhaps the Arab League should be asking itself what it has done to prevent the situation arising in the first place.[1]

But the United Nations has to rise above these problems and, collectively, confront them. One of the constraints in the collective international effort in confronting terrorism has been the ambiguity that exists in defining it. Here the panel made a worthy contribution that needs to be accepted, especially when one realizes that the recommended definition was reached by consensus.

A DEFINITION OF TERRORISM

The members of the Panel made the following recommendation to the General Assembly, as a way of breaking this long-running impasse. Because of its importance it is described here in full.

> 163. Nevertheless, we believe there is particular value in achieving a consensus definition within the General Assembly, given its unique legitimacy in normative terms,

Countering Terrorism

and that it should rapidly complete negotiations on a comprehensive convention on terrorism.

164. That definition of terrorism should include the following elements:

(a) Recognition, in the preamble, that State use of force against civilians is regulated by the Geneva Conventions and other instruments, and, if of sufficient scale, constitutes a war crime by the persons concerned or a crime against humanity;

(b) Restatement that acts under the 12 preceding antiterrorism conventions are terrorism, and a declaration that they are a crime under international law; and restatement that terrorism in time of armed conflict is prohibited by the Geneva Conventions and Protocols;

(c) Reference to the definitions contained in the 1999 International Convention for the Suppression of the Financing of Terrorism and Security Council resolution 1566 (2004);

(d) Description of terrorism as 'any action, in addition to actions already specified by the existing conventions on aspects of terrorism, the Geneva Conventions and Security Council resolution 1566 (2004), that is intended to cause death or serious bodily harm to civilians or noncombatants, when the purpose of such an act, by its nature or context, is to intimidate a population, or to compel a Government or an international organization to do or to abstain from doing any act'.

THE CLUB DE MADRID SUMMIT (2005)

It was encouraging to see the Panel's definition of terrorism being repeated, ahead of its hoped-for adoption, in the declaration from the Riyadh International Counter Terrorism Conference (5–8 February 2005) and as a basis for the 'Madrid Agenda', the statement resulting from the Club de Madrid International Summit on Democracy, Terrorism and Security (8–11 March 2005).[2]

In his keynote speech on 10 March 2005 to the Club de Madrid Summit, Kofi Annan, the United Nations Secretary-

General, outlined his 'principal, comprehensive strategy' for the UN
to deal with terrorism, based on the recommendations of the Panel.
This strategy is to be based on five elements or, as the Secretary-
General said, 'I shall call them the "five DS"'. The first two were in
fact virtually the same as the first two measures proposed by the PWG
back in August 2002, namely to *dissuade* disaffected groups from
choosing terrorism as a tactic to achieve their goals and to *deny* terrorists the means to carry out their attacks. Mr Annan then defined
the need to *deter* states from supporting terrorism, *developing* states'
capacity to prevent terrorism and *defending* human rights in the
struggle against terrorism. There are those who, while in principle
supporting this last requirement, will say that there may be times
when it is difficult to achieve without some sacrifice when cracking
down on the more extreme terrorism facing the world today. As the
Secretary-General pointed out in his speech, 'Human rights law
makes ample provision for strong counter-terrorism action, even
under the most exceptional circumstances. But compromising human
rights cannot serve the struggle against terrorism.'[3] Similarly, the
Madrid Agenda stresses that terrorism can only be ultimately defeated
by applying and working within democratic principles and upholding
the rule of law.[4]

At first glance the strategy outlined by the Secretary-General
was encouraging. Many had hoped for a more comprehensive statement, detailing not only what needs to be addressed but more of how
it was to be achieved; how the UN would be organizing itself to fulfil
the defined requirements and providing the necessary leadership. As
one has seen many times in the past, the Security Council has provided the organization with mandates to deal with terrorism, but too
often is unwilling to enforce them. Often the Secretariat has been
equally dilatory in its support. Sanctions are effective if properly
enforced and policed, but it is known that they are not popular: they
demand tough decisions and often result in discord, a situation with
which many inside the UN are uncomfortable.

'OUR SHARED RESPONSIBILITY'

If all had gone to plan, as many of the more optimistic of us had
hoped, the brave words of the High-Level Panel should have been
translated into a once-in-a-generation opportunity at the United

Nations Summit in New York in September 2005. Sadly and regrettably, but again, if one looks at the organization's track record in dealing with major security problems over the past fifteen years, not surprisingly, it failed to address effectively the problem of transnational terrorism. Many had hoped that the '2005 Summit' would have provided the vehicle for the long-awaited 'comprehensive convention on international terrorism'. Instead 'the need to . . . reach an agreement on and conclude' such an instrument was only stressed as a requirement for the General Assembly in its sixtieth session.[5]

Once again the main stumbling-block to achieving the comprehensive convention is the inability of the General Assembly to reach agreement on a definition of 'terrorism'. Most states that are totally committed to tackling international terrorism and regional bodies have adopted definitions of their own. The inability to reach agreement on a definition acceptable to the world body revolves round those Islamic states intent on wording that exempts the armed resistance against occupying forces, that is, they want the door kept open for groups such as Hamas and Hezbollah to continue with (terrorist) attacks against Israel. All the time that no acceptable definition is agreed, the loophole exists for those Islamic states that wish not to ratify or accede to 'terrorism conventions' aimed at suppressing terrorist financing. Similarly, one can expect those states that are so inclined to exploit this lacuna in other anti-terrorism matters.

'A FORK IN THE ROAD'

In his speech to the UN General Assembly in 2003, the Secretary-General said that the organization had reached a 'fork in the road'. He was, of course, referring to the acrimonious debate and significant concerns expressed by many, many member states at the decision of the US, the UK and their other allies over the invasion of Iraq outside a Security Council decision. Unfortunately, judging from the facts, it would appear that two-and-a-half years later the UN is still at that fork, and this despite the efforts of the High-Level Panel; despite the support from such an august body as the Club de Madrid; despite the growing influence and impact of transnational terrorism. Even in the Secretary-General's proposal for far-reaching change in the management of the UN – 'Investing in the United Nations: for a stronger Organization worldwide' – terrorism is not mentioned as one of the challenges facing UN staff.[6] It would seem that this metaphorical fork in the road forward has three directions that can be chosen, not two as perhaps is normally envisaged.

In other words there would appear to be three courses of action open. If all the member states of the UN are willing to face up fully to their responsibilities, then at the level of the organization itself subsidiary organs that already exist could be given stronger and more comprehensive mandates. They should then be adequately resourced and empowered to be operationally independent. They would report direct to the Security Council, which in turn would need to respond to the bodies' recommendations, however uncomfortable some of these and the supporting facts might be. How might such an improved mechanism work?

LEADERSHIP IS A RESPONSIBILITY, NOT A RIGHT!

Good, effective leadership, in any discipline or collective arrangement, whether it is among individuals or groups of people, must and can come only from the top. The United Nations has a responsibility, internationally, to lead and not just be led. In order to accept such a challenge, particularly with respect to combating transnational terrorism, the organization will have to adopt new attitudes and working practices. Such a process will prove uncomfortable for some, especially those who are accustomed to calling the shots. In a consensus-driven organization this will be difficult to achieve. It is *the* 'world body' and is in the unique position of being able to harmonize both short- and medium-term anti-terrorist measures (the *denial*) with the longer-term measures (the *dissuasion*), promoting the necessary religious and cultural tolerance and realistic but effective cooperation between states and, through capacity-building, within states. Leadership is also about taking difficult decisions and accepting the consequences, and if that means imposing sanctions for non-compliance, and making sure that they are effectively implemented, then so be it. If not, the authority of the organization will always be in doubt. It is the responsibility of the organization to take the leadership of the international community, not to leave it to any one member state, and, once again, to turn the 'trickle in the sand' into a river flowing with coordination and cooperation, willingly, towards global peace and security.

Countering Terrorism

The Security Council, for all the right reasons, looks at each scenario in which sanctions might be used on a case by case basis. When dealing with counter-terrorism measures there are the three resolutions, which complement one another as well as, in some ways, overlapping. Looking at the practicalities of how lists of designated individuals and entities are used downstream by, for example, border control services or the financial sector, there is merit in combining the counter-terrorism functions under one resolution, covering all terrorist groups. What is therefore needed is a reorganization of the present resolutions to provide one organization for countering terrorism. The difference would come in the management of the process within the United Nations.

The functions of providing advice, assistance and capacity-building would continue within one arm of the new organization assigned specifically for that purpose. Another arm would need to be responsible for maintaining and promulgating one list of designated individuals and entities. This list could still be organized into sections relevant to each of the terrorist organizations that have been designated as such, but from the point of the user it would be one list. The next requirement is to establish a counter-terrorism centre (CTC) that would maintain a comprehensive database on terrorist groups and their supporters and provide real-time research and analysis in support of the new CT organization and the CTC; a 'CTC-plus' with a broader mandate that would supersede the present CTC. In addition, such a centre could also provide information and analysis to those countries that lack the know-how, expertise and the capacity in this field. Rather than trying to run before walking, it would be prudent to establish such a centre step-by-step, starting with a cell to cover terrorist financing.[7] Other cells could then be phased in to cover measures to combat chemical, biological, radiological and nuclear (CBRN) terrorism, arms control measures and any other aspects that might be sanctioned in the international effort against terrorism.

The 'anti-terrorist information centre' would also assist the final 'arm' of the UN's comprehensive counter-terrorist organization, namely a 'sanctions monitoring group'. Sanctions monitoring mechanisms have proved their value over the past years in a number of security-related instances. The sanctions against Serbia and Montenegro (concerning the situation in Kosovo), Angola, Sierra Leone and Liberia, and against the al-Qaida network, when there was an independent monitoring group, all had a positive effect due to mechanisms established to monitor their implementation. Human nature and national interests being what they are, there will always be states and/or individuals bent on circumventing sanctions measures. That is why it is important for the implementation of sanctions to be evenly, effectively and robustly monitored. For this to work it is important that any sanctions monitoring mechanism is operationally independent, has a Chapter VII mandate from the UN Security Council and reports directly to the Council. What has not been devised and tabled by the Council, although it is a recommendation of the High-Level Panel on Threats, Challenges and Change, is a means of defining and imposing secondary sanctions 'in instances of verified, chronic violations . . . against those involved in sanctions-busting'.[8]

The terminology used here would appear to reflect the concerns over the unfortunate circumstances pertaining at the time of the Panel's report to the Iraq 'Oil-for-Food' programme. But such measures need to go further. When there are verifiable instances of non-compliance with the implementation of measures, such as those required under the resolutions directed at, for example, the al-Qaida network or even confirmed instances of incomplete implementation (as was demonstrated in the Nada and Nasreddin Case Study)[9] states need to be taken to task, even if it is inconvenient for the state concerned or its trading partners. The non-cooperation of states with a monitoring body also requires to be treated as non-compliance with the relevant resolution, and secondary sanctions applied. Then and only then will the role and authority of the Council in ensuring global peace and security 'Acting under Chapter VII of the Charter of the United Nations' regain its real meaning.

The High-Level Panel recommends that the Security Council 'should routinely establish monitoring mechanisms and provide them with the necessary authority and capacity to carry out high-quality, in-depth investigations'.[10] Such an investigatory role has in the past been extremely effective. One such instance was the ad hoc mechanism established to look into the illicit 'diamonds for arms' trading with respect to Liberia and Charles Taylor's regime. Authority for a monitoring mechanism to carry out high-quality, in-depth investigations is crucial if the panel is to be able to report effectively to the Council. Unfortunately, the provision of such authority has been contested by

Council members when drafting some sanctions resolutions, making the task of monitoring more difficult and diluting its effectiveness.

Past experience would indicate that in reality, as hard as some states might try to move in such a robust direction, vested interests will prevail and once again the process would fall short of what is needed. The process and procedures will fail. But that is realpolitik!

A VIABLE ALTERNATIVE

A possible alternative is the establishment of a smaller organization comprising experts from those countries with the resources, skills and exposure to terrorism, mandated to work on behalf of the world body. The latter is necessary if it is to be legitimized, internationally, and if it is to be funded and resourced effectively and to have the necessary authority to look hard and deep into how countries are, or are not, tackling terrorism. There exists a significant disparity in anti-terrorist capabilities and counter-terrorism capacity across the 192 members. Therefore such a body might be formed, at least initially, from and with the support of, say, NATO and EU member states. The addition of one or two participating states from South and/or Southeast Asia that are at the forefront of dealing with the current threat, such as Australia and Singapore, would also be advantageous.

The seeds of such an idea are reflected in the Club de Madrid Summit Working Papers Series as a recommendation of the Working Group on confronting terrorist financing.[11] The recommendation does carry clear qualifications, reflecting the intensity of the Working Group's discussions. It states that:

> Even if differences in their exact interpretation exist, the group is united in proposing two initiatives:
> The first aims at the establishment of a centre that will have overall responsibility in multi-lateral counter-terrorism activities.

Due to the specificity of their subject and the range of divergent views, they confined the start of such a centre to one that concentrated on tackling the financing of terrorism.

In his book *The Counter-Terrorism Puzzle: A Guide for Decision Makers*, Dr Boaz Ganor proposes a similar idea to that above to fulfil the second tine of the 'fork in the road'.[12] In the chapter 'Concerning International Cooperation on Counter-Terrorism', Dr Ganor proposes 'the establishment of a "League of Nations Fighting Terrorism" by a few countries, with others joining later on'. He stresses that this role should ideally be one for the UN, but goes on to emphasize the challenge this would be and, based on its past performance, the likely scepticism such an idea would generate, particularly when having to confront sponsors of terrorism.

The danger is that if neither of these approaches is adopted, then those states that consider themselves to be most at risk from terrorism will revert to combating it in their own way. They may do this bilaterally, when and where it suits, even regionally at times, but the overall result is likely to be a reduction in the cooperation, coordination and collaboration that are required and crucial in the long term. And with such unilateral approaches, the overall result is also likely to be less effective, an aspect the terrorist movement and its component groups will be quick to exploit. Furthermore, when states are left to their own devices, they may be inclined to work to their own rules and not necessarily within the bounds of genuine international legislation. But more importantly, as was stressed from the outset, fighting transnational terrorism cannot be achieved by any one state on its own. It requires a multi-pronged approach and it has to be responsive to more than just the immediate counter-measures, crucial as they are in the overall process. The tactical and immediate operational requirements, brought about by 9/11, other al-Qaida–related terrorist strikes around the world and the many copycat or look-alike attacks, have naturally and understandably concentrated the minds of politicians and anti-terrorist agencies alike. The longer-term and more significant challenges that face the international community, if this scourge of the twenty-first century is to be eradicated, have been brought into sharper focus by events in Iraq, those arising from the Danish cartoons, first published in September 2005, and in Lebanon in July/August 2006.

CRISIS WITHIN ISLAM

In the period since 9/11, numerous experts, academics, commentators and politicians have referred, rather alarmingly, to a 'clash of civilizations' – meaning between Western-style values and democracy and

Islam. Many people, be they Buddhist, Christian, Hindu, Jewish or Muslim, do not agree, nor do they want to see such an event unfold. However, there is an aspect of the whole situation that does not get enough airing, possibly in the interest of political correctness, and that is the situation within Islam itself. Islam is in a state of crisis, with Sunnis and Shia confronting one another in Iraq, and to a lesser degree in other parts of the world, on a daily basis. Iran is once again 'rattling its scimitars', making its Gulf States neighbours somewhat nervous. It seems that all the goodness, enlightenment and humanistic aspects of the religion have either been lost or forgotten in the current turmoil. Islam, particularly in its more extreme interpretations, is medieval. This is not just the preachings of the more radical clerics; these beliefs are those of many ordinary Muslims. Just as Christianity has learnt to evolve and change with the times, so must Islam. Islam needs to be adapted to the twenty-first century, not just for a few enlightened Muslims, but for the majority. That evolution has to come from inside the Muslim faith. It will take time, but it is one of the crucial changes that requires to be addressed if there is to be progress in re-establishing religious tolerance in the world. Freedom of religion and freedom of expression are enshrined in the United Nations Charter of Human Rights. The challenge is to ensure that these freedoms are available to all and are respected by governments and religious leaders alike. It is too easy to blame the current situation related to transnational terrorism, and sympathy for it, on the unjust prosecution of the war in Iraq and Afghanistan and the so-called 'war on terror'. Even though these events have polarized and radicalized Muslim thinking in many parts of the world, the problems confronting the international community originated long before, during the Soviet occupation of Afghanistan and its immediate aftermath. The vocal minorities, who invariably get the maximum publicity whether they need it or deserve it, tend, thanks to modern media channels, to distort the reality. Diluting their rhetoric and, eventually, silencing altogether their incitement to hatred must be done by the majority moderate Muslims. It is all part of the problem, internal to Islam. It is a problem for which Muslims must acknowledge ownership and hence find the ultimate solution. The 'West' or non-Muslim nations should be prepared to assist, but one should not ignore the likelihood that there is a limit even to their tolerance.

The approach taken by the US and UK governments to the publication of the Danish cartoons, criticizing their publication as being insensitive, was for most Christians in mainland Europe a sign of political weakness. Perhaps if there were no US or UK troops deployed in Iraq the response might have been different. It would have been much better if those administrations had highlighted the Christian and democratic values, and the rights of freedom of speech and freedom of expression. It may be blasphemous for Muslims to produce images or characterizations of the Prophet Muhammad. But there is nothing of that nature stipulated in Christianity, nor is it against the laws of the lands of that faith – a point that was not made at the time. Unfortunately, for many people in the world there are far worse matters with which they have to deal. The sectarian killings that followed the bombing of the Shia Askariya mosque in Samarra in February 2006 and Iran's belligerent attitude to uranium enrichment have, quite rightly, knocked the cartoons saga right off the television screens. Iran and the Sunni–Shia madness in Iraq are major problems for all involved, but particularly for the Muslims. This is a problem of their making to which only they must know the ultimate solution. Pluralism, when you can chose the God you worship, has many facets and the many religions and beliefs have different sects. They may not agree with one another, but they have learnt to tolerate and respect one another's beliefs. Sunnis and Shiites need to do the same: killing is not an option, with or without a functioning government. They need to look elsewhere to see how it has been made to work, even if it is not perfect.

RELIGIOUS AND CULTURAL COEXISTENCE

There are now significant minority Muslim populations in a number of European countries, particularly among the fifteen states that comprised the European Union prior to its 2004 'eastward' expansion. In the vast majority of cases the 'founding members' of these ethnic groups, which often trace their links to earlier colonies of what are now independent states or post-WWII patterns of economic expediency and migration, have integrated reasonably well into the social fabric of their country of choice. Due to many of the obvious cultural differences, there are some, especially among the younger generations, who sometimes find it difficult to integrate easily into Western

Countering Terrorism

society. This in turn produces a resentment factor towards the 'host' country, resulting in a closing of ranks within the minority Muslim communities. These attitudes have hardened since 9/11, despite calls to the contrary from many of the more moderate and senior community leaders.

The existence of al-Qaida 'sleeper' cells that came to light in so many countries, particularly within Europe, in the post-9/11 investigations, and the ongoing checks, arrests and questioning of Muslims, have made many feel persecuted, adding to their feelings of 'not belonging' or 'not being accepted'. The broadcasting by Arabic satellite television channels of scenes highlighting the daily sufferings of Arab civilians as a result of strikes by coalition forces in Iraq, or by Israeli Forces against the Palestinians, does little to develop any sympathy among Muslim communities for the more liberal and so called democratic ideals of Western nations.

Less than 1 per cent of the Muslim peoples, worldwide, is in any way involved in conducting or actively supporting terrorism. As is so often the case with minority groups, because they are vocal and active, they tend to have an impact out of all proportion to their size. What they lack in numbers they make up for with their actions and the resulting publicity.

One of the most important aspects of winning the war against Islamist transnational terrorism is to develop an effective 'hearts and minds' campaign that will overcome the current trend, as envisaged by some commentators, towards a clash of civilizations: Islam versus all the other religions. There are many facets to achieving this and they need both to be understood and followed through in a realistic sectarian context. First of all it is important to assure the vast majority of Muslims the right of coexistence, but it has to be a two-way approach. Where ethnic minorities exist, especially if they have opted to choose another country in which to live and work in order to raise their own standards of living and quality of life, they should respect the culture and customs of that country. Maintaining and/or encouraging secularity is crucial, if different ethnic groups are to become more tolerant and understanding of one another's point of view. This has to be a political decision and, in some countries, not an easy one to be implemented.

All forms of religious extremism, just as with political extremism, must be kept in its place. By rights, in a democratic society those who wish to practise a more strict form of a religion should be allowed to do so, provided that they do not violate the human rights of any individual, or try to force their form of extremism on others not so inclined. Nor for that matter should they break the law of the country of their choice, especially for cultural reasons, such as honour killings. It is after all a basic human right for all individuals to practise whatever religion they wish and to be free from persecution while they do so. Islam is often described by many Muslims as a 'compassionate' religion and for the vast majority of Muslims it is; the misrepresentation it has been given by the likes of Usama bin Laden and numerous radical clerics is out of context with the teachings of the Prophet Muhammad.

Interpretations of Islam and preaching based on the Holy Qur'an, in a number of environments, are restrictive and out of date. The religion needs to be adjusted to take account of the world in which we live; it needs to be modernized. A practical example of this out-dated approach occurred in the case of Pakistan's only woman Olympic swimmer due to compete in the 2004 Games. When a Pakistani man was asked by a TV journalist what he thought of Pakistan being represented by a woman in the Olympics, he replied that 'our religion [Islam] does not allow it'.[13] But the modern Olympics had not been thought of when Islam was started, so it would seem perfectly reasonable for some adjustments to be made to the requirements of religion that could bring it into line with modern-day practices. There are still Islamic states in which Islam is practised without extremism and in which women are encouraged to play a full part in society; in which there is female franchise and women even participate in government. Some of these same countries have encouraged secularity, without it adversely affecting the majority Muslim population.

COMMUNITIES DEFEAT TERRORISM

Just after Easter 2005 Pope John Paul II began slowly, and by all accounts peacefully, to succumb to the poor health from which he had been suffering for some time. The messages he received from around the world and the international participation at his funeral was one of the most effective, long-term antidotes to extremism and the terrorism it nurtures. Thousands and thousands of people, predominantly Catholics, travelled to St Peter's Square in Rome to be as close as

Countering Terrorism

possible to him, offering their prayers and their support. Then, after he died, millions made the pilgrimage to Rome, waiting quietly and patiently for up to twelve hours to file past his body, flanked by the Vatican Swiss Guards, as he lay in state in St Peter's Basilica. On Friday, 8 April 2005 millions more, all around the world, joined in what was described as the biggest funeral service ever seen.

Present at this Service of Resurrection in St Peter's Square were heads of state or their representatives from 200 countries from all across the globe, including those of Jordan, Syria, the Gulf States, Iran and many other Muslim countries.[14] Alongside them were the clergy, not just those from the Roman Catholic Church worldwide, but every other religion, including many of the Islamic faith. If ever there were a sign and the opportunity for a renaissance of secularity and religious tolerance, it was that day, not only in Rome but in many cities around the world. In Iraq, Lebanon, Poland, the Philippines and Syria, to name but a few, people watched on giant television screens and prayed along with the service being beamed from St Peter's Square or held services of their own.

The other long-term factor that is worthy of note was the vast number of young people who came to pray for the pope and then to pay their respects, to thank him for his leadership over the past 26 years and bid him farewell. The number of young people is very significant since they are, as the pope himself said, the future of the Church and it is they who can ensure that the religious tolerance necessary for a more peaceful world becomes a reality.

Many hoped that the passing of Pope John Paul II would mark that turning point: that politicians, the clergy of all religions and civil society, and the common man and woman in the street, would join together in a strong global campaign against terrorism. Government intelligence agencies and law enforcement authorities can lead the way, but finally it is communities that defeat terrorism. It is easy for governments, social elites and the citizens of Western industrialized countries to demonize the Muslims. Instead, Western governments and societies should work with the Muslim governments and public to build a norm and an ethic against politically and religiously motivated violence.

On Tuesday, 12 September 2006 Pope Benedict XVI gave an academic presentation to theologians at a college in Regensburg, Germany. Within the overall context of his talk about dialogues between the faiths, he quoted a criticism from a fifteenth-century Byzantine emperor, Manuel II Palaeologus, concerning the Prophet Muhammed. The reaction across many parts of the Muslim world was hysterical and, regrettably, demonstrated the depth of intolerance that exists in a number of corners of that faith. Although widely reported in the media, the latter were quick to replicate only that part of the pope's presentation on which the furore was based; none actually raised the question or appeared to investigate who had been so quick to pick on the pope's words and transmit them to rabble rousers, who exploit Friday Prayers for political purposes. It is well understood that the internet provides rapid and almost instantaneous communication across the globe. But for what purpose, other than the propagation of Islamist extremism, would such words be transmitted to initiate such intolerant and violent reactions? The generation of the reaction would appear to have similar roots to claims being transmitted daily on the internet that Islam is under attack from the 'West'. Needless to say, it is citizens of the 'West', including those of the Muslim faith, who need to be equally frank in denouncing the radical and ill-informed responses and preaching of the Muslim clerics. Furthermore, citizens of the 'West', and especially their politicians, need to be unequivocal in making it clear that whereas all faiths are welcome, everyone is expected to live and abide by the laws and traditions of the land in which he or she chooses to live, and to accept and recognize that land's culture, and not to try and change it by force to suit a minority.

When in June 2004 France's President Chirac reportedly said to US President Bush that we don't need to send missionaries to the Middle East to teach those countries democracy, he was right. It was therefore interesting to see, one or two days later, Mr Bush making a more realistic statement, saying: 'We respect the fact that these countries have their own cultural background. But we still want them to be democratic'. Although there are signs of moves towards more democratic societies and more democratic forms of government in a number of Islamic countries, the political parties benefiting from the process are not necessarily those preferred by the US and its allies. Recent examples are Hamas winning the elections in Palestine and 'conservative' Sunni Islamist parties winning control of the Baluchistan and North West Frontier Provincial Governments in Pakistan.

RESOLVING REGIONAL CONFLICTS

The international community has a collective responsibility to address the many challenges with which it is presented in and by many parts of the world. Many governments and administrations are confronted with massive problems. The virulent spread of HIV/AIDS has had a disastrous and indiscriminate impact on populations. In a number of African countries this has had an adverse effect on their economic development. The lack of clean drinking water and the effective, hygienic disposal of sewage in many under-industrialized countries present major health problems. This in turn impacts on such countries' economic progress. Malaria kills thousands of people every year in many parts of Africa with a commensurate impact on individual families and communities as a whole. Wherever deprivation and poverty exist, where peoples are unable to envisage, not just a bright and rewarding future, but even the basic necessities of life, extremism and terrorism can flourish. Much of this under-development is a product of bad economic policies, rampant corruption and bad governance. If the international community does not direct greater efforts to resolve regional conflicts, the extremist ideologies will find resonance in the hearts and minds of angry Muslims. Such ideologies will start to decay only when we stop the killing and the suffering. Regional conflicts are the primary producers of human rights violations, internal displacement, refugee flows and the production of terrorists. Increasingly, it is becoming difficult to separate some of the regional conflicts with local grievances and indigenous roots from the global jihad. Bin Laden has built an organization that functions both operationally and ideologically at local, national, regional and global levels. Defeating al-Qaida and its associated groups will be a crucial challenge that will dominate not only the international security and intelligence community, law enforcement authorities and national military forces, but a range of other actors in the foreseeable future. To win over extremism and terrorism strategically we must train practitioners both in counter-terrorism and counter-insurgency, as well as in conflict resolution and conflict management: there needs to be a move towards non-conventional approaches to traditional security concerns, especially regional conflicts. Towards achieving this goal, the future specialist centres we create must be hybrid in nature.

At national level a great deal more lateral thinking needs to be applied to counter-terrorism policies and the measures that are developed to interdict terrorist operations and the terrorists' support activities. Traditional 'barriers' between departments, agencies and services, all of whom have a part to play in dealing with the threat, need to be at least adjusted, if not demolished, to enable much closer working arrangements. These liaisons need to extend into the arena of international cooperation, providing a fast, reliable and accurate passage of information between countries. Five years after 9/11 there are still too many instances coming to light of individuals more concerned with protecting their 'turf' than working as part of a team to catch terrorists. The classification of intelligence and information is another area that often requires to be looked at more closely. The earliest possible de-classification of intelligence, converting it into actionable evidence, is a crucial ingredient for those individuals at the forefront of the law enforcement effort. This is a key ingredient if terrorists, or would-be terrorists, are to be arrested and successfully prosecuted before they can carry out attacks.

The United Nations Organization was created specifically to play a unique role in maintaining peace and stability. Since extremism and its vicious by-product, terrorism, are the most defining security threats of the early twenty-first century, the UN has a front-line role to play to reduce these threats. Unfortunately, this is proving to be a difficult task. The ability and commitment of the international community, through the UN Security Council, to assert its authority, relies to a large extent on the credibility and willingness of the five permanent members – 'P-5' – working towards common goals. A number of events since 9/11, and more so since the 2003 invasion of Iraq, have seen that credibility challenged and with it, the currency of the UN significantly devalued. Iran has defied the Security Council demands that it halt its uranium enrichment programme; Sudan is refusing to allow the presence of UN peacekeepers in Darfur in place of the African Union observer mission; and the US and UK are not in a position to contribute ground troops to the 'up-gunned' and expanded UNIFIL mission in southern Lebanon. Syria, emboldened by both Israel's inability to defeat Hezbollah quickly and in the knowledge that the US military is, like it or not, severely stretched, has also demonstrated a new-found defiance. Also China and Russia, even if it does prove to be of short-term benefit, appear to be taking advantage of the lack of support in many countries for current US foreign policies, in order to further their own national agendas.

For example, in the current global political climate neither China nor Russia is likely to support economic sanctions against either Iran or Sudan; Russia is playing a new version of the 'Great Game', trying to regain her former influence in the Caucasus and Central Asian region; China is desperate for oil and natural gas to maintain its burgeoning economy and has significant energy agreements with both countries. Such divergent attitudes will adversely impact the development of long-term strategies to reverse the growing radicalization of Muslims in many countries across the world. The on-going 'tactical' responses to the different components of the al-Qaida movement are crucial to containing the current situation in the short term. But, as has been discussed at length earlier in this book, addressing the problem in the medium and long term will require fortitude, resolve and a cohesive, comprehensive and collaborative approach if the current trends are to be effectively and sustainably reversed. The statements of individuals like bin Laden and Zawahiri have to be quietly but accurately countered. Contrary to the thinking in some circles, bin Laden is no Robin Hood or William Tell; he is nothing more than a common criminal. In some ways Zawahiri is worse. He is referred to as 'doctor'. Medical practitioners are supposed to be in the business of saving lives, not encouraging people to take the lives of others and their own. Finding effective solutions to the problems caused and perpetuated by these persons and some of their associated cohorts requires global leadership – leadership that is trusted, respected and, as a result, listened to and believed.

Crucial in this overall process is finding a durable solution to the situation between Israel, the Palestinians and Lebanon and Hezbollah. Although politicians often try to differentiate between this conflict and the activities of al-Qaida, finding a solution to this long-standing problem will remove much of the fuel that fires Islamist radicalization. Like it or not, in many other parts of the world the conflict is a source of deep resentment amongst Muslims of all persuasions, even though Palestinian leaders are often at pains not to be associated with al-Qaida or with statements emanating from bin Laden or Zawaheri. Despite this fact, in order to achieve a lasting solution the Palestinians must also make concessions between their own factions; they most of all need to find an accommodation to work together and get their own house in order.

On 8 September 2006 a glimmer of hope appeared – but it is only a glimmer. The UN General Assembly adopted a Global Counter

Terrorism Strategy. The strategy, in the form of a resolution and a Plan of Action, provides for a common strategic approach to the overall problem. As with all UN resolutions, the proof of the pudding will be in the implementation. General Assembly resolutions are not binding. The resolution is a compendium of many of the previous urgings and demands of the Security Council; there is nothing new. Despite 192 member states having reached a consensus for the resolution to be adopted, there is still no comprehensive definition of terrorism – for a long time a significant and, often, convenient loophole in the implementation of previous Security Council resolutions and adoption of anti-terrorism conventions. Consequently, it will be a miracle if anything more substantive comes of this strategy, let alone the plan producing any action.

Earlier in the book we have talked about a viable alternative. In the short to medium term, having a coalition of the willing and able – a coming together of those nations that are both interested in tackling the threat and have the resources, capabilities and, above all, the political will to make a collaborative effort a success, is probably the best way forward. The legal framework exists within which to work – the international conventions and the appropriate UN resolutions. The establishment of such a group, not hindered by the political correctness and posturing that emanates from New York, could demonstrate a new form of leadership – when things look good, others are more inclined to follow.

Unless the UN can adapt rapidly, it will fail to play that role in a fast-changing world. The world will remain in turmoil as long as the UN is unable and unwilling to manage protracted political conflicts, terrorism and proliferation. These threats pose a formidable and an enduring threat to international security. The future security and stability of our world in the early twenty-first century will depend on our ability and willingness to make the UN refocus. That means that the member states of the UN must concentrate their minds and efforts and collectively rise to the challenge. For many countries that means a change in the application of their individual political will. Where there's a will, there's a way. This saying is as pertinent to everyday challenges faced by people across the world as it is to the commitment of the world's politicians to provide a safer and more secure world, now and for future generations.

References

INTRODUCTION

1 www.londonprepared.gov.uk/relisienceteam/index.htm.
2 english.aljazeera.net/NR/exeres/554FAF3A-B267-427A-B9EC-54881BDE0A2E.htm.
3 Ibid. In addition it is believed that the Khan video was recorded by Khan earlier and combined subsequently with the Zawahiri recording.
4 Patrick Hennessy and Melissa Kite, 'Poll Reveals 40pc of Muslims Want Sharia Law in UK', and Alasdair Palmer, 'The Day is Coming When British Muslims Form a State Within a State', *Sunday Telegraph*, 19 February 2006.
5 Ministerpräsident Dr Edmund Stoiber, MdL, speech to the conference of the Christlich-Sozialen Union (CSU), *Politischer Aschermittwoch*, 1 March 2006.
6 See en.wikipedia.org/wiki/Jyllands-Posten_Muhammad_cartoons.
7 Boris Kalnoky, 'Ein später Aufschrei', *Die Welt*, 11 February 2006.
8 www.pm.gov.uk/output/Page7999.asp. See 'Questions and Answers': answer to second question.

1 THE CURRENT AND FUTURE TERRORIST THREAT

1 For a survey of Islamist fundamentalism, see Lawrence Davidson, *Islamic Fundamentalism* (Westport, CT, 1998).
2 Reuven Paz, 'Al-Qa'idah al-Sulbah', Appendix 1 of *Tangled Web: International Networking of the Islamist Struggle* (Washington Institute for Near East Policy, Washington, DC, 2002).
3 Interview with Investigative Judge Brugière, February 2004.
4 It was to this group, Ansar al-Islam and al-Zarqawi and his connections to al-Qaida that Colin Powell was referring in his notorious briefing to the UN Security Council in February 2003 when making the case for going to war in Iraq.
5 Among the CNN recoveries from the al-Qaida registry in

Afghanistan, the author identified and examined two videotapes by the Islamic Movement of Iraqi Kurdistan.

6 Ibn-ul-Khattab, 'Europe: We Are Still at the Beginning of Jihad in this Region', Azzam Publications, 27 September 1999.
7 See the Introduction above.
8 See en.wikipedia.org/wiki/2005_Sharm_el-Sheikh_attacks.
9 www.alertnet.org/thenews/newsdesk/L05832405.htm.

2 TO KNOW AND UNDERSTAND ONE'S ENEMY

1 Sun Tzu, *The Art of War*, ed. Samuel and B. Griffin (Oxford, 1963).
2 'The Jemaah Islamiyah Arrests and the Threat of Terrorism', Ministry of Home Affairs, Republic of Singapore, 2003. See www.2mha.gov.sg/mha/detailed.jsp?artid=667&type=4&root=0&pa rent=0&cat=0&mode=arc.
3 'Al-Qaeda tape archives', as obtained and held by CNN.
4 Robert Leiken, *Bearers of Global Jihad? Immigration and National Security after 9/11* (The Nixon Center, Washington, DC).
5 On 15 March 2005 a French court sentenced six men to prison for attempting to blow up the US Embassy in Paris.
6 UN Security Council document S/2003/669.
7 See www.dw-world.de/dw/article/0,,802558,00.html.
8 See www.voltairenet.org/article30084.html.
9 Bertrand Benoit, 'German police swoop on suspected Islamist terror network', *Financial Times*, 13 January 2005: www.ft.com/cms/s/ba06d4be-6507-11d9-9f8b-00000e2511c8.html
10 Briefing to Senate Armed Services Committee, 28 January 2004.
11 See www.wmd.gov/20050329.pdf.
12 Commission on the Intelligence Capabilities of the United States Regarding Weapons of Mass Destruction, dated 31 March 2005.
13 See Section 10.3: '"Phase Two" and the Question of Iraq', *Final Report of the National Commission on Terrorist Attacks upon the United States.*
14 See en.wikipedia.org/wiki/Baʾath_Party.
15 http://english.aljazeera.net/NR/exeres/FC8750D0-908D-4272-953D-EA27523A47AE.htm.

3 IRAQ: A STRATEGIC DEFEAT?

1 www.whitehouse.gov/news/releases/2003/05/20030501-15.html.
2 See paragraph 10 of the UN Security Council al-Qaida Sanctions Monitoring Group report, UN document S/2002/1338. See also http://en.wikipedia.org/wiki/Taliban_insurgency.
3 See www.fas.org/irp/crs/RS21658.pdf and Carlotta Gall, 'Taliban May Be Planning Larger Attacks, US Envoy Says', *New York Times*, 7 October 2003.
4 The NATO formation that deployed for the first year of the Dayton

Accord was known as the 'Implementation Force' – hence the acronym I-FOR. The name was then changed to S-FOR, which stood for the 'Stabilization Force', the title it retained until its mandate ended in November 2004.

5 Sean Rayment, '1,000 more troops will drive the Taliban out, says British command', e-Telegraph, 10 September 2006.
6 Armando J. Ramirez, *From Bosnia to Baghdad: The Evolution of US Army Special Forces from 1995–2004* (US Naval Post Graduate School, Monterey, CA, September 2004).
7 See http://news.bbc.co.uk/go/pr/fr//2/hi/middle_east/ 3483089.stm
8 The two 'biblical rivers' – Tigris and Euphrates – running through the centre of Iraq.
9 www.iraqbodycount.org/.
10 David S. Cloud, 'Iraq Rebels Build Their Bomb Skills Against Armor', *International Herald Tribune*, 23 June 2005, p. 4.
11 Peter Fray, 'Al-Qaeda Ace May Have Been Arrested in UK', *Sydney Morning Herald*, 6 August 2004.
12 David Leppard, '400 Terror Suspects on the Loose in UK', *Sunday Times*, 9 April 2006.
13 wwwc.house.gov/international_relations/109/eu042705.htm.
14 Bruce Hoffman, 'The enemy is closer than we think', Salon Media Group, 2006, http://dir.salon.com/story/news/feature/2005/07 /19/london_attacks/index.html
15 See http://observer.guardian.co.uk/international/story/ 0,,1120629,00.html
16 Alan Cowell, 'UK Raid Links Iraq Bombings – Arrest Reveals Pool of Terrorist Recruits', *International Herald Tribune*, 22 June 2005, p. 3.
17 Paolo Blondini, 'Kamikaze contro i marines, non è terrorismo', *Corriere della Sera*, 16 February 2006; available at www.corriere.it /Primo_Piano/Esteri/2006/02_Febbraio/16/biondan.shtml.
18 See www.counterterrorismblog.org/2006/02/recruiting_for_iraq_ not_a_crim.php/.
19 See http://www.nytimes.com/2005/01/26/international/europe/ 28cnd-fran.html?ei=5088&en=0d5241a05f24042d&ex=1264482000 &pagewanted=print&position.
20 Elaine Sciolino, 'French Detain Group Said to Recruit Iraq Rebels', *New York Times*, 26 January 2005.
21 Susan B. Glasser, 'Global Terrorism Statistics Debated: New Report Leaves Some Wondering How To Measure the Number of Attacks', *Washington Post*, 1 May 2005.

4 IRAN – THE OPEN FLANK

1 www.whitehouse.gov/news/releases/2002/01/20020129-11.html.
2 In 2001 Iran had an estimated 2 million heroin addicts.

3 UN Radio interviews at Sarajevo Airport with young Iranian passengers arriving on Mehan Air flights.
4 See UN document S/AC.37/2003/(1455)/73.
5 Ibid.
6 Faye Bowers, 'Iran holds Al Qaeda's top leaders', *Christian Science Monitor*, 28 July 2003.
7 Matthew A. Levitt, 'Heart of the Axis – Al Qaeda has long called Iran home', *National Review Online* (NRO), 29 May 2003, 8:45 a.m.
8 Bill Samii, 'Iranian Mujahideen at the Crossroads', Radio Free Europe/Radio Liberty Inc., 1201 Connecticut Ave NW, Washington, DC 20036, Copyright © 2004, RFE/RL Inc.
9 'Facing Fresh US allegations, Iran Claims It Has Dismantled al-Qaeda Groups', AFP – World News (via Yahoo), 17 July 2004.
10 Thomas Joscelyn, 'The Unholy Alliance', *Weekly Standard*, 3 March 2006.
11 http://www.weeklystandard.com/Content/Public/Articles /000/000/011/939xcmif.asp.
12 'Rice: Iran "Central Bank for Terrorism"', MSNBC staff and news service reports, 9 March 2006.
13 Michael Slackman and David E. Sanger, 'US and Iranians Agree to Discuss Violence in Iraq', *New York Times*, 17 March 2006.
14 See news.bbc.co.uk/go/pr/fr/-1/hi/world/middle_east /4821618.stm, published 19 March 2006.

5 TERRORISM: AN ENDURING THREAT

1 This expansion included armoured cars, artillery and medical services, and an air force equipped with ground-attack fighters and helicopters, the latter playing a crucial role for resupply and casualty evacuation.
2 The NFD was the administrative title given to this area of Kenya, some 50,000 square miles of arid bush, during the British colonial administration. After Independence the name of the area was changed to the North East Province, with its Provincial HQ in Garissa.
3 *Shifta*, a Kiswahili word, originally used to refer to tribal bandits that attacked caravans and made cattle raids into Kenya from across the borders with Abyssinia (later to become Ethiopia).
4 It will be interesting to see if this problem resurfaces once the 'Council for Islamic Courts' has consolidated its hold on power in Somalia and seeks to expand its extremist ideology to the Somali tribes in northeastern Kenya.
5 The truces offered by bin Laden should not be read as a serious attempt to establish a meaningful dialogue; rather they appear to be an excuse by which to justify his continued clamouring for violent action from his 'followers'.
6 See http://news.sky.com/skynews/video/videoplayer/0,,31200-

lebanon_ 0900,00.html

7 In the local Basque language, ETA translates literally into 'Basque Fatherland and Liberty'.

8 Group Islamique Combattant Marocain (GICM).

9 Jessica Stern, 'The Protean Enemy', *Foreign Affairs* (July–August 2003).

10 Author's interview, Federal Bureau of Investigation, Washington, DC, May 2005. See www.canadafreepress.com/2006/paul-williams 091806.htm

11 'FBI seeking public's assistance in locating individual suspected of planning terrorist activities', FBI National Press Office, Washington, DC, 25 March 2003: www.fbi.gov/terrorinfo/elshuk rijumah.htm

12 http://www.globalsecurity.org/security/library/congress/ 1995_h/h950928w.htm.

13 See untreaty.un.org/English/Terrorism.asp.

6 THE UNITED NATIONS: RISING TO THE CHALLENGE

1 The Krajina and Western Slavonia were, for the most part, contiguous with the Serb dominated areas of northern and western Bosnia and Hercegovina, these areas also having been a part of the *vojna krajina*. Eastern Slavonia backed onto Serbia, albeit the other side of the River Danube. Collectively, they were seen by their inhabitants and Serbs at large as all part of a 'Greater Serbia'.

2 See Christopher Bennett, *Yugoslavia's Bloody Collapse* (London, 1995), chapter 7 ('Countdown to War').

3 United Nations Security Council document S/RES/743 (1992), dated 21 February 1992

4 United Nations Security Council document S/RES/758 (1992), dated 8 June 1992.

5 United Nations Security Council document S/RES/824 (1993), dated 6 May 1993.

6 Rakia, a local distillation from grapes, and slivovic, an indigenous plum brandy, often 'brewed' in the backyard, were staple ingredients for many of the belligerents throughout the republics of the former Yugoslavia.

7 The Second Nordic Battalion Group (NORBAT2) was composed of a Swedish mechanized infantry battalion, a Danish tank squadron, a Norwegian field hospital (60 beds) and aviation flight (4 ? Bell 412 helicopters). The first NORBAT, a composite force composed of units from the Nordic countries, had deployed earlier to the Former Yugoslav Republic of Macedonia (FYROM) pursuant to UN Security Council resolution 795, dated 11 December 1992, to prevent confrontation between the Former Republic of Yugoslavia (FRY – Serbia and Montenegro) and FYROM.

8 End of Mission Report of the Force Commander HQ UNPF, dated 31 January 1996.

9   The RRF, an Anglo–French initiative, deployed into Bosnia through the Dalmatian Littoral in June 1995 under UN resolution 998. It also included Dutch troops. The RRF had artillery, mortars and attack helicopters, and retained its camouflage markings. Consequently, it was treated with considerable suspicion by both the Bosniaks and the Bosnian Croats, and its deployment into Bosnia was subject to numerous obstructions.

10 The Dayton Accord was signed in Paris on 14 December 1995.

11 UN Security Council document s/RES/836 (1993), dated 4 June 1993.

12 Evan F. Kholmann, *Al-Qaida's Jihad in Europe* (Oxford and New York, 2004), p. xii.

13 Pakistan responded to calls from the UN Secretary-General in 1994 for extra peacekeeping troops by sending two infantry battalions. With two battalions the contingent was accorded the title of a brigade, especially as they were deployed adjacent to one another. But they could only be deployed on Muslim-held territory: neither the Serbs nor the Croats would have tolerated their presence in the areas they controlled.

14 MND North: the Multi-National Division of the NATO-led Stabilization Force based in the northern Bosnian city of Tuzla. At the time referred to in the text, MND North was under US command.

15 Since the implementation of the Dayton Agreement, Bosnia and Hercegovina has benefited from the influence of the Peace Implementation Council (PIC), and the efforts on the ground of the UNMIBH, the UN International Police Task Force (IPTF), other UN agencies, the Office of the High Representative (OHR), the European Union and numerous NGOs.

16 This initiative, proposed during the London Conference on the Former Yugoslavia in August 1992, established the BH Command (BHC) of UNPROFOR with its Main HQ in Kiseljak. BHC was initially commanded by France's Major-General Philippe Morrillon who established a Forward HQ in Sarajevo, in order to be 'in touch' with the situation there and close to the political leadership.

17 UN General Assembly document A/54/549, dated 15 November 1999.

18 UN General Assembly document A/55/305 of 21 August 2000.

19 UN Security Council documents s/RES/1547, 1556 and 1564 of June, July and September 2004 respectively.

20 UN Security Council document s/RES/1574 (2004) dated 19 November 2004.

21 'Powell Declares Genocide in Sudan', BBC World Service Television, 9 September 2004; see news.bbc.co.uk/2/hi/africa/3641820.stm.

22 UN Security Council document s/2005/60, dated Geneva, 25 January 2005.

23 See House of Commons International Development Committee Fifth Report of Session 2004–5, volume I, HC 67-1, published on 30

March 2005 by authority of the House of Commons, London: The Stationery Office Limited.

24 Lydia Polgreen, 'A Shadowy Sheik Denies Leading a Miltia in Darfur', *New York Times*, republished in *Süddeutsche Zeitung*, 19 June 2006.

25 Douglas Farah, 'Intelligence Report Links Al Qaeda to Janjaweed in Sudan', 10 July 2006, www.douglasfarah.com/.

26 See english.aljazeera.net/ Aljazeera_Net - Transcript Bin Laden accuses West.htm, 24 April 2006.

27 See UN Security Council document S/RES/1593 (2005).

28 'Special Report – United Nations – Fighting for Survival', *The Economist*, 20–26 November 2004, p. 24.

29 www.un.org/apps/news/story.asp?NewsID=17934&Cr=sudan&Cr1.

30 The 9/11 Commission Report, *Final Report of the National Commission on Terrorist Attacks upon the United States*, p. 170.

7 AFGHANISTAN: THE TALIBAN AND THE THREAT BEYOND

1 Debriefing of jihadists including John Walker Lindh, 2002.

2 See UN General Assembly document A/RES/52/165, dated 19 January 1998.

3 See UN Security Council documents S/RES/1189, 1193 and 1214, all of 1998.

4 UN Security Council document S/RES/1267 (1999), dated 15 October 1999.

5 Briefing in Peshawar to the panel of experts established by the UN Secretary-General under Security Council resolution 1333 (2000).

6 See Ahmed Rashid, *Taliban: Militant Islam, Oil and Fundamentalism in Central Asia* (New Haven, CT, and London, 2001), pp 189–93, for a detailed description of the ATTA and its impact on the Pakistani economy in the late 1990s.

7 UN Security Council document S/2001/511, dated 22 May 2001.

8 In June 2001 forces of the recognized government, under the command of their charismatic leader, Ahmed Shah Masood, controlled only 20 per cent of northeastern Afghanistan, centred on the Panshir valley.

9 UN document S/RES/1363 (2001), dated 30 July 2001.

8 INITIAL REACTIONS TO 9/11

1 North Atlantic Treaty Organization – Chronology Update, Week 10–16 September 2001, www.nato.int.

2 UN Security Council document S/RES/1368 (2001), dated 12 September 2001.

3 See UN Security Council document S/2002/875 (or General Assembly document A/57/273).

4 Ibid.

5 All member states are obligated under international law to comply fully with Security Council resolutions, adopted under Chapter VII of the United Nations Charter.

6 See www.un.org/News/Press/docs/2002/sgsm8105.doc.htm.

7 UN Security Council document S/RES/1456 (2003), dated 20 January 2003.

8 UN document S/2004/124, dated 19 February 2004.

9 UN Security Council resolutions S/RES/1390 (2002) and S/RES/1455(2003).

10 UN Security Council documents S/RES/1386 (2001) and S/RES/1401 (2002), respectively.

11 UN Security Council document S/RES/1390 (2002), dated 16 January 2002.

12 The sanctions committee was originally established pursuant to resolution 1267, hence the '1267' Committee.

13 UN Security Council document, S/RES/1455 (2003), dated 17 January 2003.

9 TOWARDS TOUGHER SANCTIONS

1 Rohan Gunaratna, 'The New Al-Qaeda: Developments in the Post-9/11 Evolution of al-Qaeda', Paper presented at the Conference on Bin Laden and Beyond, CIA Headquarters, Langley, VA, 2 September 2003.

2 The 9/11 Commission Report, Chapter 2: 'The Foundation of the New Terrorism'.

3 One year after the adoption of UN Security Council resolution 1455, less than half of the UN membership had submitted the required report on the steps taken to implement the resolution.

4 Resolution 1456 [S/RES/1456 (2003)] was adopted on 20 January 2003 by the Security Council meeting at the level of Ministers of Foreign Affairs, when France held the Presidency of the Council, and stressed the obligations of all states to comply with resolutions 1373, 1390 and 1455. The Council also stated that the CTC should intensify its efforts with regard to states' implementation of 1373.

5 UN Security Council document S/2003/1070, dated 2 December 2003.

6 UN document S/AC.37/2003/(1455)/63, dated 28 July 2003.

7 Report of the UN Secretary-General to the General Assembly: 'Measures to eliminate international terrorism' – UN document A/59/210, dated 5 August 2004.

8 *Hawala*, one of the oldest 'informal remittance systems', is believed to be used extensively by members of the al-Qaida network and

their supporters to position funds for the network's operations and
logistics.

10 LIFE-BLOOD OF TERRORISM

1 Personal communication, Reuven Paz, December 2001. Dr Paz, a
   former head of research of the Internal Security Agency (Shin bet)
   of Israel, was the first to bring the founding charter of al-Qaida to
   the attention of the operational and academic communities. The
   charter, written by Azzam, was published in *al-Jihad*, the principal
   journal of the Arab *mujāhidīn*, in Peshawar, 1988.
2 Ayman al-Zawahiri, 'The Knights under the Prophet's Banner',
   unpublished MS, December 2001.
3 Al-Qaida detainee commenting on Tareekh, al-Musadat, 86, 87, 88,
   Folder 8, Documents 301–47, recovered from Benevolence
   International Foundation's Bosnia Office, 19 March 2002, p. 5.
4 Al-Qaida detainee commenting on Tareekh, al-Musadat, 86, 87, 88,
   Folder 8, Documents 301–47, recovered from Benevolence
   International Foundation's Bosnia Office, 19 March 2002, p. 5
5 Considerable speculation has taken place as to Usama bin Laden's
   personal wealth. Bin Laden was alleged to have inherited upwards of
   $300 million when his father died, funds thought to have formed the
   basis for al-Qaida financing in Sudan and Afghanistan. Such exagger-
   ations have been discredited, and his personal wealth has been estimated closer to $30–40 million – about a million dollars per year from
   about 1970 to 1994, according to the '9-11' Commission Monograph
   on Terrorist Financing. In 1994 the Saudi government forced the
   bin Laden family to sell Usama's share of the family company and
   to freeze the proceeds, thereby depriving him of what could have
   been a $300 million fortune. John Roth, Douglas Greenberg and
   Serena Wille, *Monograph on Terrorist Financing (Staff Report to the
   Commission)*, National Commission on Terrorist Attacks upon the
   United States (2004).
6 On him see www.ustreas.gov/press/releases/po3397.htm. The IIRO
   functioned under Rabita al-Islami, also known as MWLKA.
7 http://fl1.findlaw.com/news.findlaw.com/hdocs/docs/binladen
   /usbinladen1.pdf.
8 For a more detailed description of al Qaeda's financial network, see
   Rohan Gunaratna, *Inside Al Qaeda* (New York, 2002), pp. 81–93.
9 Al-Qaida detainee commenting on Tareekh, al-Musadat, 86, 87, 88,
   Folder 8, Documents 301–47, recovered from Benevolence
   International Foundation's Bosnia Office, 19 March 2002.
10 'Posing as a journalist, Al-Roomi visited with Jamil Ur Rahman and
   while interviewing him about his relationship with the Saudi government pulled out a small handgun and killed him. Al-Roomi was

killed by Jamil Ur Rahman's bodyguard. Jamil Ur Rahman was killed after Abdullah Azzam, the ideological father of al Qaeda was killed, also by al Qaeda.' Ibid.

11 Ibid.

12 Ibid.

13 Al-Qaida detainee commenting on Tareekh Osama, Folder 56, Document 136, recovered from Benevolence International Foundation's Bosnia Office, 19 March 2002, p. 7.

14 http://fl1.findlaw.com/news.findlaw.com/hdocs/docs/binladen/usbinladen1.pdf.

15 Al-Iraqi attempted to procure a uranium canister for $1.5 million, but al-Qaida was duped. The canister had been irradiated from outside and sold. While in detention, Abu Hajir al-Iraqi used a sharpened comb to stab a US corrections officer in the eye.

16 See http://www.cbc.ca/news/background/osamabinladen/. In 1996 bin Laden was forced to leave Sudan for Afghanistan following intense pressure from the US on the government. While in Sudan, bin Laden met a man who was probably a key ally, Imad Mugniyah, a Lebanese said to be a leader of Hezbollah, wanted by the US for kidnappings and killings during the civil war in Lebanon in the 1980s.

17 Gunaratna, *Inside Al Qaeda*, p. 54.

18 http://www.cooperativeresearch.org/context.jsp?item=a121694 khalifaarr

19 http://experts.about.com/e/m/mo/Mohammed_Jamal_Khalifa.htm.

20 Rohan Gunaratna, 'The Lifeblood of Terrorist Organisations: Evolving Terrorist financing Strategies', in *Countering Terrorism through International Cooperation*, ed. Alex Schmid, International Scientific and Professional Advisory Council of the UN Cooperation and the UN Terrorism Prevention Branch, 2001, pp. 180–205; see also Gunaratna, *Inside Al Qaeda*, p. 61.

21 http://en.wikipedia.org/wiki/Wood_Green_no-ricin_plot.

22 This figure is a summation of accounts in US$ and other currencies, converted into US$.

23 See Appendix III to UN document S/2003/1070, dated 2 December 2003.

24 *The 9/11 Commission Report: Final Report of the National Commission on Terrorist Attacks upon the United States*, p. 170.

25 Ibid., p. 169.

26 Scheherezade Faramarzi, 'Terrorists using cash machine scheme to fund networks', Associated Press, 10 December 2004.

27 Statement of David D. Aufhauser, former US Treasury General Counsel, before the Senate Committee on Governmental Affairs: 'An Assessment of Current Efforts to Combat Terrorism Financing', 15 June 2004.

28 The Golden Chain list (or list of wealthy Saudi sponsors) was pre-

sented by the US Government as Exhibit 5 in the Department of Justice 'Government's Evidentiary Proffer Supporting the Admissibility of Co-conspirator Statements' in the case of USA v. Arnaout (USDC, Northern District of Illinois, Eastern Division) filed on 29 January 2003. The list was also mentioned in the Indictment of Enaam Arnaout on 9 October 2002 (02 CR 892). According to the US Government, the document is 'a list of people referred to within al-Qaida as the "Golden Chain", wealthy donors to mujahideen efforts'. See http://www.libertyforum.org/showflat.php?Cat=& Board=news_history&Number=294254324.

29 Nick Fielding, 'Al-Qaida origins and the Golden Chain', in 'The Evolving Threat – International Terrorism in the Post 9/11 Era', Globe Research and publishing Srl, Rome 2006.

30 '9/11 Boost to Islamic Finance', Aljazeera.net, 28 September 2004, quoting Rushdi Siddique, Global Director of Dow Jones Islamic indexes.

31 Abdul Wahab Bashir, 'The Kingdom Has No Plans to Close Down Charities', *Arab News*, 1 January 2005 [21, Dhul Qaʾdah, 1425].

32 Ibid.

33 Travnik, a large town in Central Bosnia, boasted the most mosques in the country and had been the Bosnian capital during the Ottoman occupation. During the 1992 5 conflict Travnik had seen some of the fiercest inter-ethnic fighting, with Serbs to the north and Croats to the south and southwest of the town.

34 Resolution 1390 was reviewed after twelve months, primarily at the insistence of France. It was reinforced by resolution 1455 on 17 January 2003, this resolution extending the Monitoring Group's mandate for a further twelve months.

35 Resolution 1452 (2002) had been adopted by the UN Security Council specifically to allow individuals designated on the List a means of obtaining the release of assets for a number of clearly defined humanitarian reasons, such as payment for 'foodstuffs, rent or mortgage, medicines and medical treatment, taxes', etc. For full details, see UN document S/RES/1452 (2002), dated 20 December 2002.

36 Taken from the translated version of the request (the original was in French), submitted by the Swiss Permanent Mission to the UN to the Chairman of the 1267 Committee.

37 UN document S/2004/10, letter dated 9 January 2004, from the Chargé d'affaires a.i. of the Permanent Mission of Switzerland to the United Nations addressed to the President of the Security Council.

38 'JI: The threat remains . . .': presentation prepared by the International Centre for Political Violence and Terrorism Research, IDSS, Singapore, and shown to the UN Al-Qaida and Taliban Sanctions Monitoring Group in New York, December 2003.

39 IIRO website information, available at www.arriyadh.com.

40 P. K. Abdul Ghafour, 'SR40m Saudi Aid for Darfur', *Arab News*, Jeddah, 15 August 2004.
41 http://www.tharwaproject.com/node/1876.
42 See Christopher Bennett, *Yugoslavia's Bloody Collapse* (London, 1995), chapter 7 ('Countdown to War').
43 See www1.oecd.org/fatf/TerFinance_en.htm.
44 UN document S/RES/1526 (2004), dated 30 January 2004.

11 TERRORISM AND MODERN COMMUNICATIONS

1 Walid M. Abdelnasser, 'Islamic Organizations in Egypt and the Iranian Revolution of 1979: The Experience of the First Few Years', *Arab Studies Quarterly*, XIX (1997). Walid documents the impact of the recorded cassette on spawning and sustaining the protests that led to the fall of the Shah and the rise of the Islamic revolution in Iran in 1979.
2 Interview with Madeleine Gruen, Counter Terrorism Analyst, Counter Terrorism Bureau, New York City Police Department, June 2006.
3 Gabriel Weimann, 'How Modern Terrorism Uses the Internet', *Journal of International Security Affairs*, no. 8 (Spring 2005), pp. 1–5.
4 UN Security Council document S/2002/541, dated 15 May 2002.
5 See muaskar-al-battar.cjb.net/.
6 'Steganography Instructions to Conceal a File Within the Contents of Another for Secret Data Transmission explained by Jihadist Forum Member', siteinstitute.org/news.html.
7 Dr Udo Ufkotte, 'Telefonieren für den Terror', *Park Avenue Magazine*, 2 (February 2006).
8 See www.intelligence.org.il/eng/memri/sep_e_04.htm.
9 Javid Hassan, 'Women Come Out Against Extremist Internet magazine', *Arab News*, 7 September 2004. See arabnews.com/.
10 See en.wikipedia.org/wiki/2006_Toronto_terrorism_arrests.
11 For details of his arrest and where it is leading counter-terrorism measures, see Rita Katz and Michael Kern, 'Terrorist 007, Exposed', *Washington Post*, 26 March 2006, B01; and see also 'SITE Institute in the News', siteinstitute.org/. See also http://www.laura-mansfield.com/j/007.asp and http://mypetjawa.mu.nu/archives/160985.php.
12 Evan Kohlman, 'American Greases al-Qaida Media Machine', msnbc.msn.com/id/13842265/, posted 14 July 2006.
13 UN Security Council document S/2005/572, dated 9 September 2005.
14 Gabriel Weimann, *Terror on the Internet*, United States Institute of Peace, Washington, DC, April 2006.
15 Statt Sicherheits Dienst (State Security Service).
16 www.iwar.org.uk/law/resources/cybercrime/stanford/cisac-draft.htm.

17 www.homeoffice.gov.uk/security/terrorism-and-the-law/terrorism-act-2006/.

18 See untreaty.un.org/English/Terrorism/Conv12.pdf.

12 THE RELUCTANT LEADERSHIP

1 See UN Security Council document S/RES/1526 (2004), dated 30 January 2004.

2 After 1,200 hostages had been taken, the school was stormed. Around 350 people were killed in the ensuing explosions and fire-fight, half of them children. Once again it is the innocent who suffer at the hands of the terrorists.

3 'Without a tougher and more comprehensive resolution – a resolution that obliges States to take the mandated measures – the role of the United Nations in this important battle risks becoming marginalised'.

4 UN General Assembly document A/59/565, dated 2 December 2004.

13 PATHWAYS OUT OF VIOLENCE

1 See abcnews.go.com/International/wireStory?id=2196269&CMP–OTC-RSSFeedso312.

2 See english.safe-democracy.org/agenda/the-madrid-agenda.html.

3 See english.safe-democracy.org/keynotes/a-global-strategy-for-fighting-terrorism.html.

4 Ibid.

5 www.un.org/summit2005/. See Paragraph 83, 'Outcome Document'.

6 See paragraph 22 of UN document A/60/692, dated 7 March 2006.

7 See p. 31 of http://media.clubmadrid.org/docs/CdM Series on Terrorism Vol 2.pdf.

8 Ibid.

9 See final report of the UN Monitoring Group – document S/2003/1070, dated 2 December 2003.

10 See paragraph 180 (a) of UN General Assembly document A/59/565, dated 2 December 2004.

11 See media.clubmadrid.org/docs/CdM-Series-om-Terrorism-Vol-2.pdf.

12 Boaz Ganor, *The Counter-Terrorism Puzzle: A Guide for Decision Makers* (New Brunswick, NJ, and London, 2005)

13 BBC World TV News, 5 August 2004.

14 Pope John Paul II had specifically requested that he not be given a 'funeral service'.

Acknowledgements

In recognizing the many people whose support and encouragement has been invaluable to us in writing this book, we would like to start by thanking Hemant H. Shah, the President and CEO of Risk Management Solutions Inc., California. Mr Shah awarded Michael Chandler a RMS Fellowship at the International Centre for Political Violence and Terrorism Research (ICPVTR) at the Institute for Defence and Strategic Studies (IDSS), Singapore, to research and write a book on the international response to terrorism. Peter Ulrich, Senior Vice-President, Model Management, RMS; Dr Andrew Coburn, the director of terrorism research at RMS; and Dr Gordon Woo, who was the chief architect for the RMS Terrorism Model, supported the creation of the RMS Fellowship in Singapore. We would also like to thank Ambassador Barry Desker, the Director of the Institute of Defence and Strategic Studies (IDSS), for his support in providing Rohan Gunaratna with sufficient time to co-author the book.

We have been encouraged throughout our endeavours by many other friends and colleagues who share our concerns and vision in dealing with the current threat from trans-national terrorism and to whom we would like to express our appreciation for their support: Benny Lim, Permanent Secretary, Ministry of Home Affairs, Singapore; Bruce Hoffman, Professor, Georgetown University; Brigadier (Retd) Russ Howard, Director, Jebsen Centre for Counter Terrorism Studies, Fletcher School of Law and Diplomacy; Michael E. Elsner, Trial Attorney, Motley Rice, LLC; Donald Hamilton, Executive Director, and Chip Ellis, Research and Program Director, National Memorial Institute for the Prevention of Terrorism in Oklahoma City; Dr Josef Bollag; Dr Boaz Ganor, Deputy Dean, Lauder School of Government, Diplomacy and Strategy, Interdisciplinary Centre, Herzliya; Andy Clarke, Producer, CBS News, London; Mati Kochavi, CEO Asia Global Inc, and Ofer Dektal, former Deputy Head of Shin Bet, deserve a special thanks for their guidance and friendship; Vic Comras, former US Diplomat, Attorney and Consultant on Terrorist Financing for his expert advice, ideas and assistance with our research; Loretta Napoleoni for her advice and detailed critiques; Elmar Thevessen of Germany's *Zweites Deutsches*

Fernsehen (ZDF) and journalist Souad Mehkennet; Swati Parashar, Crystal Mariah Schautz, Mohamed bin Ali, and Nadeeka Withana, ICPVTR-IDSS research analysts, and Anders Nielsen, Research Fellow on the Middle East, reviewed the typescript. Also, in the early days of writing the book, the advice and ideas of Catarina Aanderud of Hamburg in helping to 'get the ball rolling', were extremely valuable.

That the book has been possible in the first place owes much to the commitment, dedication, unswerving resolve and teamwork, despite myriad bureaucratic and other obstacles, of the members of the UN Monitoring Group (from 2001 to 2004) on sanctions against al-Qaeda and the Taliban: Hasan Abaza, Vic Comras (and before him Mike Langan), Philippe Graver and Surendra Shah, and the members of the Group's dedicated research and analysis team at the United Nations.

A special mention must go to our families for their ideas, encouragement and patience with us, throughout the phases of travel, research and writing. In particular Michael would like to thank his wife, Alix, and daughter, Alexandra; and Rohan his wife, Anne, and their sons Kevin and Ryan, as well as his parents, his brother Keith and sister Malkanthi.

Finally, a big thank you to Michael Leaman, Emily Berry, Maria Kilcoyne and the rest of the team at Reaktion for their ideas, thoughts and guidance.

Index